Cricut
Design Space
Handbook for Newbies

Conquer The Design Space Beast
Once And For All

By Delara Chowdhury and

_____

(YOUR name goes on that line!)

For Zabed and my baby girl, Aliya.
your support throughout my journey means more than you will ever know.
Love you, always.

Claim Your FREE Gift Right Now

Hey, Crafter!

Thank you so much for investing in yourself with this book. You're going to love every second you spend in these pages. Remember, though, knowledge means nothing without implementation, so be sure to open your Design Space program and follow along every step of the way.

To make your journey as a Cricut crafter as smooth as possible, and as a token of my appreciation, I'd like to invite you to my exclusive and private Design Space for Newbies newsletter. As a valued subscriber, you'll also receive a **FREE** copy of *The Must Have Design Space Cheat Sheet for Cricut Newbies.* Follow the link below to join the newsletter and receive your gift.

www.cricutfornewbies.com

Table of Contents

Introduction

My first Cricut machine was the Explore Air 2. It terrified me, so I tucked it away safely where it couldn't intimidate me. But it haunted me. Whatever I did, wherever I went, it was on my mind, begging to be used.

I know you know what I'm talking about.

It would be *months* before I scraped together the courage to rescue the poor thing from the company of darkness and cobwebs. But by then, I had a new flame of determination to become a serious Cricut crafter. I was, after all, a self-proclaimed crafting queen and had never shied away from the latest and greatest anything, so I *had* to make this work.

Armed with the knowledge from a YouTube video, I opened the box, took out the machine and all the goodies that came with it, and opened the *Welcome Book* like a boss.

"Design Space is the free design layout application at the heart of the Cricut experience. We created Design Space to be simple for people new to crafting, but with enough power for our most experienced makers, too," I read in the Welcome Book.

Oh, good! I thought, *I'm a seasoned crafter, so this will actually be easy! Don't know Why I felt so scared in the first place. Pfft...*

You know what happened next, don't you?

Reality struck.

They lied.

It. Was. Not. Simple.

The predicament left me with a choice: accept defeat and give up, or persist and make it work. Now, it's not like there weren't a ton of other crafting options out there, so would moving on *really* mean defeat? Well, I'm like you in that regard: If I had accepted defeat, I'd be sitting in my craft room right now, wondering... *What if I made a mistake by walking away from that Cricut thing?*

And you know what? It would indeed have been the worst mistake of my crafting life and career. And if you give up, it's going to be the worst mistake of *your* crafting life and career. Seriously.

You're here, which means you're not ready to give up.

Sure, you're frustrated, overwhelmed, questioning your sanity, and so-so close to dumping that damn machine in the trash, all because Design Space has yet *another* update... (Just when you thought you finally understood something, right?) But, above all that, the determined crafter in you *knows* that Cricut crafting is awesome.

If only you could figure out Design Space.

If only you had access to a resource that would help you navigate those hair-raising updates without demanding a ton of money every time those updates come along—do they not realize you need every precious penny for craft supplies?! Some people...

If only someone could take you through every little function, step-by-step, so you could conquer Design Space once and for all and craft to your heart's content.

Jokes aside, I really do know what you're going through. It hurts and it sucks. My overwhelm was so bad, I sat and sobbed in my craft room one day. My machine was a gift, and I felt like a fraud for not being able to use it. More than anything, I just wanted to prove to myself that I would not let such a hearty and beautiful gift go to waste. After all, I was the one who fell in love with the idea of Cricut crafting after discovering it and continually expressed my desire to get a machine. Well, I got what I wished for—I had to prove that my newfound love wasn't a fad.

Whether you got your machine as a gift from yourself to yourself, or someone else gifted it to you, it's a pretty crappy feeling to have to say "not yet..." whenever anyone asks if you've made something with it yet.

This book will turn things around for you. It's packed with everything I wish I had access to when I first got my machine—and more! If you put in the time to study it, I guarantee you're not only going to conquer Design Space, you'll master it.

Meet the Author

Hi, I'm Delara Chowdhury, an unapologetic craft addict. I've been using my own Cricut since 2017 and have been through more bumps on my journey than I care to remember, because the important part is that I figured it out, so you don't have to!

You may know me from my debut book, *Cricut for Newbies*. If you're here for more Cricut magic, I'd like to take a moment to thank you and express how humbling it is to have you back. For you, this book will be an extension of the one you already read. It's the perfect companion book to help you put everything you learned into practice. You can continue reading below, or skip ahead to the *what you'll learn in this book* section.

If you are new to the *Cricut for Newbies* family, welcome! And please continue reading. I have important information to share with you.

My guess is that you are either brand new to the exciting world of Cricut crafting, or you know the basics already and are ready to soak your feet into the magic with more Design Space knowledge. If you fall into the former category, I definitely want to encourage you to get your hands on a copy of my previous book. It's a treasure trove of Cricut tips and tricks that dives deep into what Cricut is, how to use each machine, which tools you need to get started, how to troubleshoot your machine, where to get materials and tools, where to source free design resources, and much, much more.

The first book also has a chapter on the bare basics of Design Space. Through guided illustrations, it explains the fundamentals of navigating the program and how to use its most popular functions. It also explains what each program function is and when and why to use it. Furthermore, it explores how to use Cricut Access, upload external design files, and use the *Print Then Cut* feature. Finally, the book offers three in-depth project tutorials to help you get familiar with the creative process.

While I highly recommend the first book for all Newbies, you don't *need* it to get value out of this book if you are familiar with the bare basics of your Cricut machine and Design Space. I do want you to take note, though, that for the most part, this book's goal is not to explain concepts. Here, I will assume you have a basic understanding of Design Space and Cricut machine functions. For example, you'll come across exercises that show you how to *Weld* and *Slice* forms. But the exercises will not explain what *Weld* and *Slice* mean or when and why you'll want to use them. My first book explains all those things in detail.

If you want to check out *Cricut for Newbies*, you can find it here: https://www.amazon.com/dp/B09ZSGLQVX/

Now, some pros won't admit it, but I'll let you in on a secret: we were *all* in the exact dilemma you are facing right now. You owe it to yourself not to give up on Cricut crafting. There *is* light at the end of this dark tunnel, and it shines on endless creativity, fun, and Cricut projects.

What you'll learn in this book:

The *Cricut Design Space Handbook for Newbies* is a practical guide that will help you explore Design Space in-depth with exercises so you can truly master it and flex your creative muscles.

Actually, you will be co-authoring this book with me and make it your own through your personal training notes as you work through it. That's why there is a space for you to put your name on the title page. While my words will give you guidance, you will be the true mastermind behind this book once you have worked through it.

The book breaks Design Space into digestible chunks. Although each chapter will focus on a specific part of the program's interface, you will still have a holistic view of what goes where and how the parts interact with each other and influence your final design. You'll explore both the desktop version and mobile version of Design Space. The guiding illustrations will represent an Apple computer for the desktop version and an Apple iPhone for the mobile version. However, there is no difference between the Apple and Windows desktop apps, and if there are significant differences between the Apple and Android mobile apps, I'll be sure to tell you about it. If you are using a tablet, you have a mobile version of the app. Your interface might have slight visual differences compared to the iOS or Android mobile app for cell phones because your screen is bigger, but the functions remain the same. Again, if there is a significant difference between the mobile interface of a tablet and cell phone, I'll be sure to tell you.

Chapter 5 is dedicated to helping you understand layers in Design Space. When you're done with the layers chapter, you'll never again be left wondering how the heck to tackle a design. Better yet, you'll feel like you actually know exactly what you're talking about when layers come up in conversations. And, of course, you'll be able to share your new, in-depth knowledge with those who are still struggling with layers. **But please don't skip ahead to Chapter 5** before working through Chapters 1–4. The book's structure will help you get the most out of the learning experience if you tackle it chronologically.

Finally, you'll find a mega glossary of crafting terms at the back of the book. So, if you ever come across a term and find yourself lost because you don't know what it means, simply consult your trusty Design Space Handbook; chances are you'll find its definition in here. I've also included an index in the back so you can easily find the sections you're looking for.

How to interpret the screenshots in this book:

To give you the best learning experience, the book contains screenshots of each step and an explanation. Where applicable, the screenshot will contain additional information to help you navigate the Design Space interface with more ease.

Please note that even as I write this book, Design Space is probably undergoing another update. Since it is a never-ending process, you might see something different on your screen compared to the screenshot you are looking at, depending on when you bought your copy of this book. However, the book itself undergoes yearly updates to ensure it stays current and gives you the best learning experience; so, it doesn't matter when you buy your copy, you can rest assured it is the latest version that covers the most recent Design Space software updates.

Finally, to make your learning journey a fun-filled experience with the support of fellow Newbie crafters, consider joining the *Cricut for Newbies* private community on Facebook. There, you can ask questions and connect with like-minded people who will have your back every step of the way. Visit the following link to get join to the community now:

https://www.facebook.com/groups/cricutfornewbies

This book will help you discover that Design Space is, after all, not *that* intimidating. If your creative spirit has taken a knock for whatever reason lately, it's time to revive it by inviting balance and joy into your life once more, one page at a time.

Ready to rekindle your creativity and get those ideas flowing abundantly again? See you in Chapter 1, then!

Chapter 1
Overview of the Design Interface

The aim of this chapter is to help you get familiar with the overall Design Space interface so that, when we dive into specifics in the upcoming chapters, you'll know exactly where to look for features and functions. We're also going to explore the differences between the desktop and mobile versions of the program.

Note: This book will exclusively focus on the Canvas interface and some other features that are relevant to the design process. If you're interested in learning more about the theory of the *entire* Design Space interface and its functions, I recommend my first book, *Cricut for Newbies*.

By "theory," I don't mean endless definitions that will bore you and help you set up a new world-record for the most yawns in a single reading session.

Rather, it takes a more in-depth look at what each function means and entails, but in a fun way. When we dive into using the different Design Space functions in this handbook, and you find yourself wondering, *"Huh... I wonder what 'Slice' actually means and why I would use it,"* you will probably benefit from a book like *Cricut for Newbies*.

That said, **I don't want you to think that you're missing out** if you choose not to get the first book. You're all set if you have a basic understanding of Cricut machines and Design Space. Besides, you can consult the Glossary at the back of the book for helpful definitions on the most popular Cricut (and general) crafting terms. If you already own *Cricut for Newbies*, but haven't used Design Space since reading it, this is your chance to practice what you learned. On the other hand, if you started using Design Space already, everything you learn here will serve as a refresher and help you get those pesky things you've been struggling with right—once and for all.

Let's get started.

Parts of the Interface

The Canvas

On both the desktop and mobile versions of Design Space, the Canvas takes up most of the screen, as that's where your design will take shape. The Canvas is the area where you see the grid on your screen. In both versions, you can make adjustments to design elements directly from this area by clicking on those elements and interacting with them. We'll explore everything you can do directly in the Canvas area in Chapter 3.

Whenever you start a new project on the **desktop version**, you'll see the blank Canvas in the middle, two panels on each side of the Canvas, and a bar at the top of the Canvas. On the **mobile version**, you'll see the blank Canvas taking up most of the screen and a single bar with various functions at the bottom of the screen.

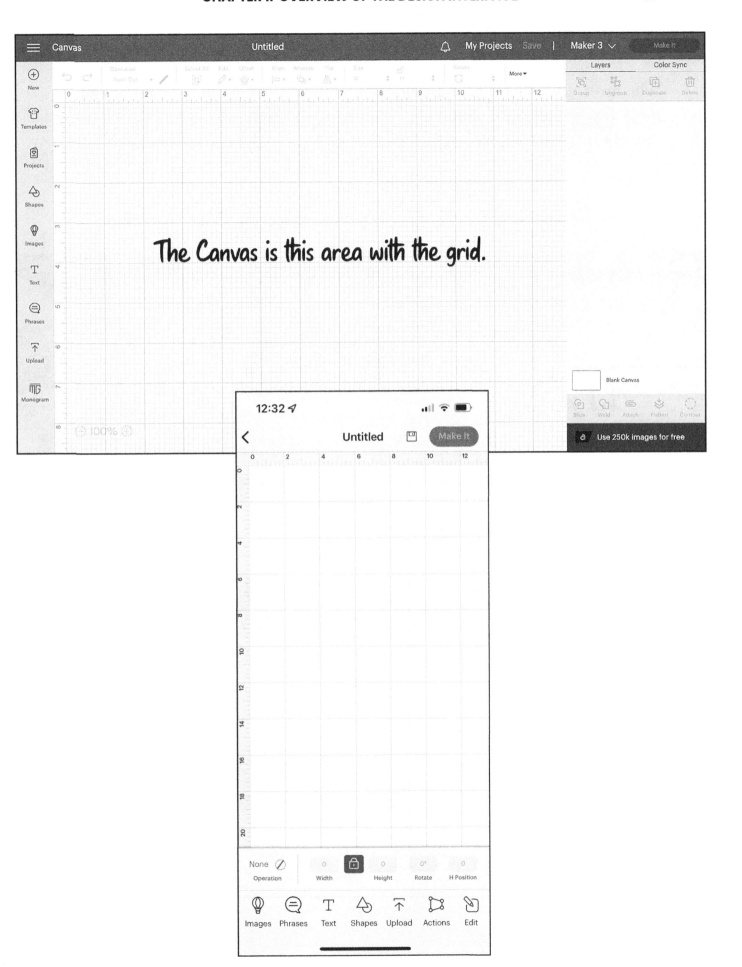

How To Open a Blank Canvas

Whenever you launch your Design Space app, you'll be met with the Home page. If you have the **desktop app**, you can open a new (or blank) Canvas using one of the following methods:

Option 1

Click on the hamburger menu in the top-left corner and select "Canvas."

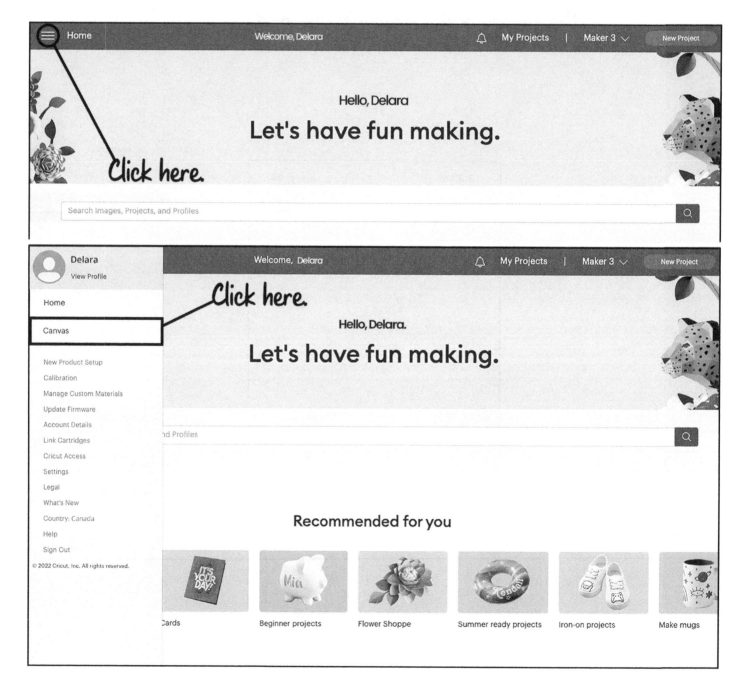

Option 2

Click on *My Projects/My Stuff* in the menu bar. In the new window that opens, click on the very first option (*New*) you see in the right-hand panel.

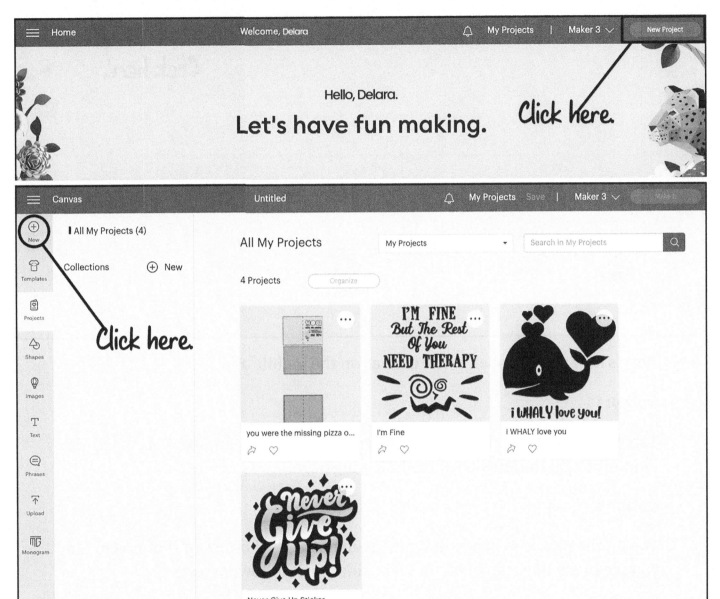

Option 3

This is the quickest way, as you simply click on that inviting green button in the upper-left corner of the menu bar that says "New Project."

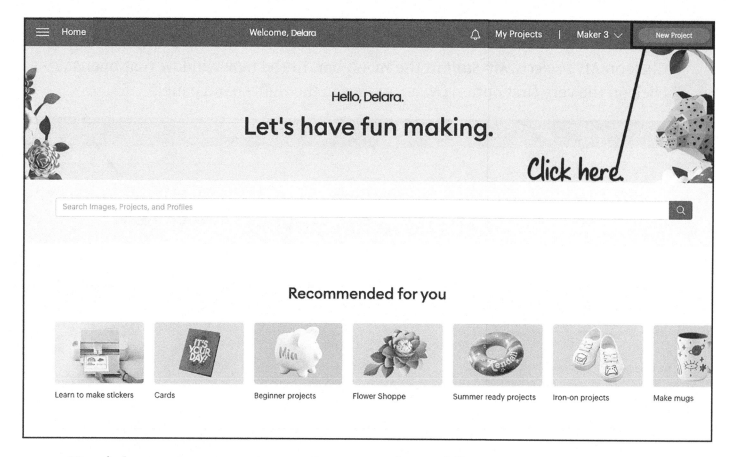

Here's how you can open a new Canvas on the **mobile app**:

Option 1

Tap on "Canvas" in the upper-right corner of the screen, like you see in the illustration on the left side of the following page.

Option 2

Tap on the plus icon inside that big green dot at the bottom of the screen, like you see in the illustration on the right side of the following page.

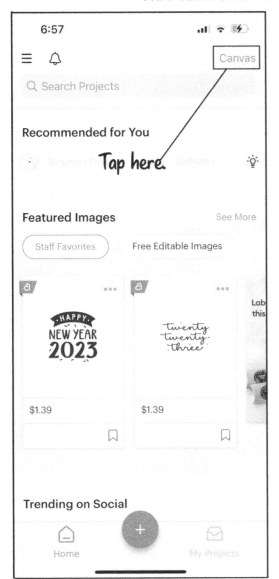

How to Hide and Show the Grid on the Canvas

The grid on the Canvas works kind of like criss-crossing rulers. It's super useful for helping you line design elements up perfectly and gives you a good idea of a design's size. However, if you find yourself annoyed by all those lines, there is an option to hide the grid partially or completely. While I don't recommend turning the grid off when you're just starting out, it's good to know you can do it. And, of course, it's your choice!

I'll show you how to hide the grid below. However, for the rest of the screenshots in the book, the grid will be fully visible.

We'll start with the **desktop app**. First, click on the hamburger menu, like you learned in option 1 in the *How To Open a Blank Canvas* section. Next, select *Settings*. When the pop-up window appears, choose *Canvas*.

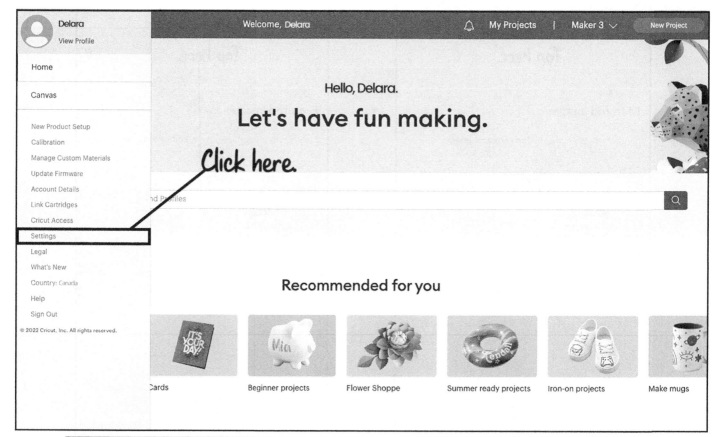

Next to *Canvas Grid*, you'll see three options:

- *Full Grid*
- *Partial Grid*
- *No Grid*

The default setting is *Full Grid*. Let's change it to *Partial Grid* to see what happens. Select *Partial Grid* and click on *Done* in the bottom-right corner of the window. As you can see, the smaller lines in between the larger blocks of the grid have now disappeared.

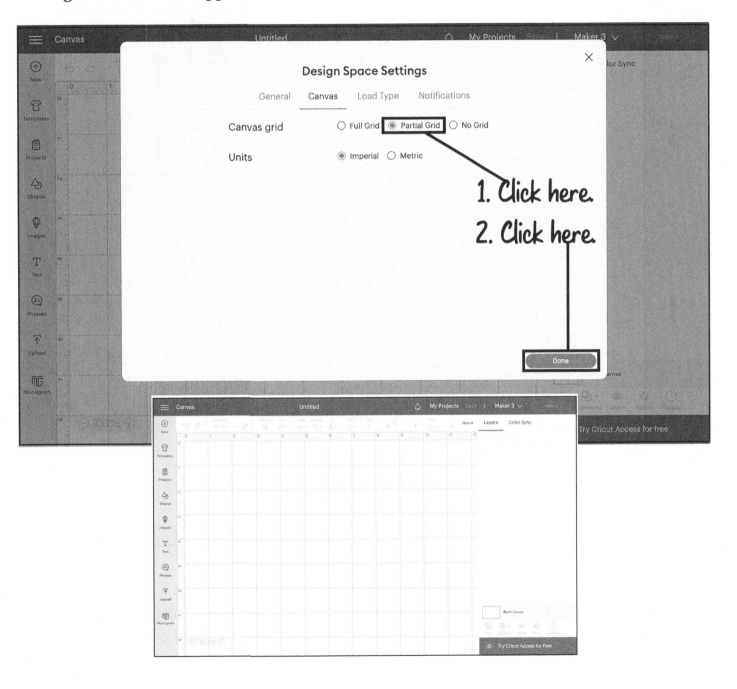

Go into the Canvas again. This time, choose *No Grid* and click on Done. This time, your Canvas shows a white background only.

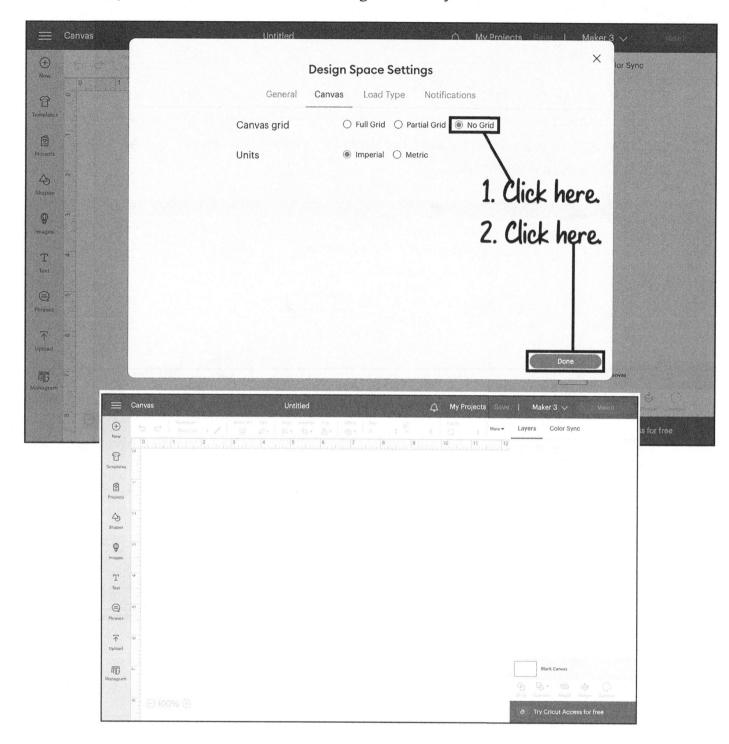

To show or hide the grid on the **mobile app**, you'll have to open a new Canvas first. Once there, swipe the bar at the bottom of the screen until you see *Settings*. Tap on *Settings* and toggle the *Grid* switch. There is no *Partial Grid* setting on the mobile app, meaning you can work on a Canvas with either a *Full Grid* or *No Grid* at all.

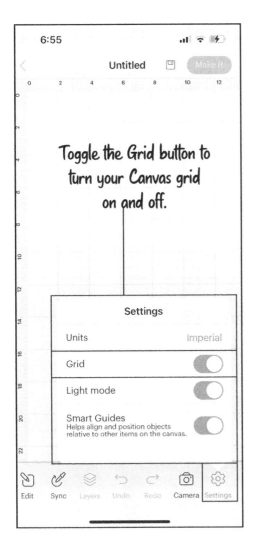
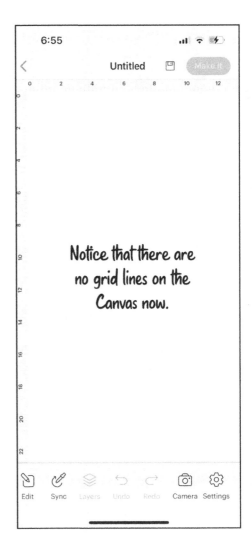

If you want your screen to look exactly as mine as you work through the rest of the book (whether you're following along with your desktop or mobile app), go ahead and change the Canvas grid's settings back to *Full Grid*.

How to Search for a Ready-to-Make Project

If you saw something cool at the shops, maybe a t-shirt that inspired you or a mug that made you happy, and thought, *"Mm... I can make something like that with my Cricut!"* but you're not sure where to start, it might be worth your while to look for some inspiration from the Design Space library. There are two ways to go about this:

Option 1

On the **desktop app's** Home page, you'll see a search bar right underneath the top banner. If you type in a word or phrase and then hit enter, the program will take you to a new window full of (mostly) relevant results.

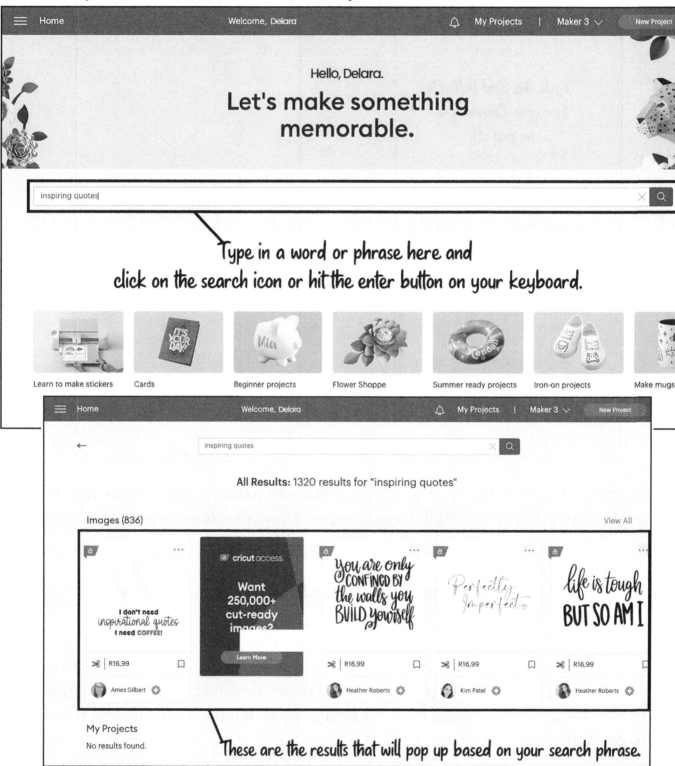

On the **mobile app**, there is a search bar right underneath *Canvas* at the top of the screen. Tap on the icon, enter some words to describe what you're looking for, and then tap on the search icon or Enter key on your keypad.

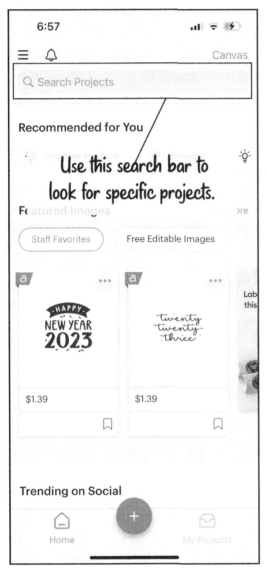
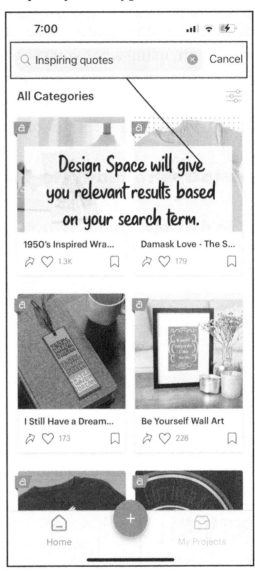

With the mobile app, you might want to refine your search a little further. On the results page, right underneath your search term at the top of the screen, you'll see *All Categories* on the left and a *Filters* icon on the right. Tap on the *Filters* icon to see what options are available for more relevant results.

Option 2

If you have absolutely no idea what you are looking for, this is the way to go. Your Design Space Home page is full of gems, whether you're using the desktop or mobile app. All you have to do is scroll.

You'll be met with *Featured images*, *Trending on social*, *From idea to I-did-it*, and many more categories. Browse through those until you see something that talks with your inner creative genius.

With both options 1 and 2 above, you can use what you see as is or go make your own design, using what you see as inspiration. If you opt to use a project as is, you can open the file on your Canvas and tweak it however you like. However, to cut the project, you will either need an active Cricut Access subscription or you can purchase the design for a once-off fee.

How to Open a Ready-to-Make Project

In the **desktop app**, hover over the image or design you like. A button will appear that says *Add to Canvas*.

*In the **mobile app,** tap on the project you like. On the screen that opens, tap the Customize button at the bottom of the screen.*

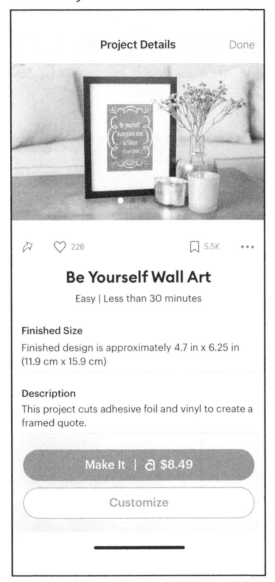

Once you have chosen a design to work with, Design Space will take you straight to the Canvas and display it. You can now add your own flair to the design with extra shapes, images, or an extra word or two.

Note: Even if you change the design to make it unique, you will still need to buy the base project you chose from the library. You can do a once-off purchase or, if you have a Cricut Access subscription, you should be able to use the design.

The Design Panel

The vertical column way on the left side of the **desktop version** is called the Design Panel, where you'll find design elements to work with. To put something on the Canvas area to work with, you need to choose something from this panel.

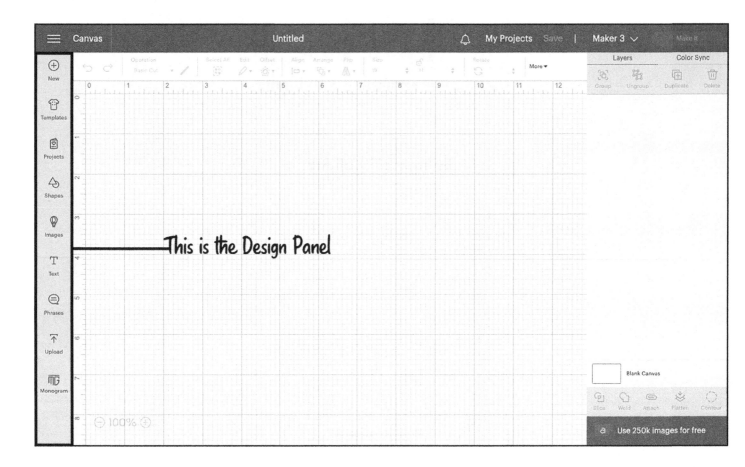

Unlike the desktop version, the **mobile version** does not have distinct areas where you can find design functions. Instead, everything you need is located in that bar at the bottom of the Canvas. For example, while you can use the Design Panel of the desktop version to add an image to the Canvas, you can simply search for the *Image* option in that bottom bar when using the mobile version.

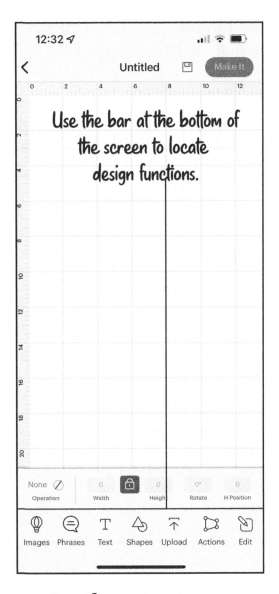

The Menu Bar and Edit Bar

At the top of the **desktop app's** screen, you'll see two distinct horizontal bars. The first one is called the Menu Bar. From there, you can navigate to other Design Space windows (like the Home page, Calibration page, Cricut Access, etc.,), save your current project, and move on to the Make It screen when you're ready to cut your new design with your Cricut machine. On the **mobile app**, the bar you see at the top of the screen represents the Menu Bar. Here, if you want to navigate to other Design Space windows, you have to leave the Canvas by tapping on the "back" arrow. The only other options available on the Canvas Menu Bar in the mobile app are the *Save* icon and the *Make It* button.

The second bar on the **desktop app**, called the Edit Bar, is a lighter shade of gray and contains functions that will help you tweak design elements on your Canvas.

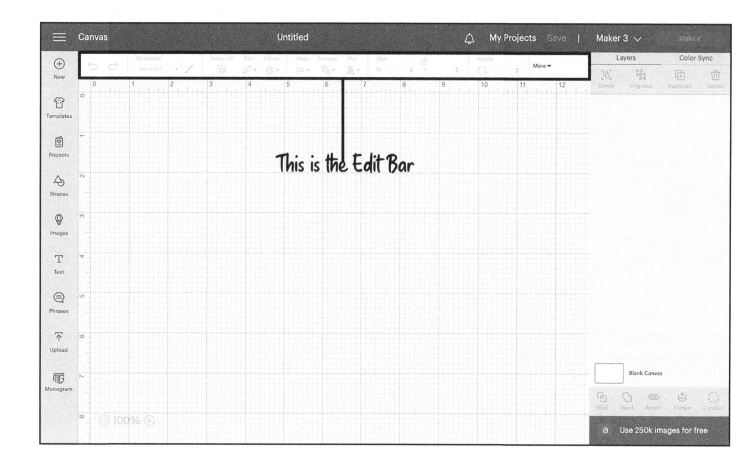

You will notice that all the options in there are currently grayed out if you have your app open. The reason for this is that you have no design elements to work with yet. Once you add something, the Edit Bar functions will become active.

On the **mobile app**, when you tap on *Edit* in the bottom bar, a secondary bar will appear on top of it, containing the same functions you'll find in the desktop version's Edit Bar. As with the desktop version, you'll see that all the *Edit* functions are currently grayed out, as there are no design elements to tweak.

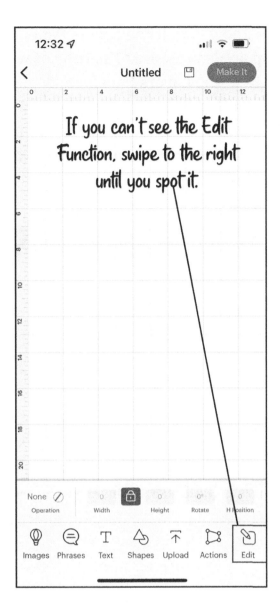

The Layers Panel

The word "layers" strikes fear into any Newbie when it comes to this program. I remember having sleepless nights over it! Not even the intimidation of having to learn all the functions of Design Space could beat the sheer frustration I experienced with layers. *What are they? How do they work? Why can't I see that other thingy I had on the Canvas just now?!*

Urgh...

I know how you feel. But soon, all that frustration is gonna be a thing of the past—this book has your back!

For now, all you need to know is that the Layers Panel is the far-right vertical column on your **desktop app's** screen. At the time of writing this book, Cricut rolled out a major update to the Layers Panel; so, depending on when you got your copy of Cricut Design Space for Newbies, your layer's panel might look slightly different from the one you see used for the most part of this book. When we get to Chapter 5, though, we'll explore this update and the new Layers Panel functions. The screenshot below shows you where the Layers Panel is located on the desktop app.

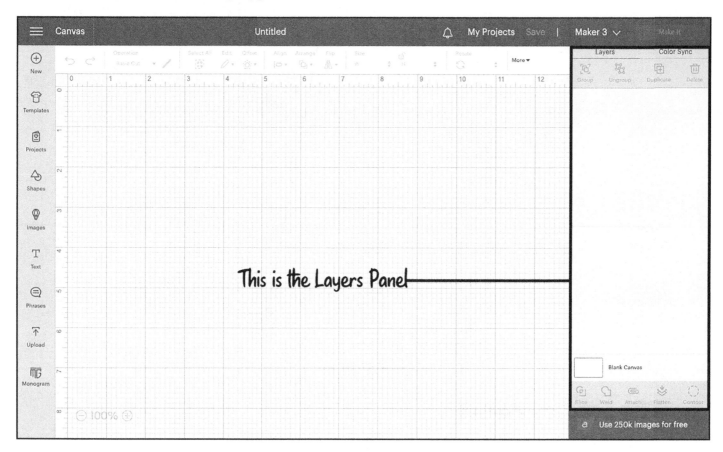

This panel gives you an eagle's eye view of all the design elements on your Canvas and allows you to hide or show elements, change their hierarchical positions on the Canvas, and apply handy functions to make your designs unique.

The **mobile app** has its own version of the Layers Panel, which we'll explore in Chapter 5.

The Make It Screen

When you have completed a design and want your Cricut machine to go ahead with the cutting process, you'll click on the *Make It* button on the top-right corner of the Canvas interface page on both the desktop and mobile apps of Design Space.

If there is nothing on the Canvas, the *Make It* button will be grayed out. For now, I'll add a simple shape to my Canvas and go ahead to the Make It screen so you can see what it looks like.

If you own a Cricut Joy, Explore 3, or Maker 3, the program will ask you if you want your machine to cut without a mat, on a mat, or on a card mat. Your choice will depend on whether you're using normal materials or Smart Materials. If you own a Cricut Explore Air 2 or Maker, the program will take you to the preview screen straight away.

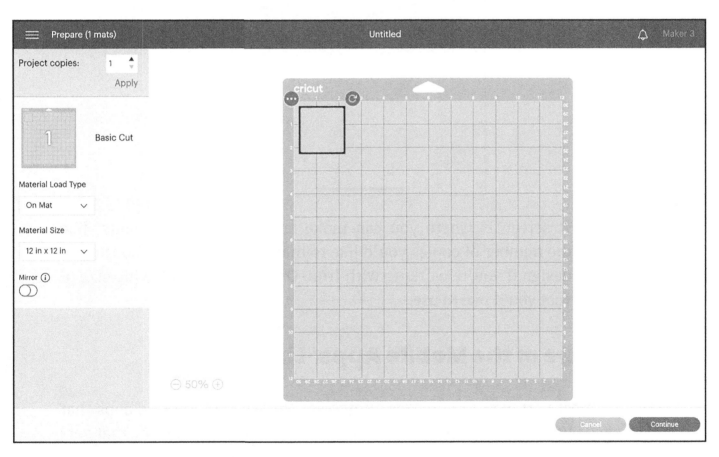

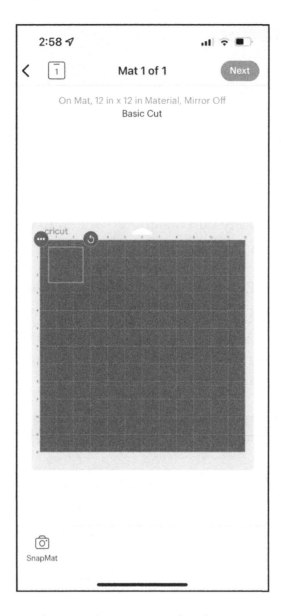

The Make It screen is where you can make last-minute adjustments, like increasing the number of copies you'd like to make of the design, choosing to mirror the design if you're working with Iron-On (HTV), or specifying size of the cutting mat you'd like to use.

Be Aware of the Mobile Apps' Limitations

For the most part, you can do everything with the iOS and Android apps that you can do with the desktop app. That said, the desktop app is the one that gets the most developmental updates, so it has a few features you won't find on either version of the mobile app. Then again, there are a few iOS features you won't get on the desktop or Android app. The Android app draws the short straw, as it lacks the most features compared to the desktop and iOS apps. If you're a serious crafter who takes on projects at least twice a week, you should really consider saving up for a laptop or desktop computer. Having access to the desktop app will really enhance your Cricut crafting capabilities. From a practical viewpoint, it's a lot more convenient to create designs on a larger screen. That said, you can achieve a lot with the mobile apps as a Newbie, so don't get too discouraged about what you can't do if you only have a tablet or cell phone to work with at this stage.

What You Can't Do with the iOS App

Pattern Fills

Pattern fills allow you to fill your designs with special patterns, backgrounds, or images as opposed to filling them with standard colors. They're great for making custom *Print Then Cut* projects. However, few pros use the *Pattern Fill* feature, let alone Newbies! Point in case: you're not missing out on anything here.

Use Templates

Templates are outlined representations of real-life objects you plan on applying your designs to, for example, a tumbler or a coffee mug. While templates are useful to help you visualize what a design might look like once applied to an object, it's by no means a must-have feature.

Link Physical Cartridges

Cartridges were special memory houses that contained specific design elements before Cricut developed Design Space. If you're new to Cricut, you need not worry about this at all, as cartridges have become obsolete for the most part. If you're familiar with the older generations of Cricut machines, you will not be able to link your cartridges to Design Space with the iOS or Android app.

Knife Blade Cutting

The Knife Blade is a specialized cutting blade that allows your machine to cut through thick materials. If you plan on working with thick materials, you'll definitely want to invest in a laptop or desktop computer.

Project Collections

Project collections are just a convenient way of organizing all the projects you create in Design Space. The more you create, the more useful this feature becomes, but it's not a necessity.

Even though the iOS app has a few limitations, it brags with some features you won't find in the other versions of Design Space. These include Photo Canvas, 3D Layer Visualization, SnapMat, and Smart Guides (also available for the Android app).

What You Can't Do with the Android App

Apart from everything you can't do with the iOS app, you'll have these additional limitations if you're working with the Android app:

Curve Text

You can curve text elements to give it some cool looks and features with the desktop app, but not with the Android. Cricut might add it some time in the future, though.

Offset

The *Offset* function allows you to create a proportionally larger or smaller layer of an existing design element on the Canvas, which essentially creates an outline of the design element. It is a very useful feature to make stickers or just to make a design pop. That said, you probably won't have any real need for this feature until you're a more experienced Design Space user.

Print Then Cut

I won't lie—this limitation is not ideal. Newbies can take on *Print Then Cut* projects fairly quickly once they get familiar with Design Space. It's a very convenient feature to have, which allows you to print out a design before cutting it with your Cricut machine. So, depending on the direction you want to take your Cricut crafting, you may find yourself needing to upgrade to a laptop or desktop computer sooner than you had planned. However, there is more than enough you can achieve with your Cricut in the meantime!

Use the App Offline

If you lose your internet connection, your Android app will either give you limited functionality or not work at all, depending on your device's age and current software.

Access to the Cricut Community

Cricut Design Space has an online community where you can create a profile and share your projects with fellow crafters. At the time of writing this book, this feature is not yet available for the Android app.

Three Important functions You'll Use Often

Save

There's nothing worse than working your butt off on an amazing craft design when, out of nowhere, your design program crashes. Thank goodness for autosave these days, right?

Well, not so fast...

For all its cool capabilities, Design Space lacks this critical feature. So always, always, always save your work while designing.

Because I want you to take your work seriously and form this habit early on, this is the *only* time in the entire book you're going to see me talk about saving your projects. The best way new information sticks is when we take action and practice what we learn. I'm going to help you open a new Canvas and save it especially for what you'll learn in this book. So, whenever you get a chance to read, you can open the same project and continue where you left off, but remembering that saving your progress will be your responsibility. Seriously— I'm not going to remind you even once after this.

How To Save Your Work on the Desktop App

Let's start by opening a new Canvas. Since there's nothing on the Canvas yet, Design Space won't give you the option to save anything. So, let's add a shape.

Step 1: Click on *Shapes* in the Design Panel.

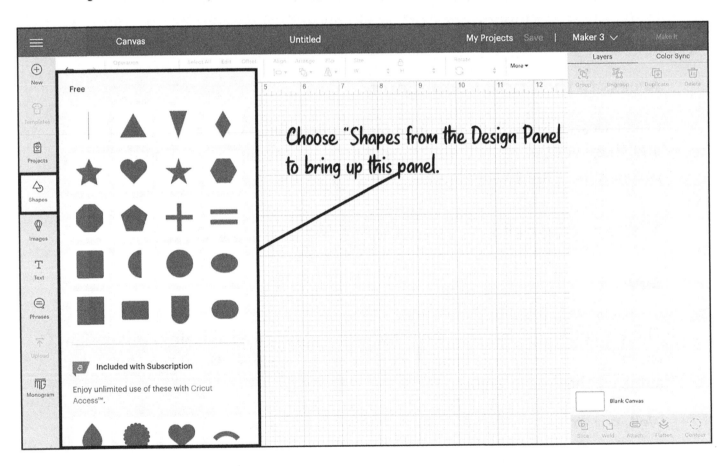

Step 2: Choose a circle.

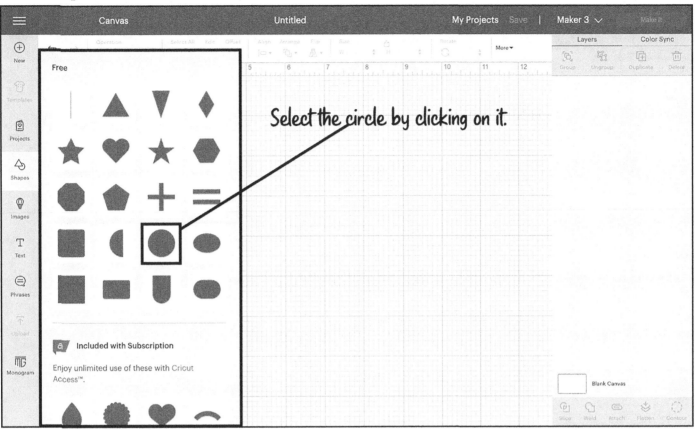

Step 3: Click on *Save* in the Menu Bar.

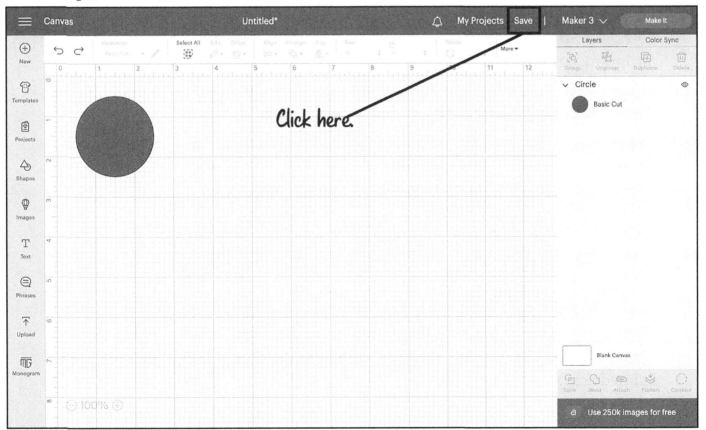

Step 4: Give your project a name (something like "Cricut Test Project" or "My Design Space Handbook Tutorials") and click on the *Save* button.

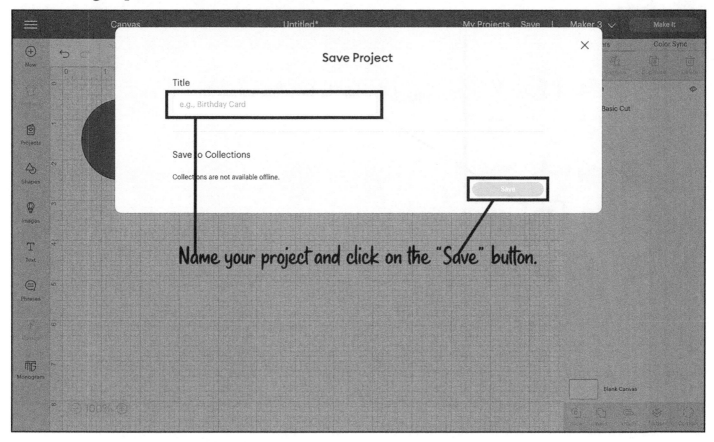

Name your project and click on the "Save" button.

Once you have saved the project, Design Space will take you to the My Projects/My Stuff screen, where you can access all the designs you save in the program.

How To Save Your Work on the Mobile App

Step 1: Open a new Canvas and tap on *Shapes* in the bar at the bottom of your Screen. (See the illustration named *Step 1* on the next page.)

Step 2: Choose a circle. (See the illustration named *Step 2* on the next page.)

Step 3: Tap on the *Save* icon at the top of the screen. (See the illustration named *Step 3* on the next page.)

Step 4: Give your project a name (something like "Cricut Test Project or "My Design Space Handbook Tutorials") and tap on *Save*. ((See the illustration named *Step 4* on the next page.)

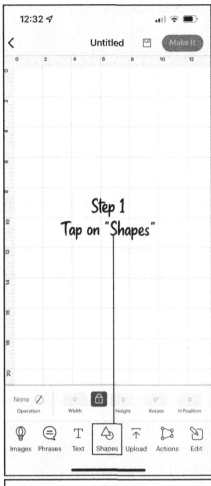

Step 1
Tap on "Shapes"

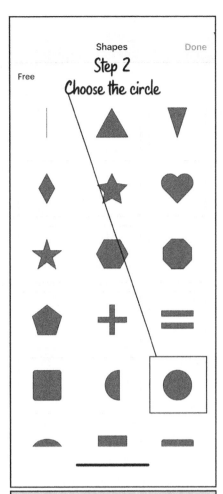

Shapes   Done

Free

Step 2
Choose the circle

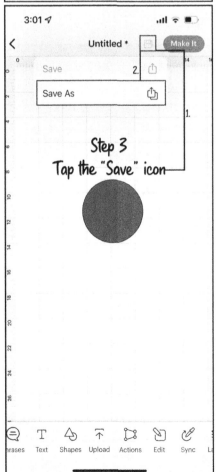

Save   2.

Save As

1.

Step 3
Tap the "Save" icon

Save Project As

Cricut Test Project

Save to the Cloud

Save to iPhone

Cancel

Step 4
Name your project and save it

That's it! Now, as you work through the book, **remember to save your progress** by clicking on *Save* in the desktop app's menu bar, or by tapping on the *Save* icon in the mobile app's menu bar regularly.

Undo/Redo

Undo is handy when you make mistakes or realize your intended change was not such a good idea after all. *Redo* gives you a convenient magic button if you change your mind and decide that, after all, the adjustment you made wasn't such a bad idea. (And—yes—you'll change your mind a *lot* while designing and crafting!)

How to Undo/Redo on the Desktop App

Way to the left of the Edit bar, you'll see two curving arrows next to each other. The one on the left is the *Undo* icon and the one on the right is the *Redo* icon. If you make a mistake or want to see what your design looked like before a change, click on the *Undo* icon. And if you used the *Undo* function but want to bring the change back, click on the *Redo* icon.

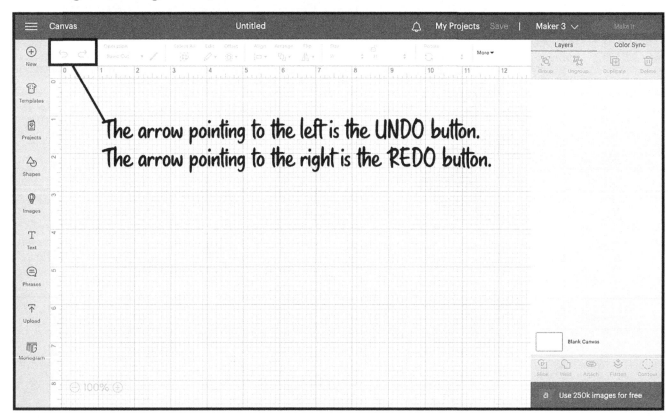

The arrow pointing to the left is the UNDO button.
The arrow pointing to the right is the REDO button.

How to Undo/Redo on the Mobile App

The bar you see at the bottom of the screen contains various options that allow you to interact with design elements. If you swipe to the right on the bar, you'll see the same icons that represent *Undo* and *Redo* as in the desktop app. Use those icons whenever and as much as you need.

Pro Tip #1: The *Undo* and *Redo* functions only work on a per-session basis, and it does not have unlimited memory to go back to a design's previous state indefinitely. Every time you close Design Space, that memory disappears, which means you can't use *Undo* or *Redo* to go back to a previous state after reopening the program. The purpose of these functions is merely to give you a quick way to go backward and forward in the moment you make changes.

Pro Tip #2: Instead of using your mouse, you can apply the *Undo* and *Redo* functions using your keyboard with the following shortcuts:

Undo

• COMMAND + Z (CMD + Z) on a Mac and

• CONTROL + Z (CTRL + Z) on a Windows computer.

Redo

• COMMAND + SHIFT + Z (CMD + ↑ + Z) on a Mac and

• CONTROL + SHIFT + Z on a Windows computer (CTRL + ↑ + Z).

Zoom In and Out of the Canvas

Depending on how many elements you have on your Canvas, or how intricate your design is, you might find yourself needing to zoom in or out for a better perspective.

How To Zoom In and Out on the Desktop App

You'll see a semi-opaque *100* with a minus sign to its left and a plus sign to its right in the bottom-left corner of the Canvas. The minus sign allows you to zoom out of the Canvas, while the plus sign allows you to zoom in. Try it out to see how the view changes.

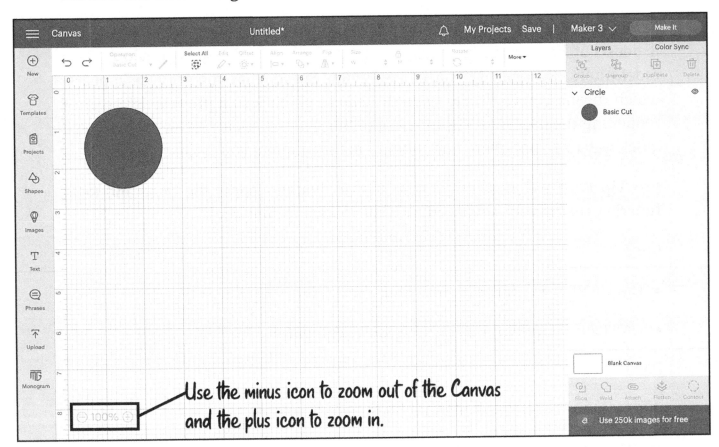

Use the minus icon to zoom out of the Canvas and the plus icon to zoom in.

How To Zoom In and Out on the Mobile App

The mobile app does not give you a percentage to show you how much in our out of the Canvas you are zoomed, but it doesn't really matter. The most important thing is the ability to move in when you need to make a detailed tweak and out when you feel like the Canvas is getting a little crowded. On a cell phone, you'll probably zoom out quite a bit, since the screen is so small.

To zoom in on the mobile app, place your thumb and index fingers against each other on the screen, kind of like you're going to pinch something, and push them away from each other. To zoom out, place your thumb and index fingers relatively far apart on the screen and drag them toward each other (again, kind of like you're going to pinch something).

Now you're ready to dive into the nitty-gritties of using each Design Space function! To limit your overwhelm while learning about everything you can achieve with the Canvas interface, the following chapters will each focus on just one part of the interface. Since the mobile version of Design Space cannot be broken up into parts like the desktop version, we'll cover the relevant mobile app functions as we work through the parts of the desktop app.

Note: If you only have a tablet or cell phone, I'd like to encourage you to work through the entire book instead of skimming for relevant bits. Skimming through will not give you the full learning experience, and you might miss out on important information.

See you in Chapter 2.

Self-Reflection

This exercise will be a fun walk down memory lane when you get to the end of the book. Better yet, it's going to help you see and appreciate the immense progress you have made later on. Take your time to answer the following questions and be as specific as possible—really dig deep into your thoughts and feelings!

How long have you been struggling with Design Space?

_____

_____

What is the one thing about Design Space that has been holding you back?

_____

_____

What do you *feel* when you think of Design Space right now?

_____

_____

_____

_____

What would it mean to you if you can conquer Design Space?

_____

_____

_____

_____

How confident are you that you can conquer Design Space? (Use a percentage or scale from 1–10 if it helps!)

_____

_____

Chapter 1 Notes

Use this space to jot down the best take-aways you learned from Chapter 1. Use these notes as your personal quick-reference guide whenever you want to refresh your memory ons something specific.

_____
_____
_____
_____
_____
_____
_____
_____
_____
_____
_____
_____
_____
_____
_____
_____
_____
_____
_____
_____
_____
_____
_____

Chapter 2
Let's Conquer the Design Panel

Unless you're working on a ready-to-make project that you opened via the Design Space library, every new project starts with help from the Design Panel when working on the **desktop app**. It's from here you will choose elements to work with to build your custom designs from scratch, or upload SVGs and other files from external sources.

The aim of this chapter is to teach you what each feature in the Design Panel does. By the time we get to the end of the chapter, you'll be free from any form of head-scratching and unwelcome feelings of nervousness when your eyes meet that left-hand panel.

Pro Tip: The Design Panel is accessible from the *My Projects/My Stuff* page, too. In fact, if you click on *Projects* in the Design Panel (third option from the top), the Design Panel will remain visible.

Let's get to know the Design Panel features, starting at the very top.

New

This option allows you to start working on a new, blank Canvas. If you click on *New* before saving the project you're working on currently on the **desktop app**, Design Space will prompt you to either save or discard it.

The **mobile app** does not have this option when you are working on the Canvas. To start something new, you will have to exit the Canvas interface and then tap on the plus icon at the bottom of the Home screen.

Exiting the Canvas on your mobile device while working on a design will not prompt you to save it. However, once you tap on that plus icon and you haven't saved the project, a pop-up box will appear, asking you whether you want to replace the current Canvas content. If you want to save it, tap on *Cancel* and go back to the Canvas by tapping on *Canvas* in the upper-right corner of the screen. When the Canvas screen opens, tap on the *Save* icon to the left of the *Make It* button at the top of the screen, name your project, and finally tap on *Save*. On the other hand, if you don't want to save whatever you were working on, tap the *Replace* button. This will immediately give you a blank Canvas on which you can start a new design.

Pro Tip #1: All the projects you save when working in the Canvas interface are accessible from the *My Projects/My Stuff* page in both the desktop and mobile versions of Design Space.

Pro Tip #2: If you have multiple devices you use for Design Space; for example, a laptop, a desktop computer, a tablet, and a cell phone, you can access projects you have saved from any of them as long as you're logged in to your Design Space account.

Templates

This feature is exclusive to the desktop app. Unlike other elements you add to the Canvas, your Cricut machine will not see templates as *design* elements. That is, it will not cut them out.

A template is merely visual aid to help you arrange design elements according to the shape of said template, so you can be sure you're creating the best design for the surface you want to apply it to.

Let's say you've bought an apron and its blandness bores you terribly. So, you switch on your Cricut machine and open Design Space to create something that will give the apron life. The first thing you want to do is measure the area on the apron where you'd like to put your design. Let's say you decide 4 by 4 inches will do the trick and you come up with a great design.

Now, before you hit that *Make It* button, you might find yourself wondering, *"Hm... I wonder if the way I did it will look good on the apron."*

That's when using a template will come in handy. Let's go to the Templates library to find a visual representation of an apron.

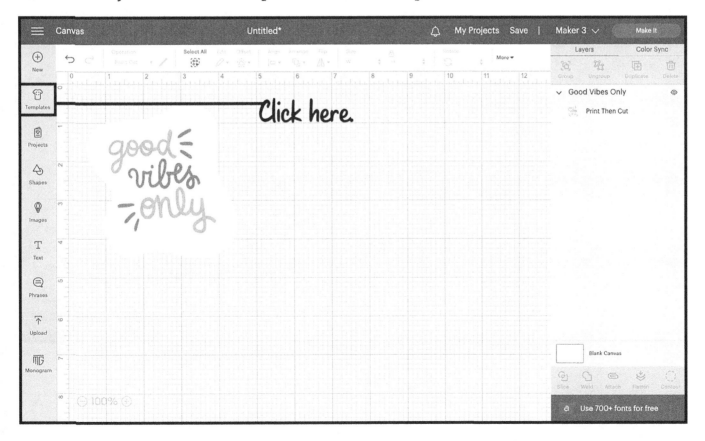

To find what you're looking for, you can scroll through the categories on the screen, or you can use the search bar in the upper-right corner of the screen. In this case, *Aprons* is the very first option, as the categories are alphabetized. When you click on *Aprons,* the program will take you back to the Canvas and display the template. Now you can play around with your design by placing it on the apron template to see if it will look good once you apply it.

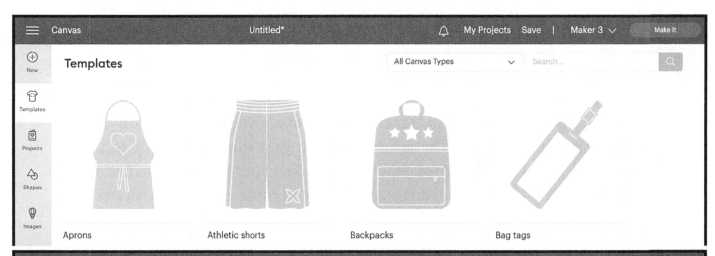

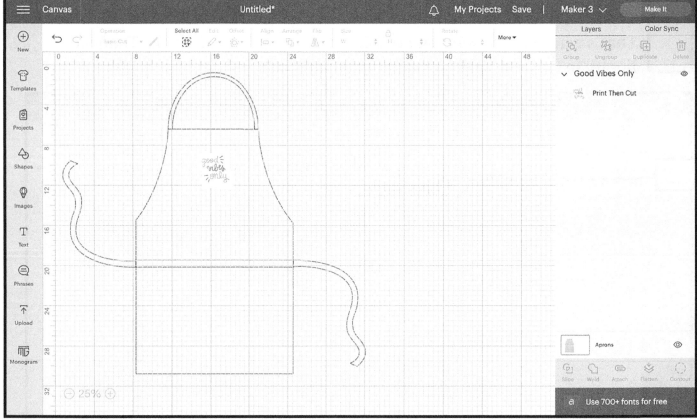

Pro Tip #1: Once you add a template to the Canvas, the Canvas will automatically zoom out so you can see the full template. When this happens, your design will look smaller. Remember that its actual size did not change, so there is no need to make it bigger.

Pro Tip #2: You cannot move the template around like you can design elements, and you cannot delete a template once you have added it to the Canvas. However, you can hide it so it's not visible, as shown in the illustrations below.

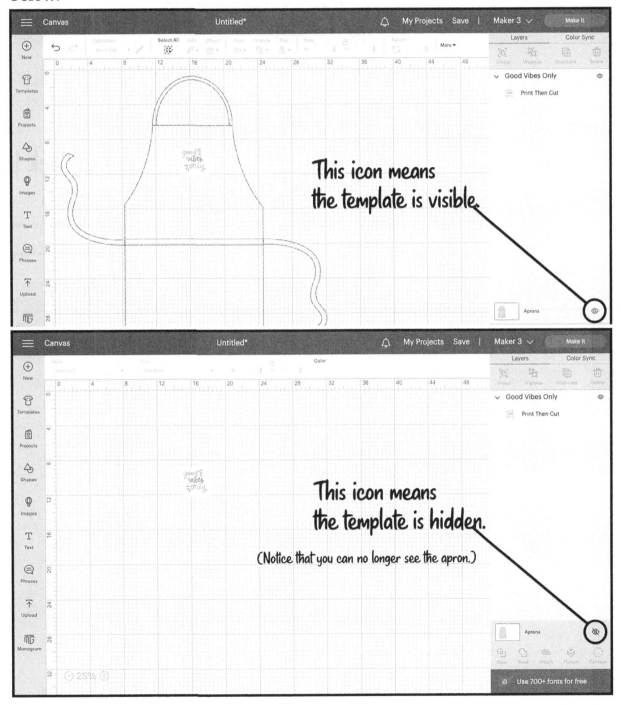

This icon means the template is visible.

This icon means the template is hidden.

(Notice that you can no longer see the apron.)

Pro Tip #3: If you click on the template layer at the bottom of the Layers Panel, the Edit Bar will change, allowing you to make some minor adjustments to the template, like changing the type of apron and its size.

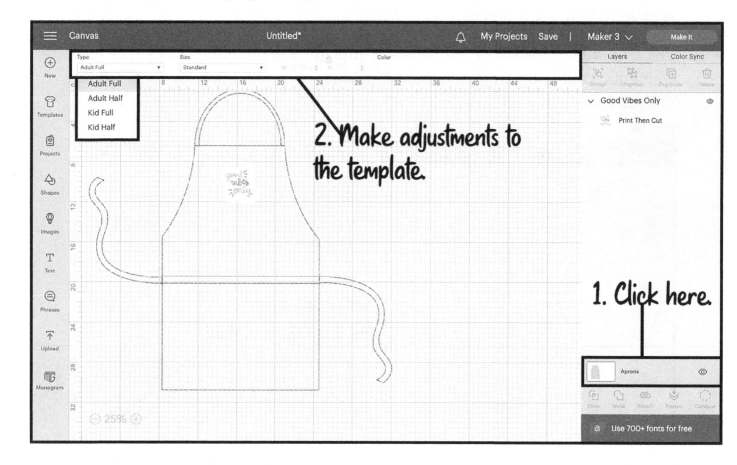

Projects

The Projects library contains the same assets you can access from the Home screen when looking for ready-to-make projects. When you open the Projects library from the Canvas, the default view will show you *All Categories.*

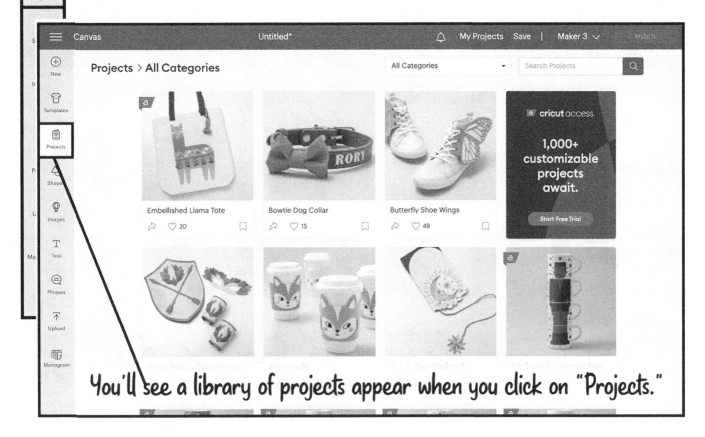

You'll see a library of projects appear when you click on "Projects."

You can also access your own projects (that is, designs you have saved previously) from here. Click on *All Categories,* and choose the very first option, *My Projects/My Stuff,* like you see in the illustrations on the next page.

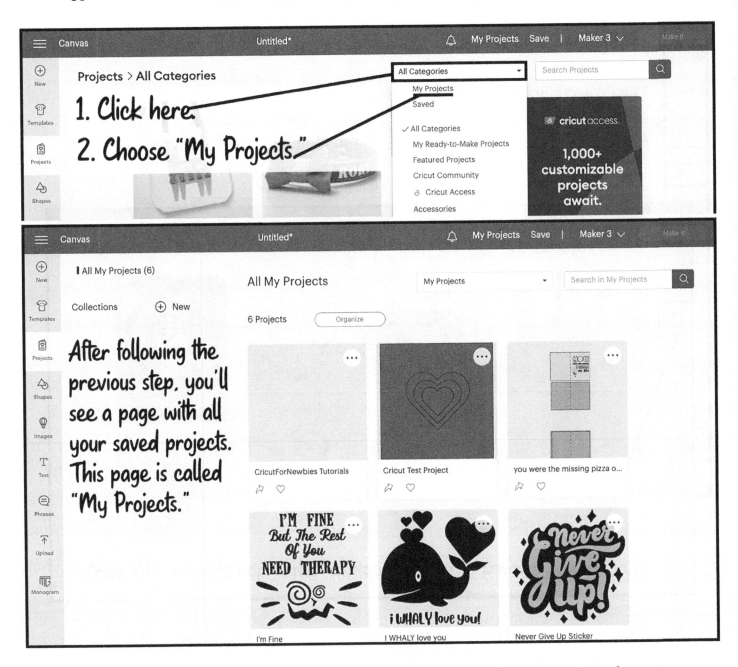

You won't find the Projects option on your mobile app's Canvas interface. To use ready-to-make projects on the mobile app, you'll need to search for something you'd like to do using the method we talked about in Chapter 1's *How to Search for a Ready-to-Make Project* and *How to Open a Ready-to-Make Project* sections. Personally, I find the *Projects* feature on the desktop app's Canvas interface a bit redundant, as I almost never use it. If you open Design Space and want to use a ready-to-make project, you can start your search immediately by simply scrolling (as opposed to opening the Canvas first and then searching for something).

Pro Tip #1: Projects are useful in the sense that they're literally ready to go. It's as easy as adding one to the Canvas and then hitting that *Make It* button. Although you can tweak those designs before cutting them, I wouldn't recommend it when you're just starting out. The saying, "Don't fix it if it's not broken," comes to mind!

Pro Tip #2: Projects come with useful instructions when you click or tap on them. Be sure to read through those before adding it to your Canvas so you know what you're getting yourself into.

Pro Tip #3: Most ready-to-make projects come with a price tag, so watch out for that. If you don't have a Cricut Access subscription or don't want to pay the once-off fee to use the project, refine your search by choosing the *Free* category when searching for projects to make.

Shapes

Shapes are surprisingly versatile and useful when creating designs from scratch. As you gain experience, you'll find yourself using them for almost all the creative ideas keeping you up at night. Design Space comes with a decent set of basic, free shapes you can use as much as you want to. In fact, we're going to play with them a lot as we get into the exercises in the coming chapters. With a Cricut Access subscription, you have more options to choose from; but as a Newbie, the basic shapes will take you quite far.

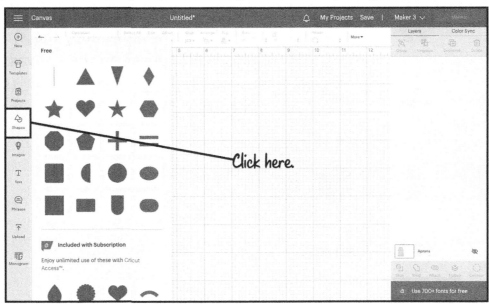

When you click on the shape you want, Design Space will add it to your Canvas.

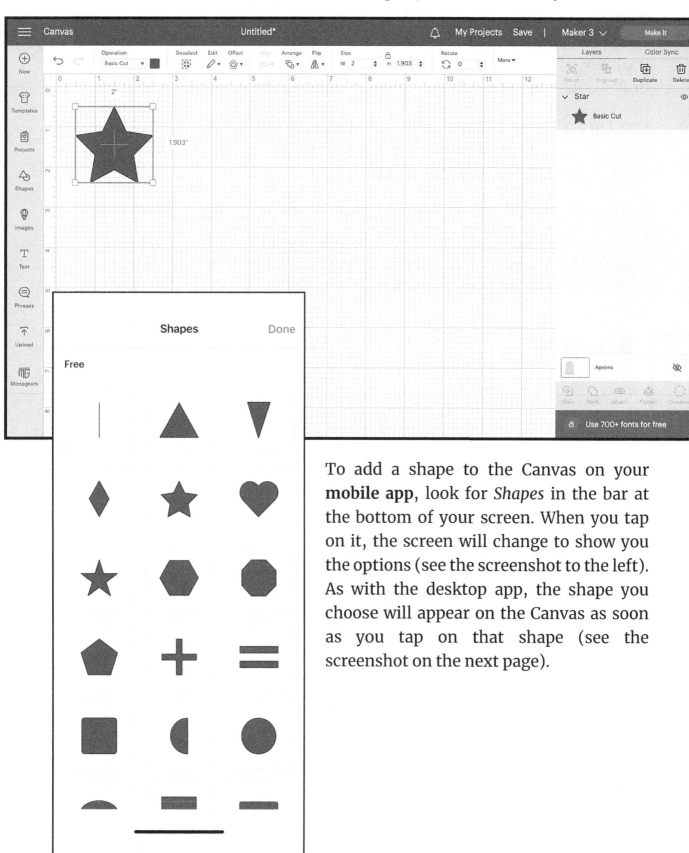

To add a shape to the Canvas on your **mobile app**, look for *Shapes* in the bar at the bottom of your screen. When you tap on it, the screen will change to show you the options (see the screenshot to the left). As with the desktop app, the shape you choose will appear on the Canvas as soon as you tap on that shape (see the screenshot on the next page).

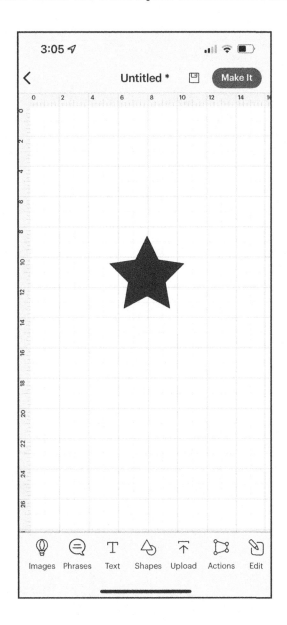

Images

The Images library contains all kinds of custom artworks you can incorporate into your design. Typically, when you activate the Images library by clicking on it, the first thing you will see is a lot of standard shapes. But scroll down, and you'll discover a treasure trove of designs. Of course, if you know what you're looking for, you can type in a keyword or phrase into the search bar and click on the search icon.

On the **desktop app,** click on *Images.* When the Images library opens, you'll see a panel to the left with useful filters. With these filters, you can tell Design space whether you're looking for single or multi-layer images, whether you're looking for designs to Cut, Draw, or Print Then Cut, and so on.

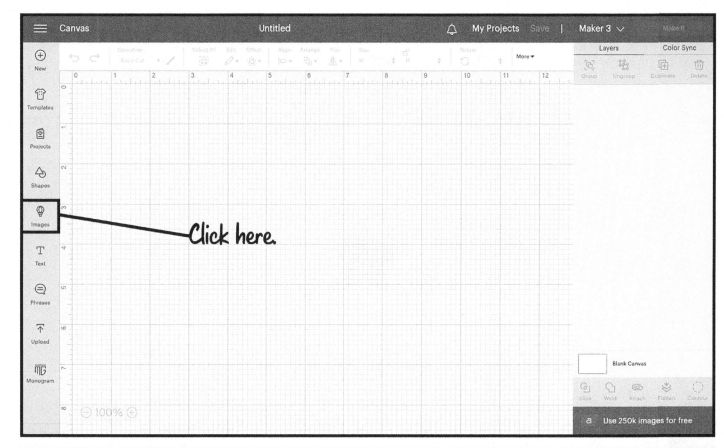

Click here.

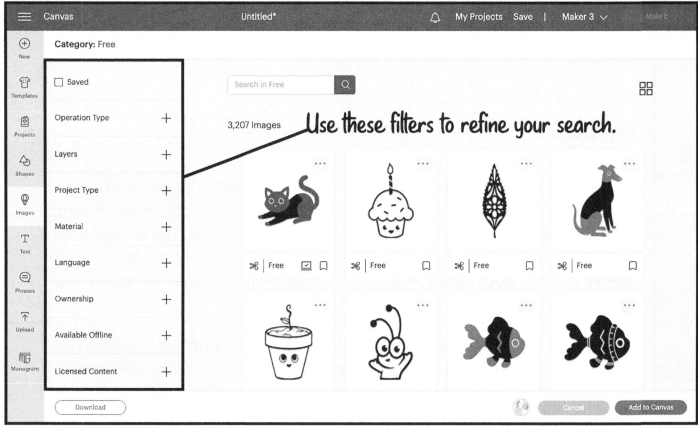

Use these filters to refine your search.

On the **mobile app**, you can activate the Images library from the bar at the bottom of the screen by tapping on *Images*. Here, too, you can refine the results by tapping on the filters icon in the top-right underneath the search bar.

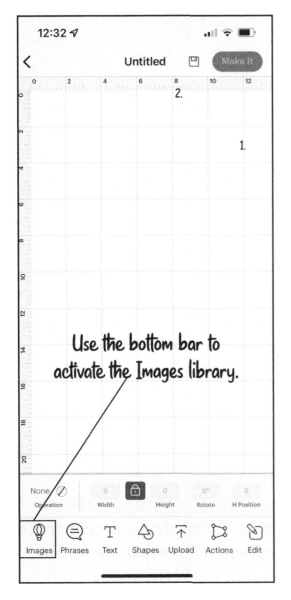

Like the Projects library, the Images library contains free and premium designs. You can access the premium designs via your Cricut Access subscription or buy them once-off.

Pro Tip: Don't let projects and images confuse you—they're not the same thing. You may say projects contain images, but images are not projects. Projects will give you information, telling you exactly what the design was made for, what you need to do the project, and how to assemble the parts after the cutting process. Images, on the other hand, are standalone design elements and do not have a specific purpose. Unlike projects, they're not ready to go, and you still have to add other elements to the canvas, get your sizing right, and so on.

Text

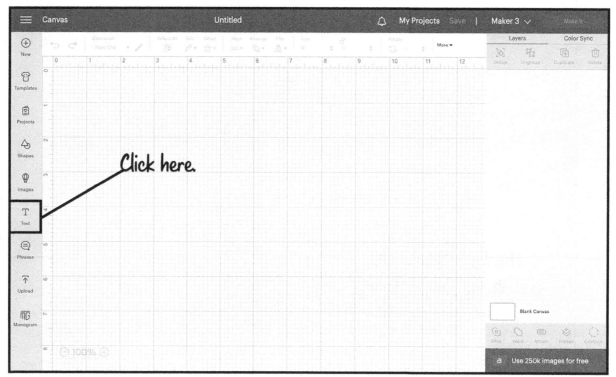

When you click on *Text* Design Space will add a text element to the Canvas for you. Initially, it just reads "Text." I know—super creative, right? With the text element selected on the **desktop app**, you'll see text-specific options appear underneath the standard Edit Bar options at the top of the screen.

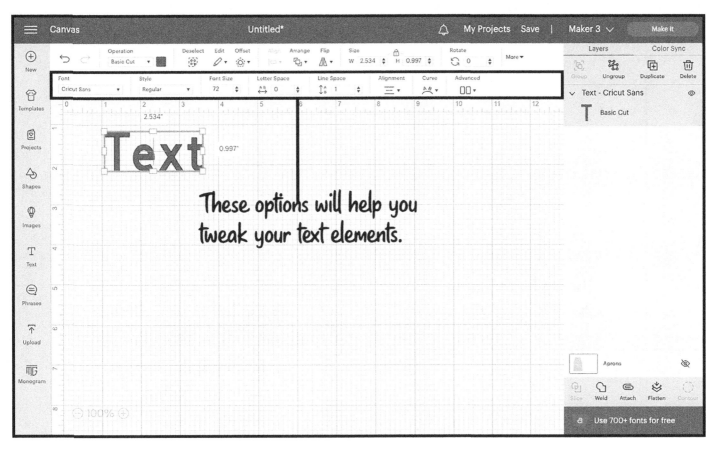

These options will help you tweak your text elements.

On the **mobile app**, you'll tap on "Text" in the bar at the bottom of the screen (see the left-hand illustration on the next page). The moment you do that, the element will appear on the Canvas and activate your device's keypad so you can edit the text. For now, just tap anywhere on the Canvas area to make the keypad disappear. Select the text element by tapping on it. To find the text-specific options mentioned above, find *Edit* in the bottom bar and tap on it. This will activate a secondary bar on top of the regular one, which shows those options (see the right-hand illustration on the next page).

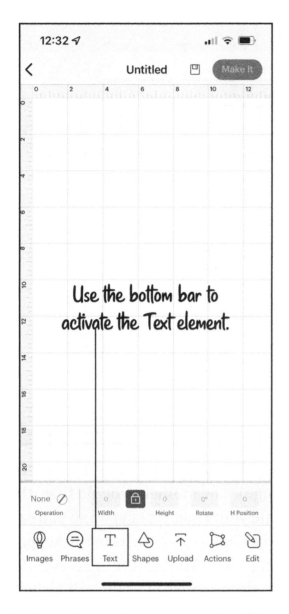

Let's explore what you can do with a text element in Design Space.

Choose Fonts via the Font Menu

In Design Space, you have a choice between Cricut fonts and System fonts for text elements. The benefit of using Cricut fonts is that you know for a fact they'll work perfectly with your Cricut machine. In other words, no unexpected hiccups will pop up. That said, you should—for the most part—not experience issues with the fonts installed on your laptop or computer, either.

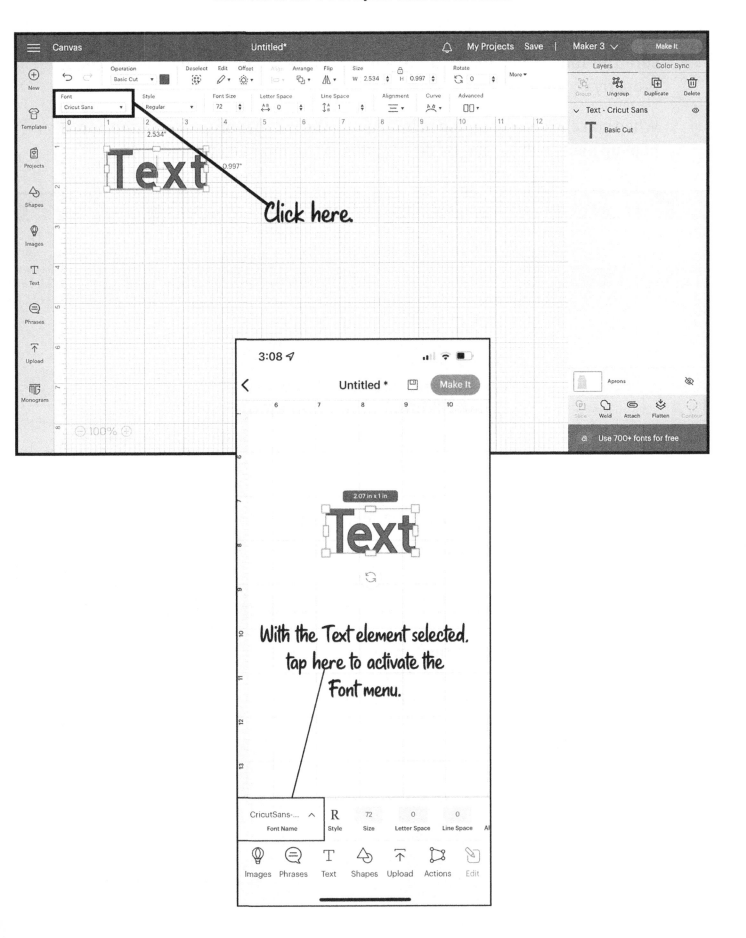

Click here.

With the Text element selected, tap here to activate the Font menu.

Pro Tip: If you want to use a font installed on your device for a Cut project, make sure the font is not too thin, as your machine might not be able to cut it properly.

When you click on the option below *Font* in the Edit bar on your **desktop app**, a pop-up menu will appear. By default, this menu shows you Cricut fonts.

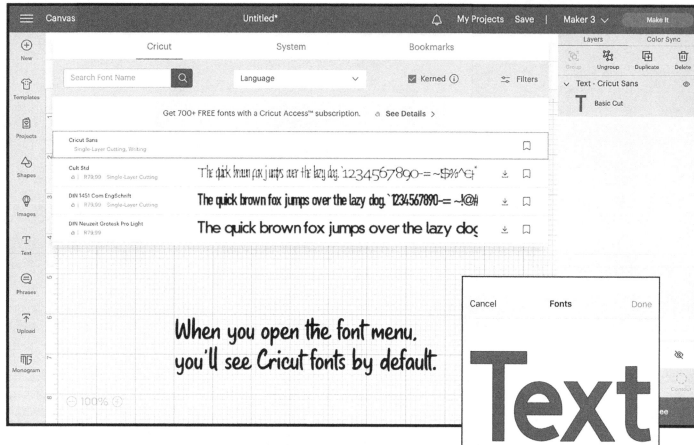

Likewise, when you tap on the first option of the text options on your **mobile device** (where it normally says "Cricut Sans" with "Font name" underneath it), the app will take you to a screen with Cricut font options.

Cricut offers free and premium fonts. As with all their design elements, you can use premium fonts if you have a Cricut Access subscription, or you can buy single fonts once-off. Fonts are pricey, so if you use them a lot, having Cricut Access just for that reason is well worth it.

If you want to see all Cricut fonts, untick the box next to *Kerned*. Kerned fonts use optimal spacing between individual letters for printing purposes, but it's not a necessity. If you're a perfectionist, keep this option activated. Otherwise, turn it off, especially when looking for free Cricut fonts!

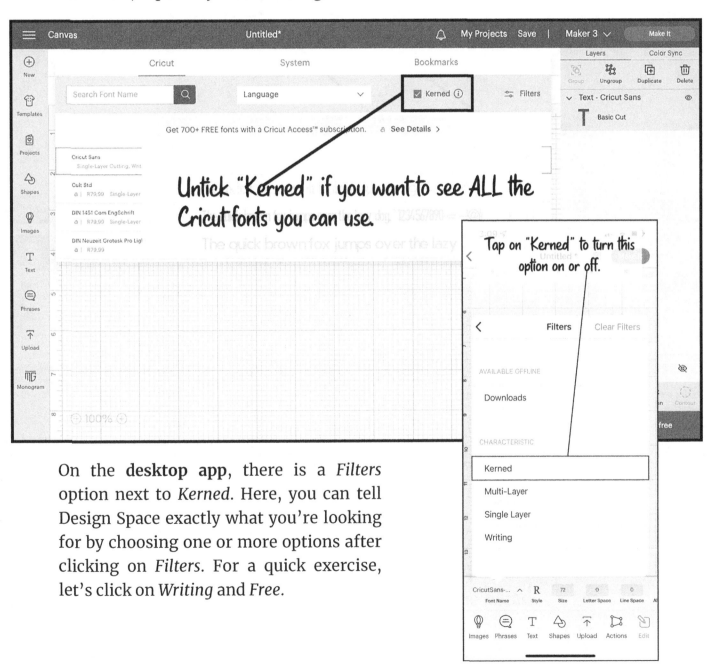

On the **desktop app**, there is a *Filters* option next to *Kerned*. Here, you can tell Design Space exactly what you're looking for by choosing one or more options after clicking on *Filters*. For a quick exercise, let's click on *Writing* and *Free*.

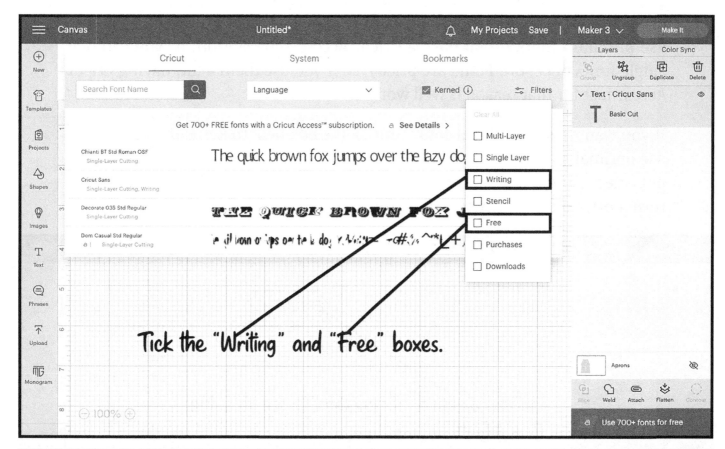

Tick the "Writing" and "Free" boxes.

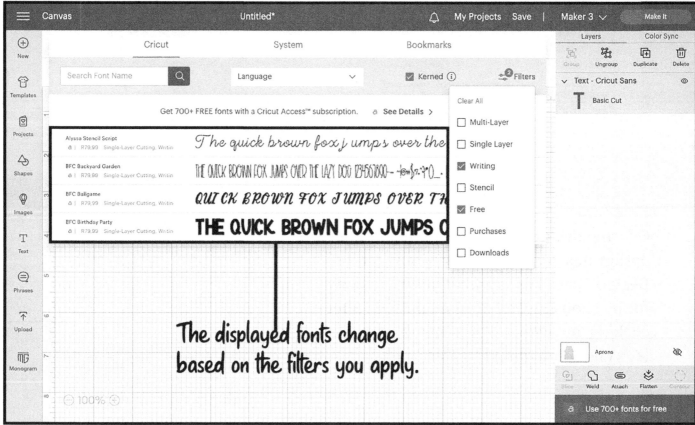

The displayed fonts change
based on the filters you apply.

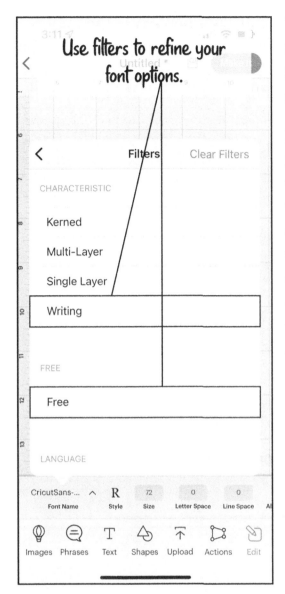

You can achieve the same results on your **mobile app** by tapping on the "Filters" icon in the top-right corner of the screen and applying the same filters as above.

Pro Tip: Different projects require different fonts. For example, you don't want to use a writing font for a Cut project, and vice versa. Writing fonts are perfect for your Cricut's Draw function, which allows it to write out or draw shapes and images using Cricut Pens, but they're way too thin and delicate to cut out. So, always be mindful of the type of project you're working on when choosing a font for your design.

Now, let's say you're not connecting with any of the Cricut fonts, and you really, really want to use that amazing font you downloaded the other day, because it's perfect for your latest project idea.

All you have to do is switch from *Cricut* to *System* in the font menu, which you'll see right next to *Cricut* at the top of the menu in your **desktop app,** like you see in the first illustration on the next page.

With *System Fonts,* you don't have the option to show or hide kerned fonts, and you can't apply filters, either. However, if you know the name of the font you want to use, simply type it into the search bar in the top-left corner of the font menu.

Pro Tip: If one of your fonts isn't showing a preview in the font menu, it means that Design Space has identified a possible compatibility issue with that font, and the program is subtly telling you not to use it. You can try, but chances are it will either do some weird stuff or not work at all. So, when searching for fonts to use, try your best to find Cricut-friendly fonts. (See the second illustration below.)

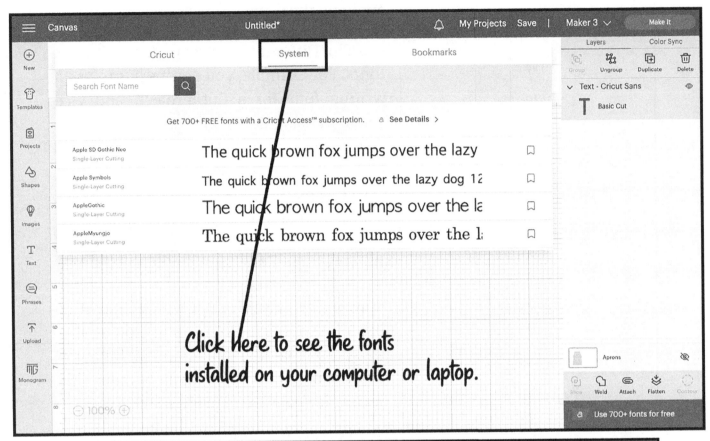

Click here to see the fonts installed on your computer or laptop.

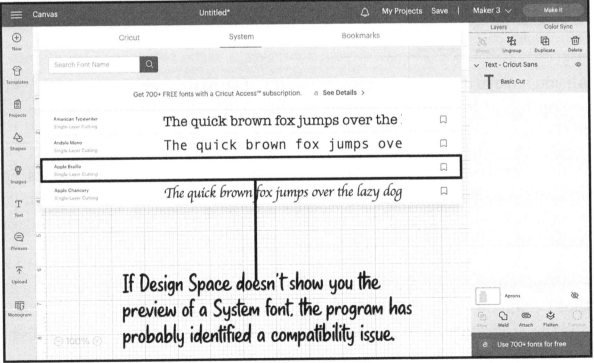

If Design Space doesn't show you the preview of a System font, the program has probably identified a compatibility issue.

If you have an iPad or Apple iPhone, you will be able to access system fonts on your mobile app, too. To see the system fonts, open the Font menu and choose *System*.

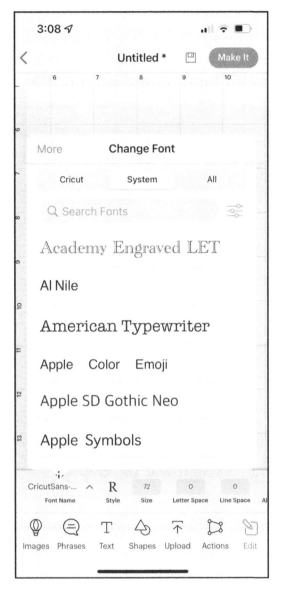

Pro Tip: If you have an Android cell phone, you'll be able to see pre-installed system fonts. However, to use custom fonts that you downloaded from the internet requires a workaround. In my book, *Cricut for Newbies*, I take you through the entire process of using that workaround step-by-step. The book also covers how to download and use custom fonts in your Design Space app for iOS devices.

The last thing about the font menu you may find useful is the *Bookmarks* option. When viewing *Cricut* and *System* fonts, you'll see a little label to the right of each font. Hover over it, and you'll see a little tooltip appear that says, "Bookmark."

If you click on that label, you're basically telling Design Space, *"This is a favorite for me!"* and it will store that font in the *Bookmarks* section for you. Now, whenever you need one of your favorite fonts, you can simply go to the *Bookmarks* option in the font menu, which is the option next to *System* on your desktop app. When you're just starting out, Design Space will have nothing to show you.

Pro Tip #1: Resist the urge to bookmark every font you fall in love with, otherwise you're defeating the object of the *Bookmarks* section! The idea is to have quick access to fonts you know you'll use almost every single time you open Design Space to create a project so you don't have to spend your precious time searching for them among the hundreds (sometimes thousands!) of options.

Pro Tip #2: The Bookmarks section is device-specific for *System* fonts. In other words, if you bookmark a *System* font installed on your iPhone, don't expect to see it when you click on *Bookmarks* when working on your computer, and vice versa. However, you'll have access to all the Cricut fonts you bookmark on any device, since they're stored on the cloud and not your device.

The *Bookmarks* section is not available on iOS or Android mobile devices yet.

Specify Your Font's Style

Style refers to the characteristics of the font you choose, like whether you want it to display bold, italic, or perhaps bold italic. The available style options depend on the font itself, so you won't see the same options for all fonts. For the most part, your options will be:

- Regular
- **Bold**
- *Italic*
- ***Bold Italic***

Pro Tip: Some Cricut fonts have a special style called *Writing*, which will work perfectly for projects that require a Cricut Pen to write or draw something.

On your **desktop app**, the *Style* option is right next to the *Font* option in the Edit Bar. The options will appear when you click on *Style*.

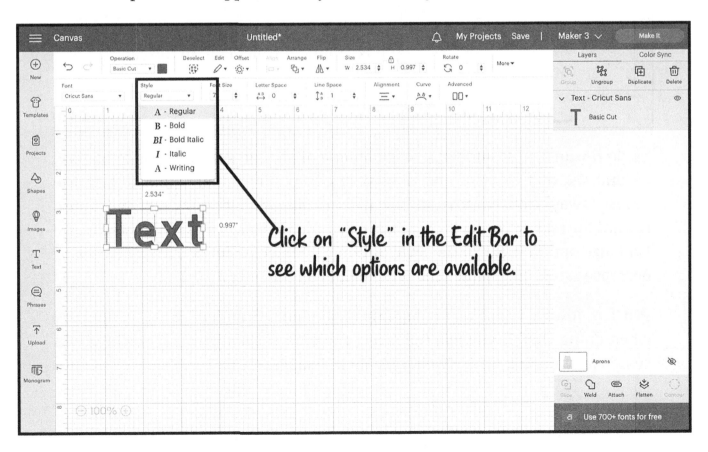

Click on "Style" in the Edit Bar to see which options are available.

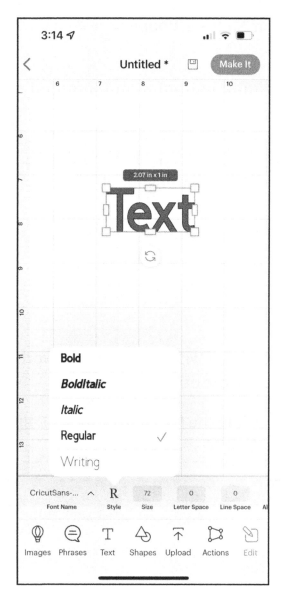

On your **mobile app**, the *Style* option is also right next to the *Font* option. Tap on it to see the available options.

Adjust Your Text's Size

You can make a text element bigger or smaller with this setting. How big or small you make it depends on the design you're working on. For example, the text for a t-shirt will be smaller than the text for a porch sign.

To adjust a text element's size, you have two options:

Option 1:

Resize it proportionally using the selection box around the element on the canvas.

To do this on the **desktop app**, click on one of the corners of the selection box around the text element and drag your computer's mouse. If you drag the mouse 'away' from the text, its size will increase, and if you 'push' the mouse toward the text, its size will decrease. As you do this, notice that the value in the *Font Size* option (next to the *Style* option we talked about above) increases or decreases accordingly. (See the screenshots on the next page.)

Pro Tip: Always resize text using one of the four corners of the selection box when doing this. If you use the sides, the element's alignment settings will switch to wrapping, which we'll talk about in a bit.

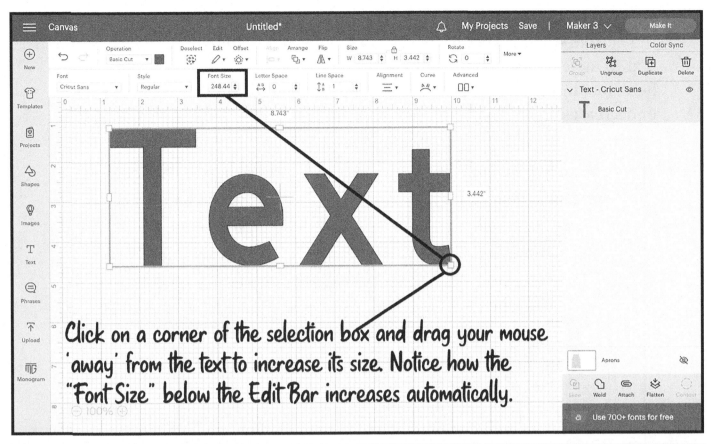

Click on a corner of the selection box and drag your mouse 'away' from the text to increase its size. Notice how the "Font Size" below the Edit Bar increases automatically.

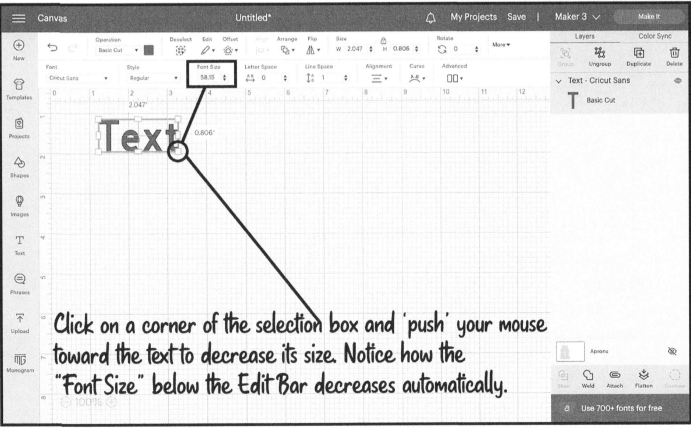

Click on a corner of the selection box and 'push' your mouse toward the text to decrease its size. Notice how the "Font Size" below the Edit Bar decreases automatically.

To resize a text element proportionally on your **mobile app**, tap and hold on to the bottom-right corner of its selection box while 'dragging' away from the text to increase its size or 'pushing' toward it to decrease its size. Notice that here, too, the information in the Size box at the bottom of the screen increases or decreases accordingly.

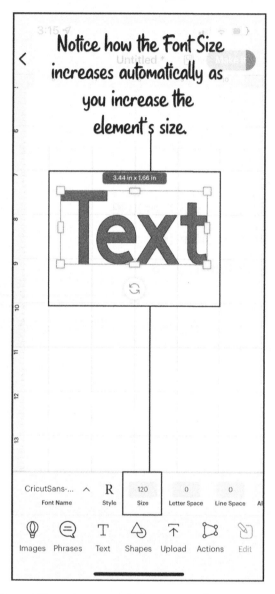 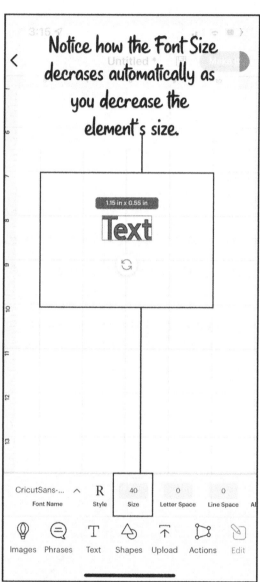

Pro Tip: Be careful not to decrease your text element too much on the mobile app with this method, as doing so can actually deactivate its proportional constraints and leave you with a weird-lookin' word.

Option 2:

Using the *Font Size* box right next to the *Style* option on your **desktop app**, enter the value you want. The larger the value, the larger your text will be; and the lower the value, the smaller your text will be.

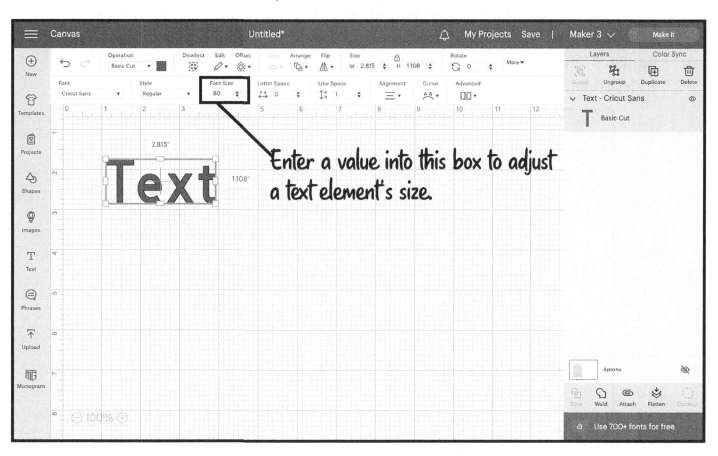

On the mobile app, you'll find the *Font Size* box next to the Alignment option in that secondary edit bar at the bottom of the screen. Tap on the little box above *Size* and enter the value you want. (See the two screenshots on the next page.)

Good to Know

If you are familiar with Photoshop or a similar program, you might think of a text *box* when working with the text element in Design Space.

However, the text element you find in Design Space works totally different from a text box you might find in other design programs. With Design Space's text element, you cannot adjust the size of the selection box around the text element without affecting the size of the text itself. If you make the text smaller, the selection box around the text will shrink with it; and if you make the text bigger, the selection box around the text will grow with it. Likewise, if you make the selection box around the text element smaller or bigger, the text will shrink or grow with the selection box.

Point in case: the text element and the selection box around it are one and the same thing in Design Space, whereas a text *box* in other design programs can be adjusted independently of the text, and the text's size can be adjusted independently of the text *box*.

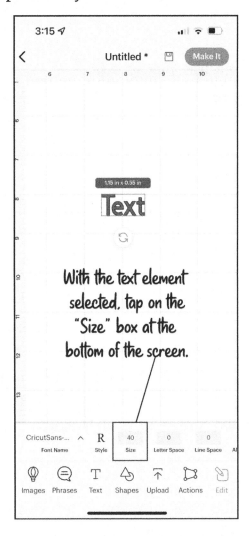

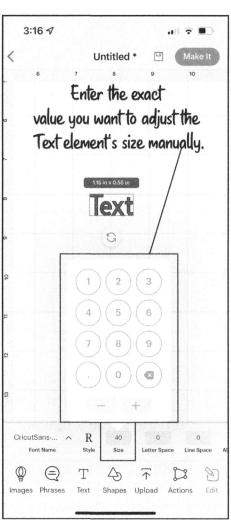

Adjust Your Text's Letter Spacing

Sometimes, you end up in situations where you wish the spacing between a word's letters was just a teeny bit bigger, or maybe a lot bigger, or even a lot smaller! Well, Design Space has your back. With the *Letter Spacing* option, you can control how far away or near to each other the individual letters in a word should be. The *Letter Spacing* settings are next to the *Font Size* settings in the Edit Bar on your **desktop app**.

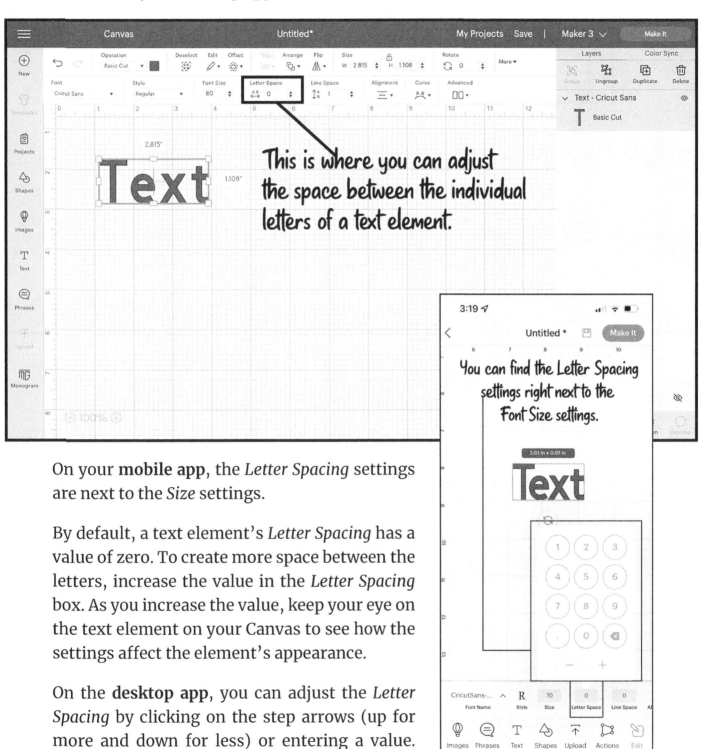

On your **mobile app**, the *Letter Spacing* settings are next to the *Size* settings.

By default, a text element's *Letter Spacing* has a value of zero. To create more space between the letters, increase the value in the *Letter Spacing* box. As you increase the value, keep your eye on the text element on your Canvas to see how the settings affect the element's appearance.

On the **desktop app**, you can adjust the *Letter Spacing* by clicking on the step arrows (up for more and down for less) or entering a value. First, let's increase the *Letter Spacing*.

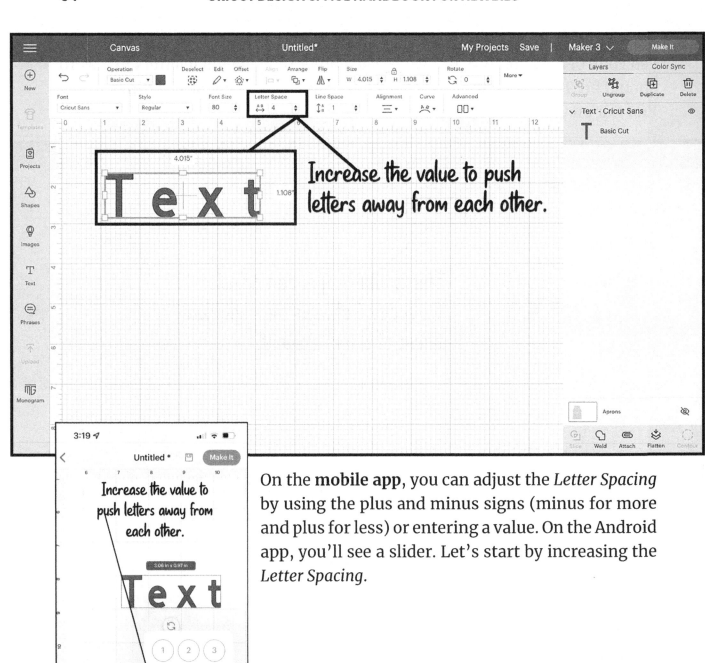

Increase the value to push letters away from each other.

Increase the value to push letters away from each other.

On the **mobile app**, you can adjust the *Letter Spacing* by using the plus and minus signs (minus for more and plus for less) or entering a value. On the Android app, you'll see a slider. Let's start by increasing the *Letter Spacing*.

To bring the letters closer to each other, decrease the value in the *Letter Spacing* box. You don't have to stop at zero—decrease it even more to see how it affects your text element's appearance.

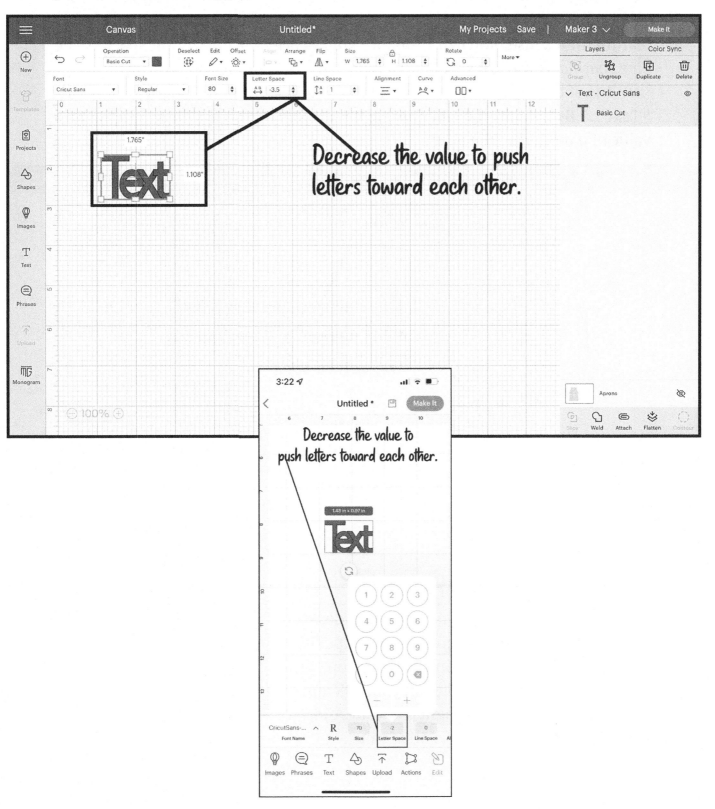

Adjust Your Text's Line Spacing

Depending on the look and feel you're trying to create with a design, you may want more or less space between lines of text, which makes this a handy feature. In a sense, you can think of *Letter Spacing* as horizontal spacing and *Line Spacing* as vertical spacing. To illustrate how *Line Spacing* works, I'll add a new line of text to my Canvas. I'll call the first line "Text 1" and the second line "Text 2." By default, the *Line Spacing* has a value of 1 on the desktop app and a value of 0 on the mobile app.

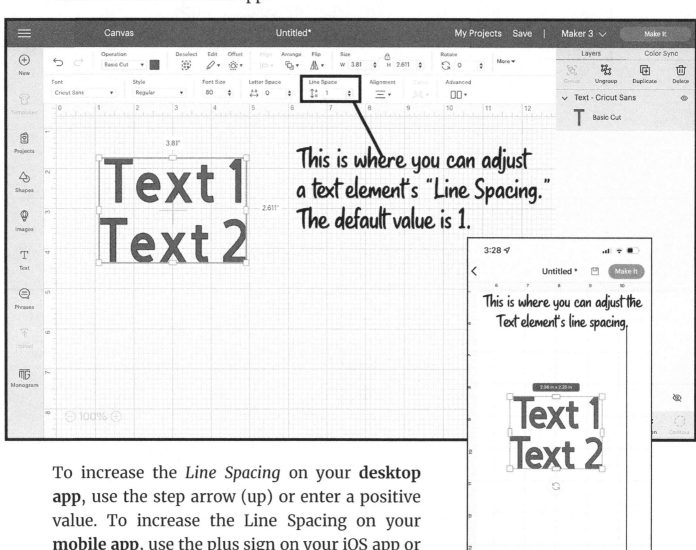

To increase the *Line Spacing* on your **desktop app**, use the step arrow (up) or enter a positive value. To increase the Line Spacing on your **mobile app**, use the plus sign on your iOS app or the slider (move it to the right) on your Android app. Alternatively, enter a positive value.

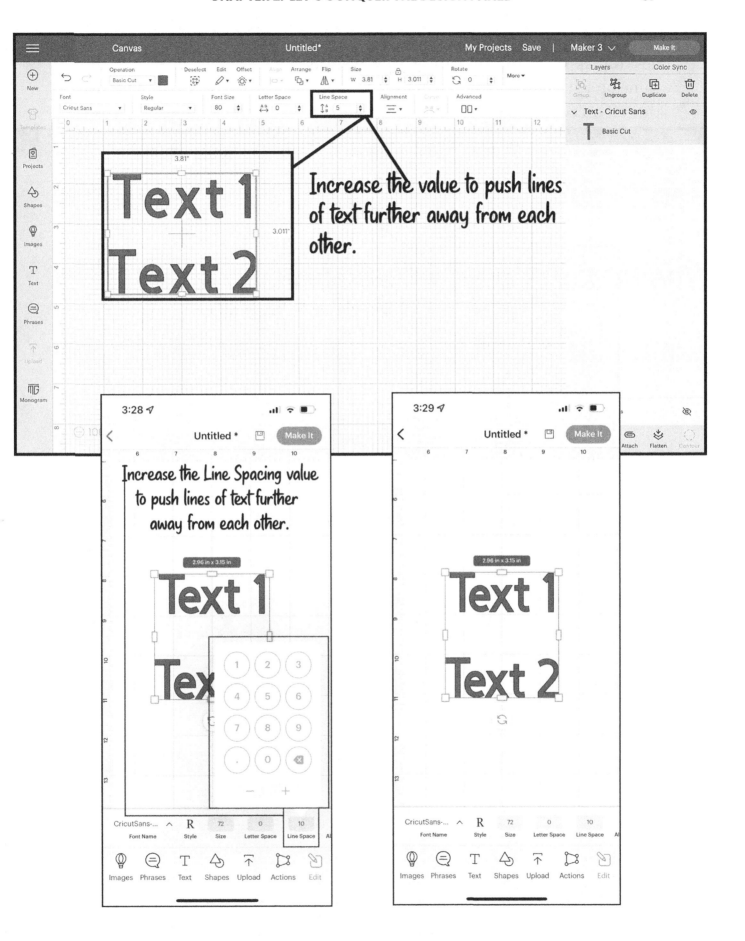

Increase the value to push lines of text further away from each other.

Increase the Line Spacing value to push lines of text further away from each other.

To bring lines of text closer to each other with the *Line Spacing* settings on your **desktop app**, use the step arrow (down) or enter a negative value. To do the same on your **mobile app**, use minus sign on the iOS app or move the slider to the left on your Android app. Alternatively, enter a negative value in the box.

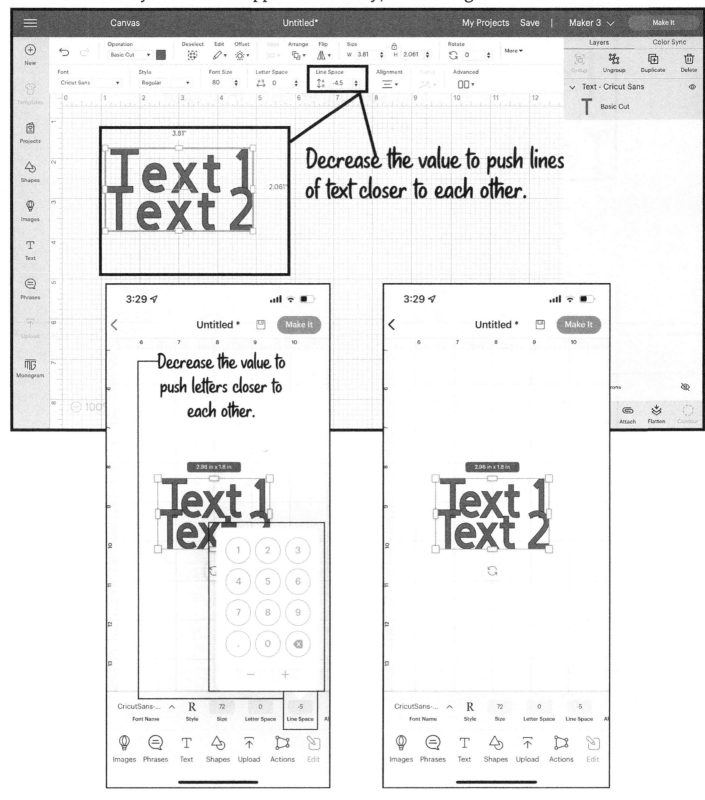

Adjust Your Text's Alignment

The *Alignment* options are next to the *Line Spacing* settings on the **desktop app**, and next to the Style options on the **mobile app**.

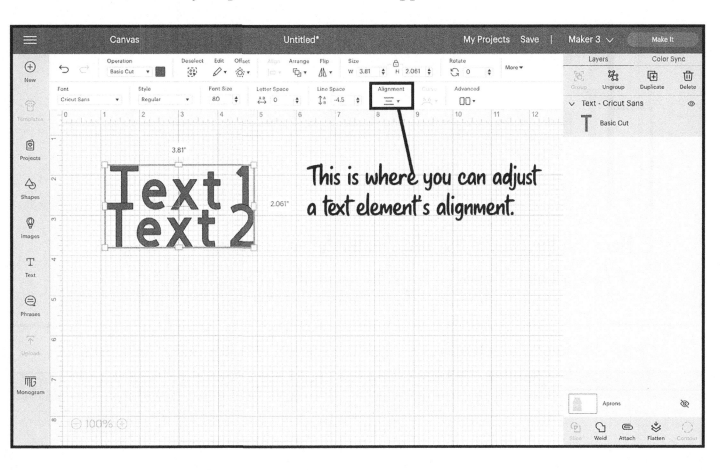

This is where you can adjust a text element's alignment.

The *Alignment* settings tell Design Space how you want lines of text within a single text element to align relative to each other. To demonstrate this feature, I'll add some more text to my text element. Next to "Text 2," I'll add "Text 3." Then I'll hit ENTER on my keyboard to add another line of text, which I'll call "Text 4."

There are three basic *Alignment* options to choose from on the **desktop app**. They are:

Left Alignment, which makes sure all the lines of text line up on the left side.

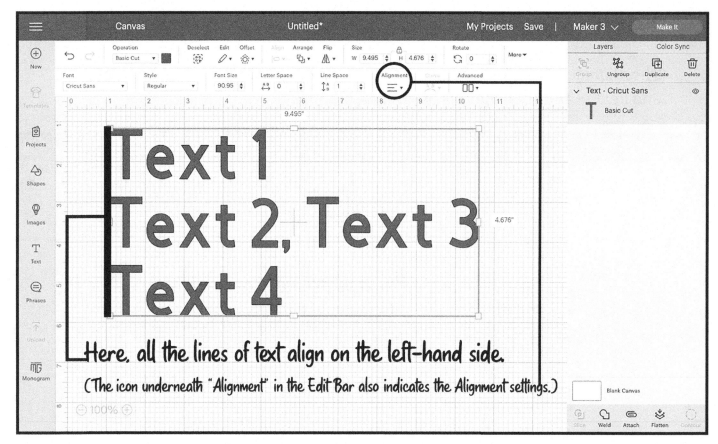

Center Alignment, which makes sure all the lines of text line up in the center.

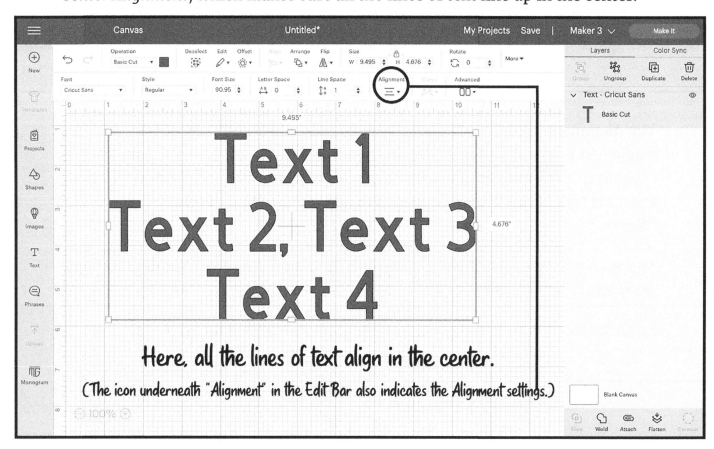

Right Alignment, which makes sure all the lines of text line up on the right side.

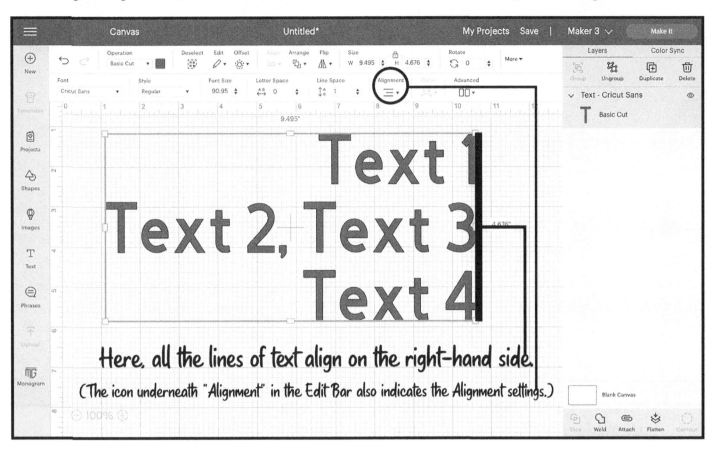

Here, all the lines of text align on the right-hand side.
(The icon underneath "Alignment" in the Edit Bar also indicates the Alignment settings.)

Pro Tip: This *Alignment* option works for individual text elements only and influences the text lines of the selected text element. Don't confuse it with the Edit Bar's *Alignment* function, which controls how multiple design elements on the Canvas line up relative to each other. We'll explore this function a bit later.

The desktop app has other *Text Alignment* options that have to do with how a single line of text flows inside the selection box that surrounds it. If you click on any of the four sides of a text element's selection box and move the pointer away from or toward the text, you'll automatically activate the program's *text wrapping*, which basically makes the text flow according to how wide or narrow you make the selection box. For this example. I'll delete my additional text lines, "Text 2," "Text 3," and "Text 4," leaving us with "Text 1" only. Now I'll grab the text element's right side by clicking on it and then 'pushing' toward the text. See how the letters get pushed onto new lines:

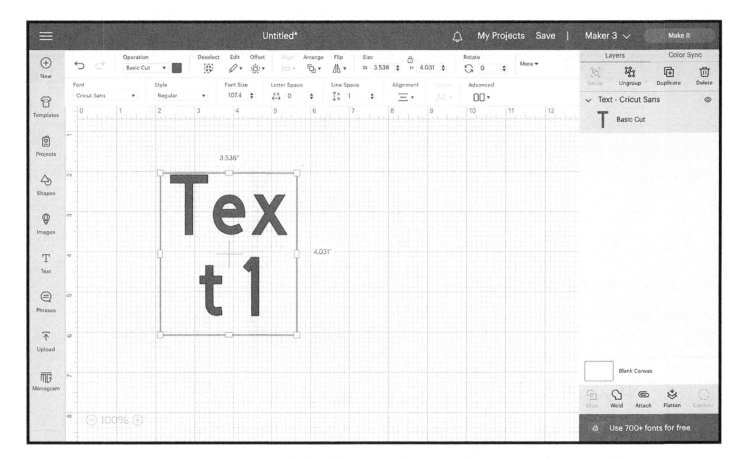

So, how does text wrapping differ from just hitting the ENTER button when you want to push letters or words onto separate lines?

For one, it's very quick and convenient if you want a word in your design to display vertically instead of horizontally; just keep pushing until all the letters sit nicely underneath each other. (See the first screenshot on the next page.)

From there, you can still apply the *Line Spacing* settings to bring the letters closer to each other or push them away from each other even further, or even apply the standard *Alignment* settings to align the letters left, right, or center.

Let's see how text wrapping differs from manually creating lines of text when dealing with more than one word. I'll add "Text 2," "Text 3," and "Text 4" to my text element again, but this time I'll write them all on the same line, like you see in the second screenshot on the next page.

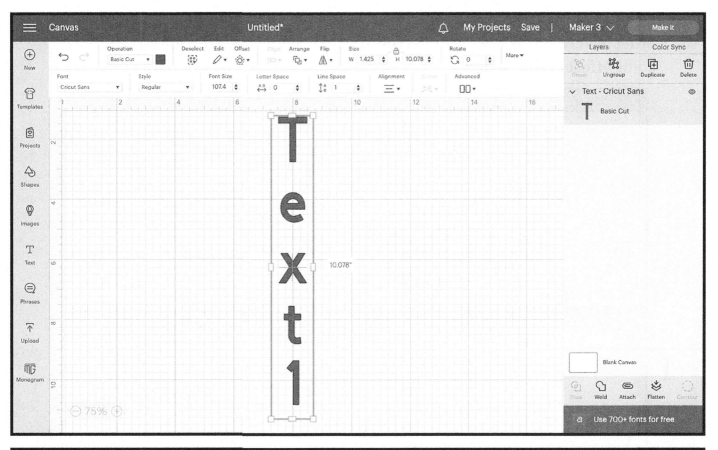

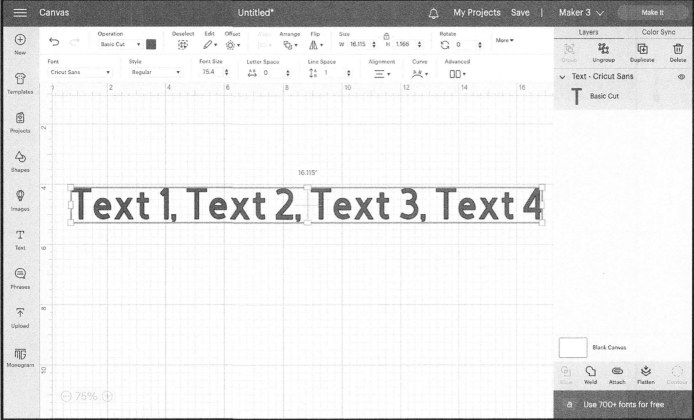

Now, when I activate text wrapping, I can control how the words stack on each other by how much I widen or narrow the text element's selection box. Here are some effects I can create:

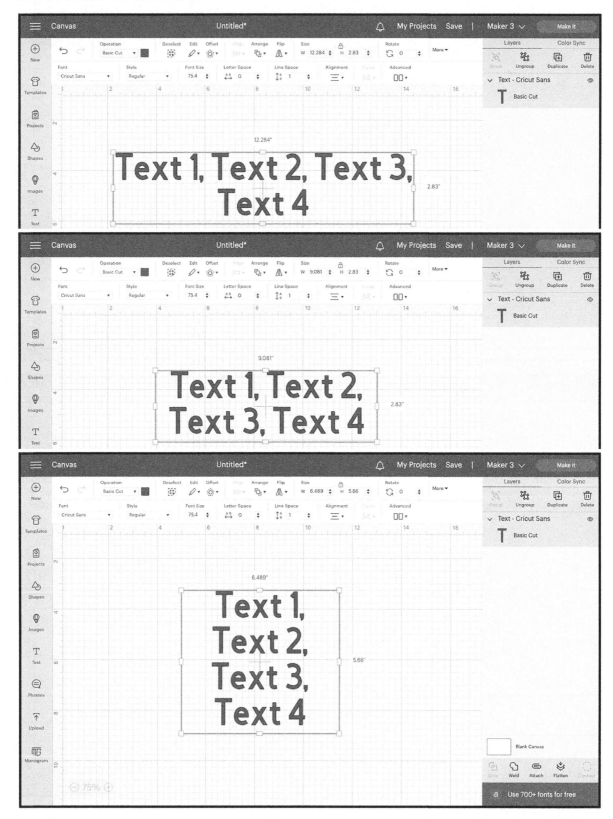

I think, if you're not sure where you want to take your design idea just yet, this feature is useful for playing around until you get that "aha!" moment.

Before we look at the *Alignment* options on the mobile app, I want to show you that you can see whether text wrapping is active for your text element when you click on *Alignment* in the Text Edit Bar above the Canvas.

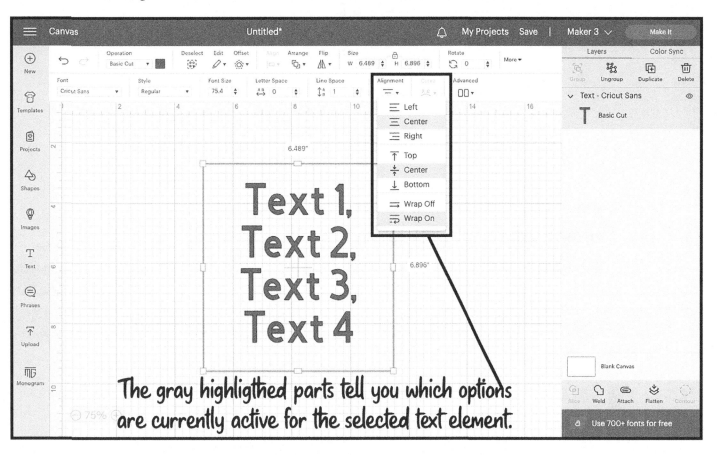

If you were playing with ideas and don't like the direction things are headed in, simply click on the second last option, *Wrap Off,* to reset the text element. (See the first screenshot on the next page.)

Finally, the settings you see in the middle, *Top*, *Center*, and *Bottom* tell Design Space how you want the text to behave within the selection box when the text wrapping is activated.

Top will push the very top line of text to the top of the selection box. (See the second screenshot on the next page.)

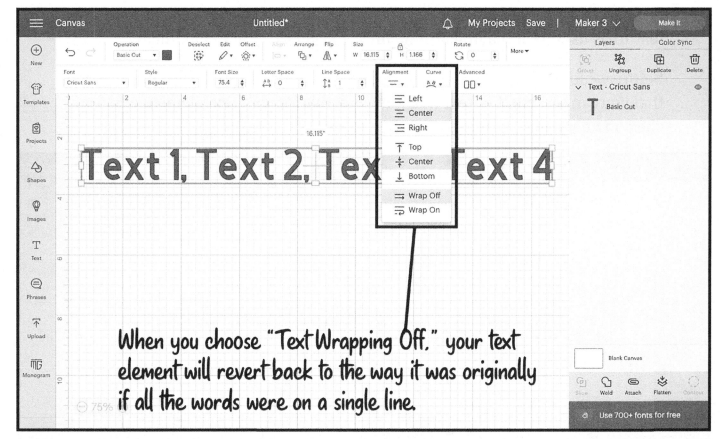

When you choose "Text Wrapping Off," your text element will revert back to the way it was originally if all the words were on a single line.

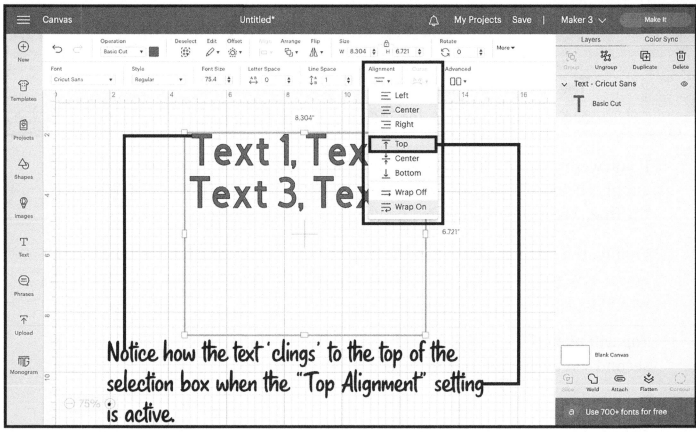

Notice how the text 'clings' to the top of the selection box when the "Top Alignment" setting is active.

Center will create an equal amount of space above the first line of text and the last line of text.

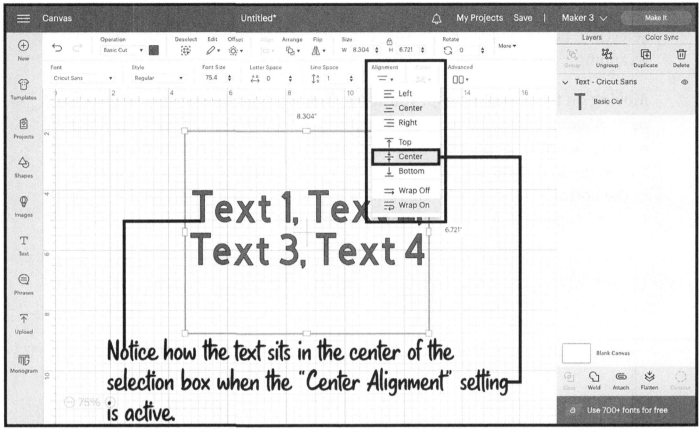

And *Bottom* will push the very last line of text to the bottom of the selection box.

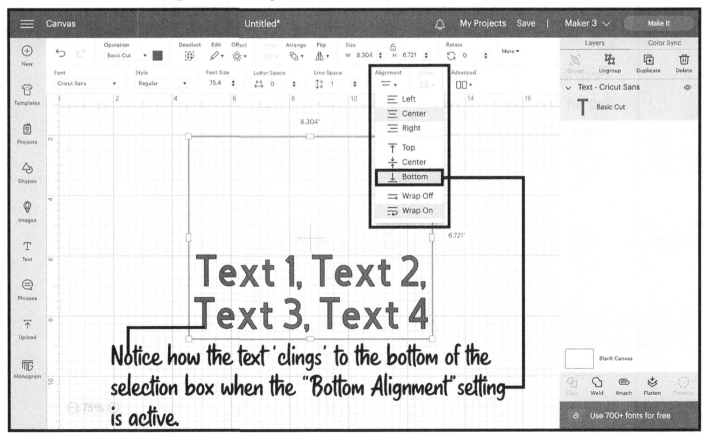

Pro Tip: Technically, there is no point in having so much space around your text inside the text selection box, so I never adjust the top and bottom sides of my text elements when I want text wrapping activated, and I always keep the selection box's *Alignment* at the default setting when working with text wrapping, which is *Center*.

Moving on to the **mobile app**, you'll see that you only have access to the three basic *Alignment* options for text elements on the Android app: left, right, and center, so there is no text wrapping available. However, you do have text wrapping on the iOS app. With the text element selected, tap on *Edit* in the bar at the bottom of the screen. This will bring up a secondary bar, where you will find the *Alignment* option; tap on it to choose your alignment preferences.

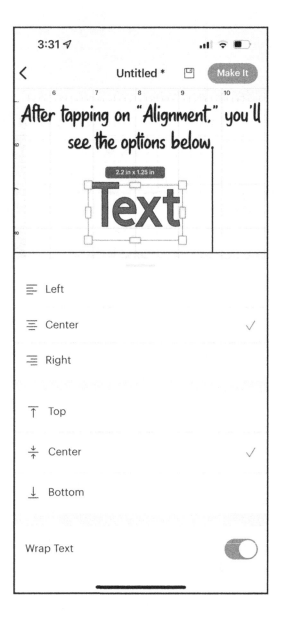

Curve Your Text

The ability to curve text is **exclusive to the desktop and iOS versions** of Design Space. Text curving only works with single lines of text and is a handy tool that allows you to bring a unique twist to your Cricut creations. You can find this option next to *Alignment* in the Text Edit bar. When you click on *Curve*, a slider will pop up and show a dot sitting in the middle of the slider.

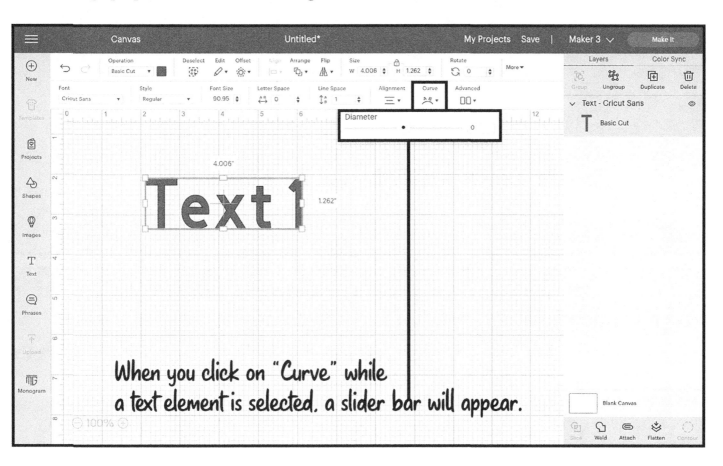

When you click on "Curve" while a text element is selected, a slider bar will appear.

Moving the slider to the right bends the ends of your text element downward. Moving the slider to the left bends the ends of your text element upward.

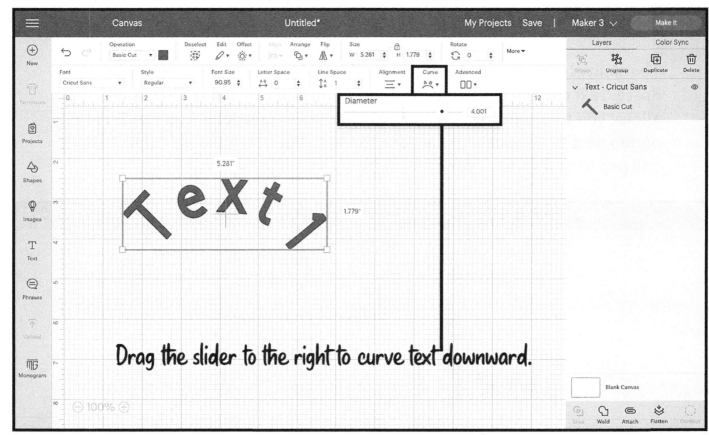

Drag the slider to the right to curve text downward.

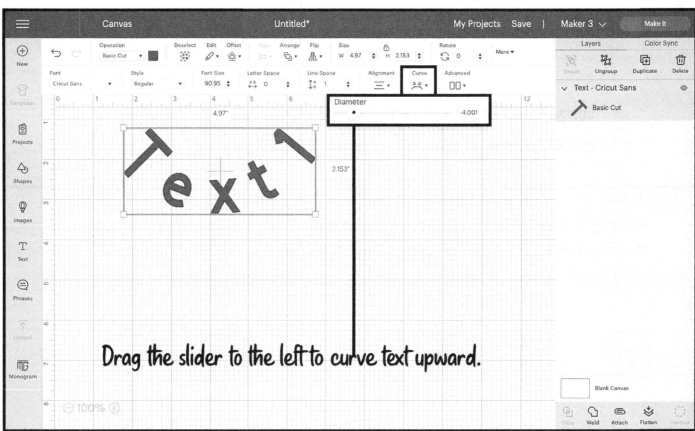

Drag the slider to the left to curve text upward.

Advanced Text Settings

The last thing you can do with a text element is to separate text into individual vector design elements. "Vector" simply refers to a type of image that you can scale to any size without negatively affecting its quality. When you save a vector graphic from a design program for later use, the saved file becomes an SVG, a term you have probably heard of in the Cricut world. When working on *Cut* projects, we mostly use SVG files.

On the **desktop app**, click on *Advanced*, which you'll see next to *Curve*. Depending on what you have going on in the text element, you'll see different options to choose from. In the example below, we can apply *Ungroup to Letters* or *Ungroup to Lines*.

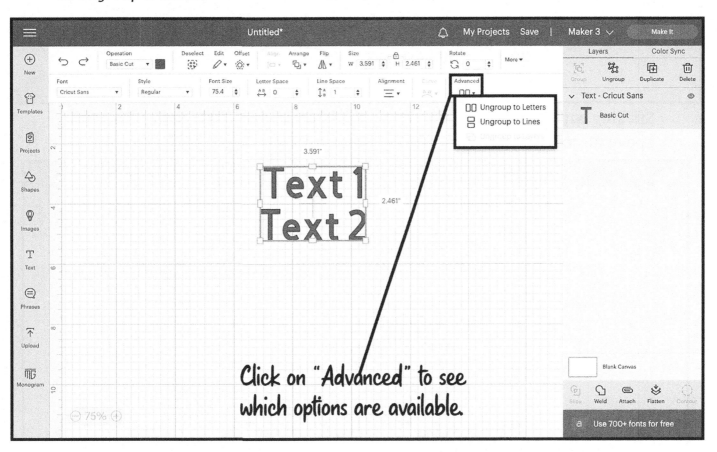

Click on "Advanced" to see which options are available.

I'll go with *Ungroup to Lines* first. As you can see on the next page, "Text 1" and "Text 2" are now each an individual text element, which I can tweak separately.

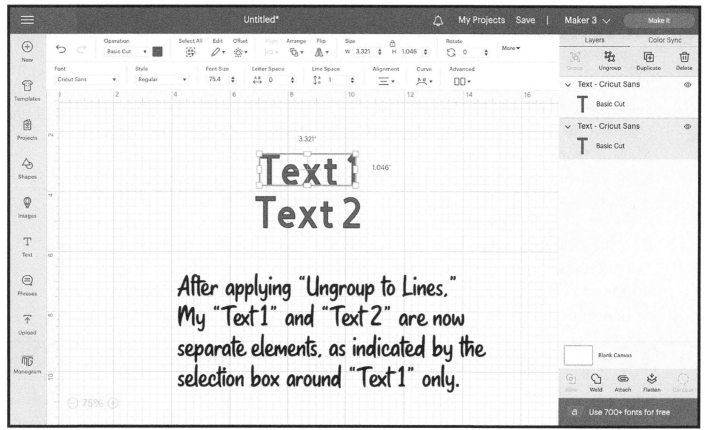

Sticking with "Text 1," I'll now apply the *Ungroup to Letters* setting. This time, I have turned every letter into its own element.

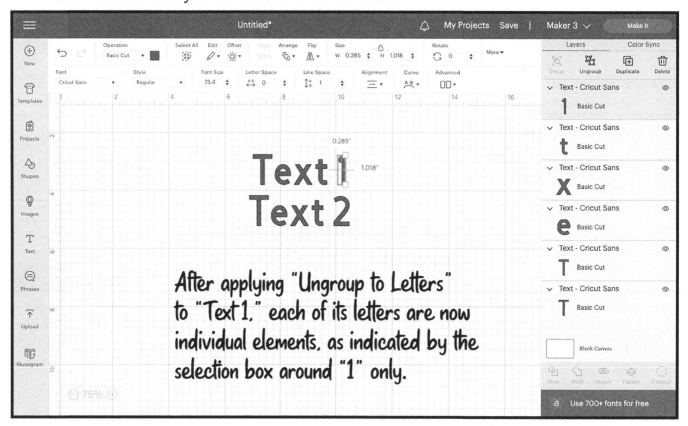

But why would you *want* to separate text into individual parts? Well, it gives you more flexibility with your design. For example, I can now exaggerate the "T" of "Text 1" by increasing its size.

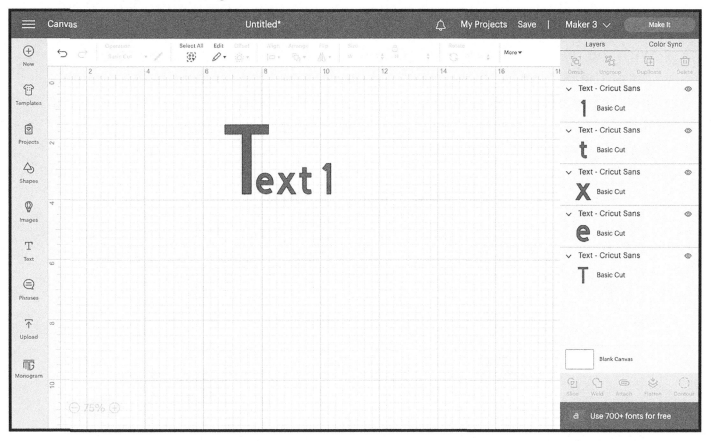

Or I can tilt the letters to create a sort of chaotic effect. (We'll talk about how to do the rotating/tilting effect later.)

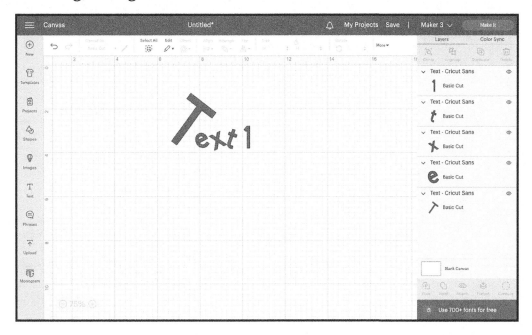

You can also separate a text element's letters when working on the **mobile app**, but the setting is available under the *Actions* function in the bottom bar and not under the *Edit* function like all the settings we've been playing with up to now. With the text element selected, tap on *Actions*. This will bring up a secondary bar at the bottom of the screen. Find *Ungroup* and tap on it. Initially, it might look as if nothing had happened. To see if the setting worked, tap on any blank spot on your Canvas and then tap on one of the letters. As you can see, each letter is now an individual element.

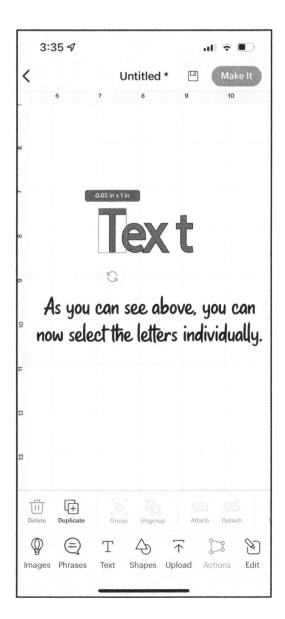

Text Element Self-Assessment Questions

Let's recap everything you can do with a humble text element before moving on to the rest of the Design Panels features.

I can change a text element's font using the _____ function. From there, I can choose between _____ fonts and _____ fonts. On my desktop app, I even have a _____ section where I can store all my favorite fonts.

If I want to change a font's characteristics from regular to **bold**, or maybe ***bold italic***, I need to use the _____ function.

The _____ function allows me to change a text element's size. I can either enter a value in the Edit Bar or resize the element using the selection box directly on the Canvas.

_____ Spacing allows me to increase or decrease the space between letters and _____ Spacing allows me to increase the space between lines of text.

If I want all the text in a text element to align in a certain way, I need to use the _____ function. The three basic alignment options are _____ Alignment, _____ Alignment, and _____ Alignment.

Yes or no: I can curve text on both the desktop version and iOS versions of Design space. _____

With the _____ text function on the desktop app, I can separate letters and tweak them individually. If I want to separate letters to tweak them individually on my mobile app, I have to tap on _____ and then choose the _____ function.

Phrases

Phrases is a fairly new Design Space feature. In the past, if you wanted inspiring words or a cool quote to add to your design, you would go searching for it in the Images library. However, the use of sayings is so popular in design projects, they really deserve their own library, which is exactly what Cricut decided to give us with recent updates to their design program.

You can access the Phrases library on the **desktop app** when you click on *Phrases.*

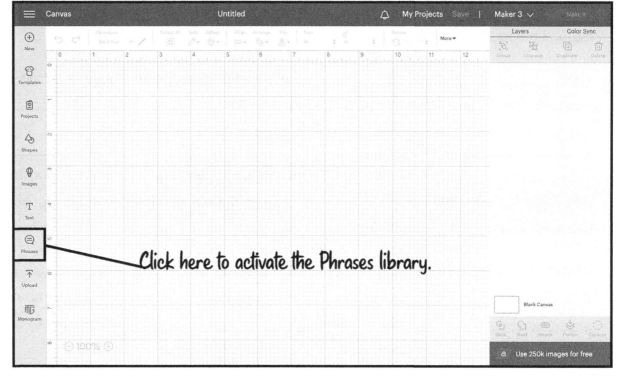

Click here to activate the Phrases library.

The library looks almost identical to the Images library, with the same filter options to refine your search. The only difference is the results you see, which consist of words for the most part. Some results in the Phrases library may contain a few design elements, but these tend to be minimal.

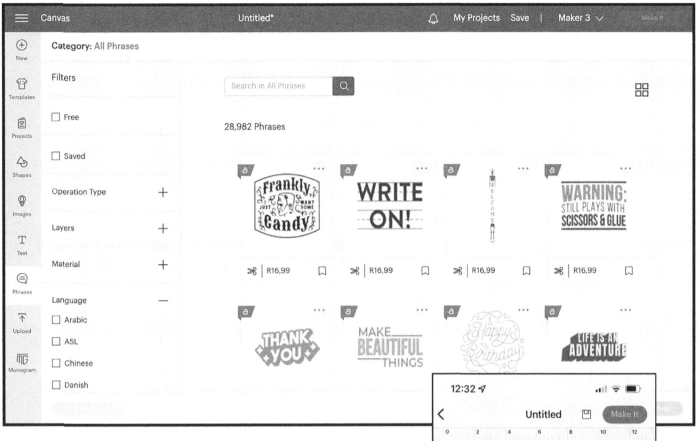

For now, the Phrases library is **not available for the Android mobile app**. However, you should be able to find cool sayings and word designs in your Images library. To activate the Phrases library on your iOS device, tap on Phrases in the bottom bar of your Canvas screen.

Although phrases are made up of words, the files you see in the library are images, so you can't change the words or tweak the designs. However, you can add extra elements to the phrases to create unique designs. Take note that some of the assets in the Phrases library are free, while most come with a price tag (which you can get with a once-off purchase or through your Cricut Access subscription).

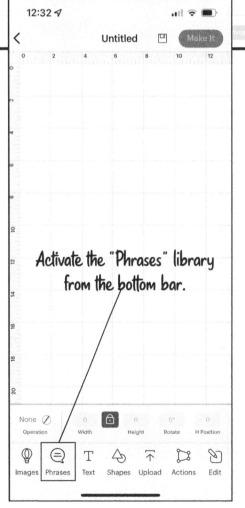

Activate the "Phrases" library from the bottom bar.

Pro Tip: Be mindful of the *Operation* settings for the design assets you want to use. When viewing the library, you'll see little icons in the bottom-left corner of each design. Those icons tell you what your Cricut will do with the design (this is true for the Images library, too).

- **Scissors:** *Cut* only project (your machine will cut out the design).
- **Pencil:** *Draw* only project (your machine will use a Cricut Pen to draw the design).
- **Printer:** *Print Then Cut* project (you will first print the design on your home printer and then let your machine cut it).
- **Scissors and Pencil:** *Cut* and *Draw* project (your machine will draw part of the project with a Cricut Pen and cut part of the project with a blade).

Upload

When you download design assets from external sources, like *Creative Fabrica*, *Design Bundles*, or *LoveSVG*, you'll use the *Upload* feature to bring them into Design Space for your Cricut projects.

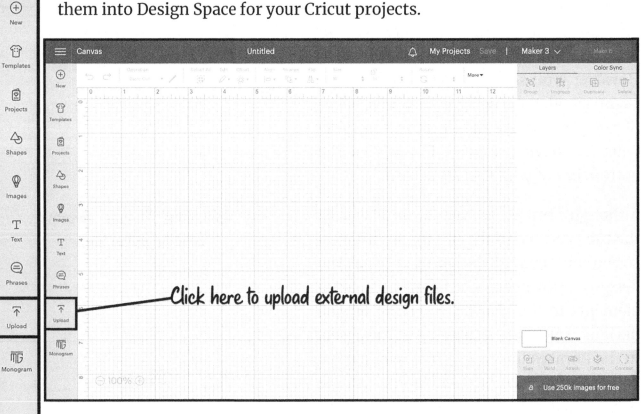

Click here to upload external design files.

My other book, *Cricut for Newbies*, covers in detail how to download SVGs and other image files on a computer, iOS device, and an Android device, so we will not talk about that here. However, if you have no idea how to download design assets, head over to the *Cricut for Newbies* Facebook Group and leave a post to ask for help. You can also look up how to do it in Google or YouTube.

When you click on *Upload* on the **desktop app**, you'll be met with a screen that displays your recent uploads at the bottom (but this part will be empty if you haven't uploaded anything yet). At the top of the screen, you'll see two *Upload* options: *Image* and *Pattern.*

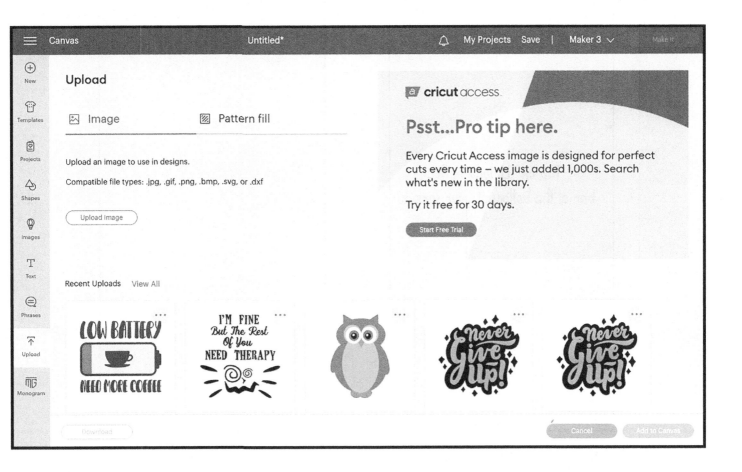

Pro Tip: Ninety-nine times out of a hundred, you'll go with the *Upload Image* option. Pattern fills allow you to fill up text and other design elements with backgrounds, images, and pattern designs instead of solid colors. Sounds cool, but it's not something you'll be bothered with much in the beginning stages of your crafting journey. For that reason, we're not going to cover this option at all.

On the **mobile app**, you'll find the *Upload* function in the bar at the bottom of the screen. When you tap on *Upload*, a pop-up menu will appear, and give you three options:

- Take a Photo
- Select from Photo Library
- Open Uploaded Images

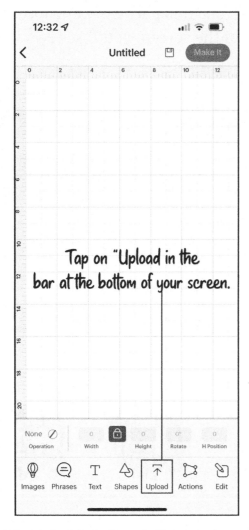
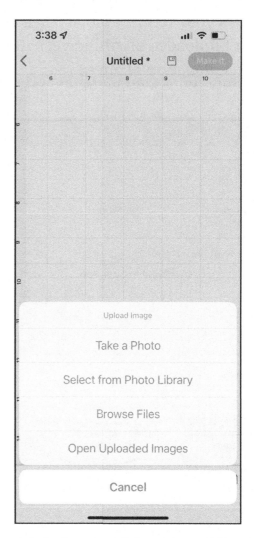

You'll probably never use the first option, and the second option is the one you'll use most often. Tapping on it will take you to your mobile device's Images library or Downloads library, from where you can find and select the design asset you want to add to Design Space. The third option will bring up all the design assets you have already added to Design Space, and this is the one you'll use most often after the *Select from Photo Library* option.

Best Practices for Uploading Files to Design Space

As you go through the upload process, you'll encounter a few steps before getting to the part where you can actually use the file for your project. To help you get the best results every time, I'll walk you through these steps. Hopefully, you can do this exercise with me, as that will make the things you learn here stick in the back of your mind.

SVG Files

By default, when you upload an SVG file, Design Space will recognize the file as a project you want to cut out with your Cricut machine. Indeed, that is the only purpose you ought to be using your SVG files for, as they're the perfect format for that. Luckily, Design Space doesn't even give you the option to upload an SVG as a *Print Then Cut* file.

Note: We'll talk more about the difference between *Cut* and *Print Then Cut* projects in Chapter 5.

Here is what you'll see when uploading an SVG on your **desktop app**:

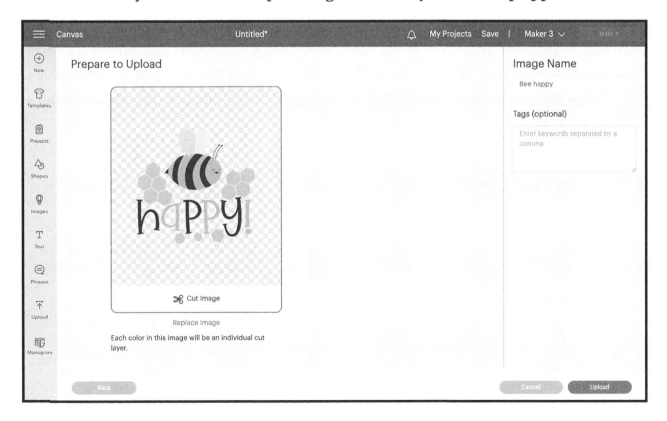

From there, all you have to do is click on the *Upload* button in the bottom-right corner of the screen. This will add the SVG to your Uploads library, allowing you to use it on the Canvas.

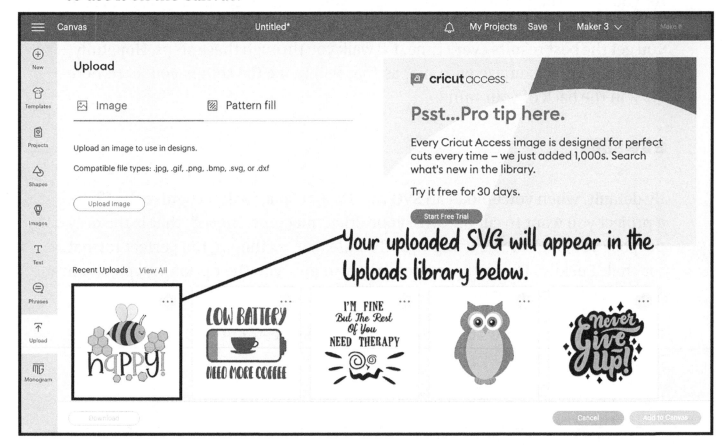

On the next page , you'll see what the screen looks like when uploading an SVG on your **mobile app**. To add the SVG to your Uploads library, you have to give the file a name and then tap on the *Next* or *Save* button in the top-right corner of the screen.

Pro Tip: Sometimes, you'll see this message when uploading an SVG on your mobile app: *Multi-layer SVGs will appear as single-layer objects in Quickstart projects.*

By this, Design Space just means that when you open the SVG in your Canvas and you tap on it, it will look like a single image. That is, a selection box will appear around the entire thing, as opposed to allowing you to select individual parts, like the bee only. All you have to do is tap on the *Actions* function at the bottom of the screen and then tap on the *Ungroup* function in the secondary bar that appears (see the left-hand screenshot on the next page). Once you have done that, you'll be able to select individual parts of the design, like you see in the right-hand illustration on the next page.

Pro Tip: If you're not planning on tweaking the SVG design you have added to the Canvas, there is no need to *Ungroup* it like I showed you above.

JPEG and PNG Files

The other types of files you'll upload to Design Space regularly are JPEGs and PNGs. What's important to know about them is that, although many of them have more than one color on the image, the file does not consist of different design elements like SVG files. What's more, these files are ideal for *Print Then Cut* projects and not the best option for *Cut* projects.

When uploading a JPEG or PNG file, Design Space will take you through more steps than it does when you're uploading a SVG file. To show you the difference between the JPEG (or PNG) and SVG uploading process, I'll use the same image from the previous example. The only difference is that I will use the JPEG version this time.

Let's start with the **desktop app**. The first difference you'll notice is that Design Space wants to know the image type. To keep things simple, always choose the *Complex* option and then click on the *Continue* button in the bottom-right corner of the screen.

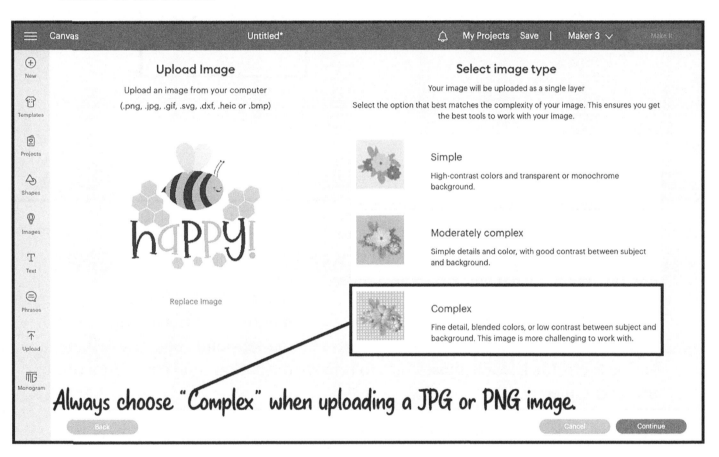

On the next screen, you have access to Design Space's Background Remover. This is important, especially when uploading JPEG files. They always have a color behind the actual image. In the case of our little bee friend, the color behind him is white. Now, if I want my Cricut to do a proper job of cutting this little bee out after printing it on my home printer, I need to remove that white background. It's easier than it sounds—I promise!

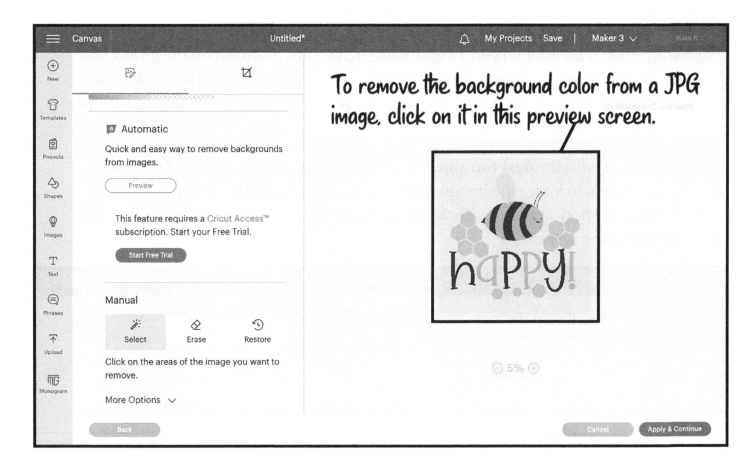

Pro Tip #1: The checkers on the checkered background are sometimes super, super tiny, giving you the impression that the background has turned a shade of blue. If that's what you're seeing, you're still good to go!

Pro Tip #2: Did you get *all* of the background? Sometimes, especially when you have letters with closed loops in an image, the background color will still be visible there. Click inside those areas to remove the background color from the image completely.

Pro Tip #3: Depending on the JPEG image's quality, some bits of white may still remain in the background after you followed the above instructions. If this happens to you, grab the eraser tool, zoom in to the preview, and use the eraser to clean up those remaining bits.

When you have removed the background, click on the *Apply and Continue* button in the bottom-right corner of the screen.

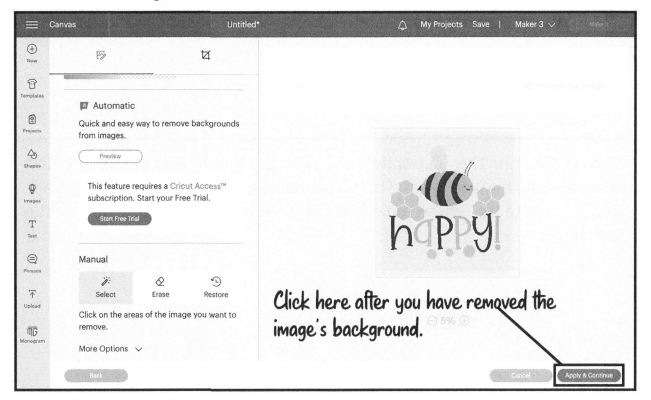

Next, Design Space is going to ask you if you want to save the file you're uploading as a *Cut Image* or a *Print Then Cut Image.* The first thing that might catch your eye is that the *Cut Image* option looks like a silhouette of the original. The reason for this is what we talked about earlier—even though you can see black, yellow, and blue when looking at a JPEG or PNG image, the image itself is flat and does not contain multiple design elements like a SVG image. Design Space cannot 'see' the different colors of a JPG or PNG file; it simply sees a shape.

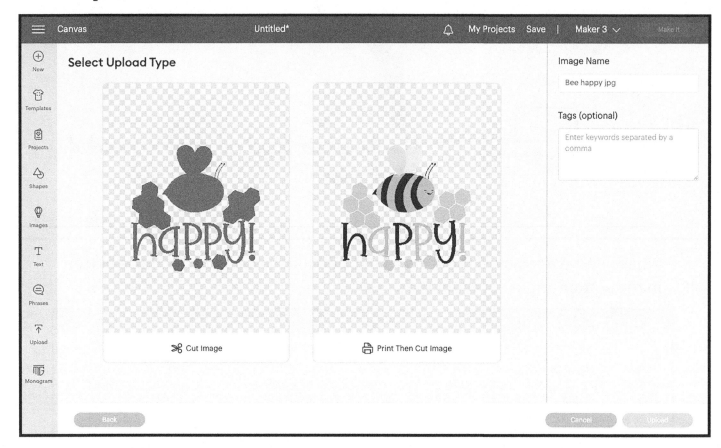

Choose the *Print Then Cut* option and click the *Upload* button (see the first screenshot on the next page). The image should now be visible in your Uploads library, next to the SVG we uploaded first (see the second screenshot on the next page).

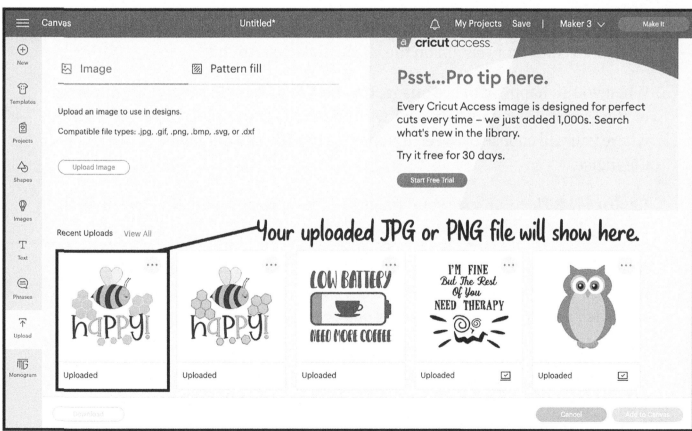

Unfortunately, Design Space doesn't give you any indication of whether uploaded files are *Cut Images* or *Print Then Cut Images*. So, if you uploaded something months ago and decide you want to use it today, you'll only know which type of image it is once you add it to your Canvas to start a new project.

Let's see how the process of uploading a JPEG or PNG works on the **mobile app**. Start by tapping on *Upload* at the bottom of your Canvas screen. Choose *Upload from Photo Library*, and then choose the JPEG or PNG you'd like to work with. Once you tap on your choice , Design Space will open the Clean Up screen, which is the equivalent of the Background Remover screen on the desktop app.

To remove the color behind the image on your mobile app, choose the *Remove* tool you see at the bottom of the screen and tap on the white area (or whatever color your image has behind it) of the image. This will remove the color and bring up the checkered background, just like you saw with the desktop app.

Pro Tip #1: If you accidentally tapped on the wrong area and removed a part you actually wanted to keep, tap the *Undo* icon at the bottom of the screen and try again.

Pro Tip #2: Use the Eraser tool next to the Remove tool to clean up any bits of unwanted color that remain on the checkered background.

When you're happy with the image, tap the *Next* button in the top-right corner of the screen. Next, you'll be met with the Prepare to Upload screen, which is where you will choose between uploading your file as a *Cut Image* or a *Print then Cut Image*.

Choose *Print Then Cut*, give your image a name, and tap on the *Next* button in the top-right corner of the screen.

Note: If you're doing this on an Android device, you'll get the following pop-up message when you tap that *Next* button: *Usage Notification: Print Then Cut is not supported on this app. Save this project and open it from a desktop computer to make it.*

If you don't have a laptop or computer, you won't be able to do anything with this image unless you change it to a *Cut* file later on; but even then, you'll only have the silhouette to work with. However, if you do have a laptop or computer, you'll be able to go ahead with your project once you're able to open your desktop app.

By keeping the above best practices in mind when uploading images to Design Space, you'll save yourself a lot of frustration as you learn to conquer the program. With that, here's a last tip to keep in mind:

Pro Tip: Although I just walked you through the process of removing the background of a JPEG image on both the desktop and mobile apps, you can save yourself a lot of trouble by *always* choosing PNG images to upload instead. A PNG image's background has already been removed, so you don't have to go through the trouble of getting the image ready to use.

Upload Process Self-Assessment Questions

What type of image file is best for Cut projects?

_____

What type of image files are best for Print Then Cut projects?

_____

Why will uploading a PNG image instead of a JPEG image save your sanity?

_____

_____

_____

_____

Monogram

This new feature is still in the Beta phase, which means it's still being tested and might give you a hiccup or three should you decide to give it a go. Unlike Projects, Shapes, Images, and Phrases, everything in the Monogram library comes with a price tag. You can open the Monogram Panel, play around, and add your idea to the Canvas, but that's as far as you can go. If you'd like to make a project using a monogram, you'll have to subscribe to Cricut Access.

The Monogram feature is exclusive to the desktop app at this stage.

I think the only reason you may be interested in this feature is if you're going to make a lot of logos, which is typically the purpose of monograms. For example, if I enter my initials in the top of the Monogram Panel, opt for a *Thematic* look, and choose *Botanical*, Design Space will give me a few options to choose from.

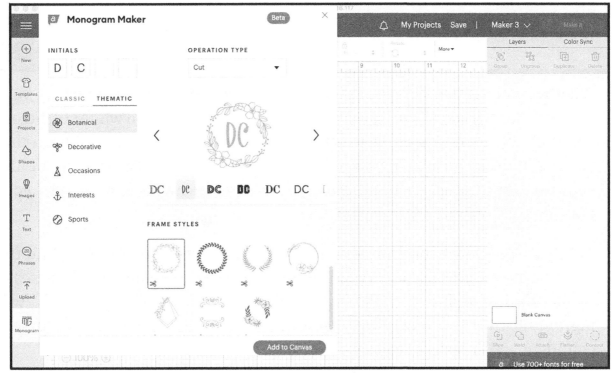

And if I add it to the Canvas, this is what I'll see:

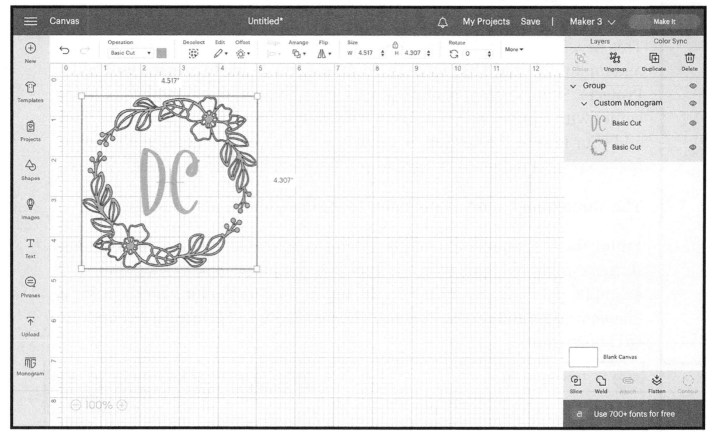

Whether you use the Monogram feature will, of course, depend on where your crafting journey takes you. However, it will probably be a good while still before you think of where you'd like to take your crafting skills. By that, I mean that you might decide to stick to it as a hobby to get away from the stresses of life, venture into making crafts on the side for some extra money, or turn your crafting passion into a thriving business.

That's it! You now know the Design Panel inside-out. Before we dive into the other parts of Design Space, spend some time with the following self-assessment. It's important to challenge yourself with these questions, as it will ingrain all this new knowledge deep into your mind so you can become a confident and knowledgeable crafter.

Design Panel Self-Assessment Questions

How would you explain the process of opening a new Canvas on the Design Space desktop app?

_____

_____

_____

_____

_____

How would you explain the process of opening a new Canvas on the Design space mobile app?

_____

_____

_____

_____

_____

Can you access the Templates feature on a mobile app?

_____

Will your Cricut machine recognize a template from the Templates library as a design element it needs to Cut or Draw?

_____

True or false: The Projects feature in the desktop app's Design Panel gives you access to the same ready-to-make projects that you find on Design Space's Home page when opening the program.

_____

In your own words, explain why ready-to-make projects are useful for a New-bie Cricut crafter.

_____

_____

_____

_____

_____

If I'd like to add a basic shape to my design on the Canvas, where can I go to find one? Explain this for the desktop app and the mobile app.

_____

_____

_____

_____

_____

How would you explain the difference between Projects and Images?

_____

_____

_____

_____

Are all the Projects, Images, and Phrases in Design Space free to use?

_____

When choosing Images or Phrases for my design, I see little icons underneath each one. I've seen some with scissors, some with printers, some with pencils, and some with scissors and pencils. What do each of those icons mean?

Scissors:

_____

_____

Printer:

_____

_____

Pencil:

_____

_____

Scissors and Pencil:

_____

_____

If I want to add external design assets to Design Space, like SVG or PNG images, what function can I use?

_____

If I want to add my own words to the Canvas, what function can I use?

_____

Chapter 2 Notes

Use this space to jot down the best take-aways you learned from Chapter 2. Use these notes as your personal quick-reference guide whenever you want to refresh your memory ons something specific.

_____

_____

_____

_____

_____

_____

Chapter 3
Let's Conquer the "All-Rounder" Functions

Now that you know where to find design elements to add to the Canvas, it's time to see what you can actually do with those design elements. The ability to tweak (or edit) a design element is what will set your own designs apart and help you add your personal flair to your Cricut creations.

First up, we're going to look at functions you can apply to design elements from different parts of the Canvas interface, hence the term "all-rounder functions." It's not an official Cricut term, though, just something I came up with.

I decided to walk you through these first, because it will give you the perfect holistic view of how everything in your Canvas interface works together and influences each other. So, in this chapter, you'll learn to look at the broader picture while designing.

Let's do this!

Select All

For this example, I'll add two circles to my Canvas. You can do the same or add any other shapes you prefer.

How To Use it on the Desktop App

"Select All" means that you want to grab *all* the design elements on the Canvas. There are different reasons for wanting to do this, such as grouping elements together or changing all the shapes' colors at the same time.

To use this function via the **Edit Bar**, click on *Select All*. This will form a single selection box around all the elements on the Canvas.

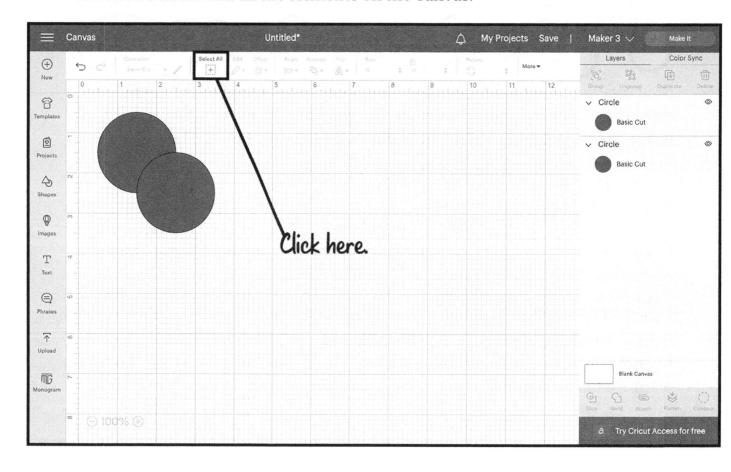

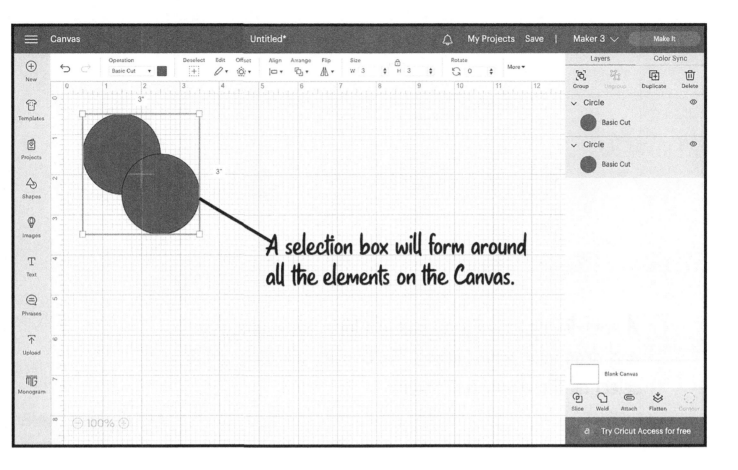

To select all the elements **directly on the Canvas**, click in the Canvas Grid's upper-left corner and drag your mouse. You'll see a gray box appear as you drag, which indicates the selection area. To grab all the elements, drag the box until it covers everything. Once you've got everything, you can let go of the click. As with the *Select All* option in the Edit bar, you'll now see a single box around all the elements on the Canvas. (See the screenshot at the top of the next page.)

Pro Tip: You can also select multiple elements directly in the Canvas by holding your keyboard's SHIFT button while you click on the individual elements you want to select. Once you have everything you want, you can let go of the SHIFT button.

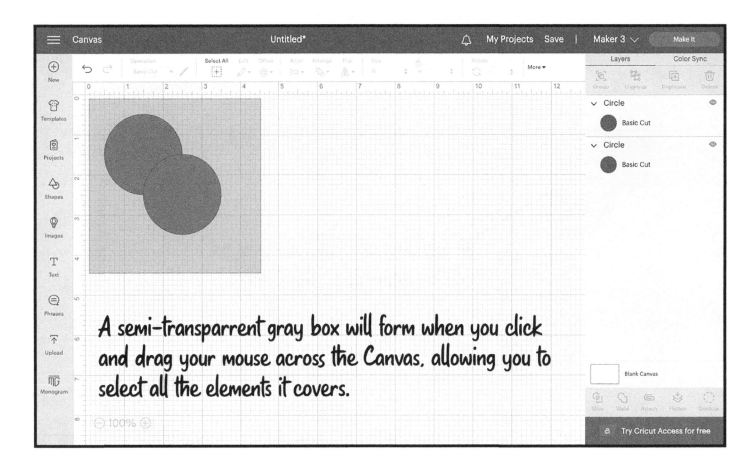

A semi-transparrent gray box will form when you click and drag your mouse across the Canvas, allowing you to select all the elements it covers.

To select all the elements on the Canvas via the **Layers Panel**, click on the first layer you see in the Layers Panel (the one at the very top), hold the SHIFT key on your keyboard, and select each of the layers underneath the first one until you have all of them. Only let go of the SHIFT key when you have everything you want. You'll know that you've got everything when (a) a single selection box forms around all the elements on the Canvas and (b) all the layers in the Layers Panel are highlighted in a darker shade of gray. (See the screenshot at the top of the next page.)

By the way, working in the Layers Panel is also the best way to select multiple elements on the Canvas. For example, if you have words, squares, and hearts, but you want to select the hearts only, hold your keyboard's SHIFT key and only click on all the layers that say "Heart" in the Layers Panel. In doing so, you will grab the hearts only while ignoring the words and squares.

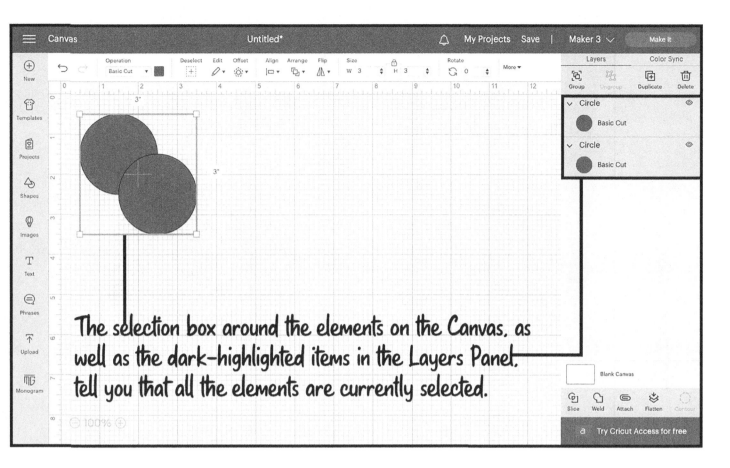

The selection box around the elements on the Canvas, as well as the dark-highlighted items in the Layers Panel, tell you that all the elements are currently selected.

Pro Tip: The quickest way to apply *Select All* is with a keyboard shortcut.

- On a Mac, the shortcut is Command + A (CMD + A).
- On a Windows computer, the shortcut is CONTROL + A (CTRL + A)

Try it out to see how quick and easy it is.

How To Use it on the Mobile App

Option 1:

Similar to how you can select all the design elements directly from the Canvas on the desktop app, you can place your finger in the upper-left corner of the Canvas on your mobile app and drag your finger toward the bottom-right corner of the Canvas. This will create the outline of a box as you drag. Cover everything you see on the Canvas with that outline and, once you have everything in it, lift your finger. Now you'll see a selection box all around the elements on your Canvas.

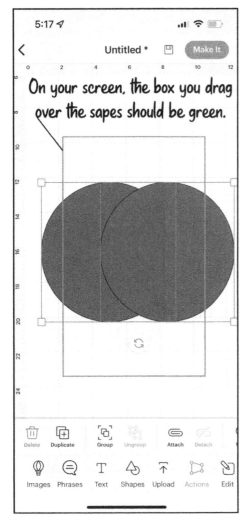

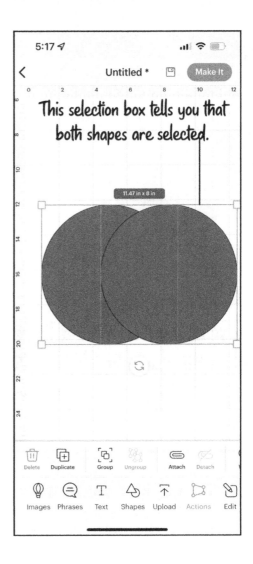

Option 2:

Locate the *Layers* function in the bar at the bottom of your screen and tap on it (see the left-hand screenshot at the top of the next page). If you don't see the *Layers* function, swipe to the right until you spot it.

This will open a screen, which is the mobile app's equivalent of the desktop app's Layers Panel. Tap and hold the top layer until it turns gray (see the right-hand screenshot at the top of the next page).

After that, tap and hold the second layer until it turns gray, too. You will continue doing this until all the layers in the Layers Panel are gray (see the screenshot right below the other two two on the next page).

Now, when you go back to the Canvas, you'll see a selection box around all the design elements, just like you saw in option 1.

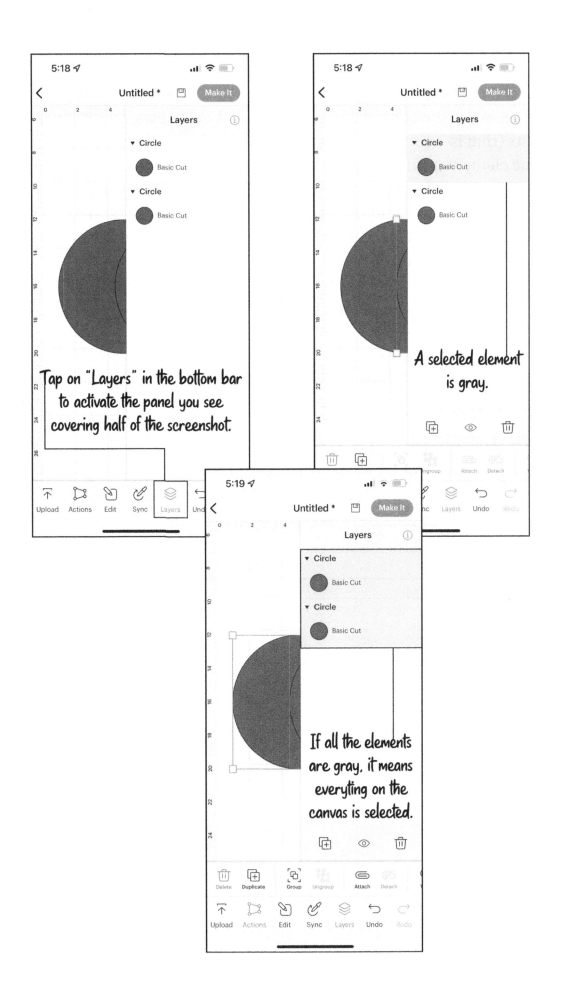

Tap on "Layers" in the bottom bar to activate the panel you see covering half of the screenshot.

A selected element is gray.

If all the elements are gray, it means everyting on the canvas is selected.

Pro Tip

You can also use the Canvas or Layers Panel when you want to select multiple elements (that is—some elements, but not all of them). **On the Canvas**, tap and hold one element until a selection box forms around it. To add another element to the selection, tap and hold on the one you want until you see the selection box expand to include it. **In the Layers Panel**, follow the same steps as you did in option 2 above, but this time only tapping and holding the layers you want to include in your selection.

Select All Function Self-Assessment

After trying all the available options to apply the Select All function on my desktop app, I think I like using the _____most.

The fastest way to select all the elements on my mobile app's Canvas is to:

_____

_____

_____

_____

_____

Edit

How To Use it on the Desktop App

"Edit" is an umbrella term for the following actions you can apply to a design element:

- Copy
- Cut
- Paste
- Duplicate
- Delete

Let's continue with the circles we started working with when we talked about the Select All function. To complete any of the above actions using the **Edit Bar**, select one of the circles by clicking on it. Now click on *Edit* in the Edit Bar. This will activate a pop-up menu containing all the actions I mentioned above, but *Paste* will be grayed-out. This is because we have not yet cut or copied the shape. When we do, the pop-up menu will make the *Paste* action active.

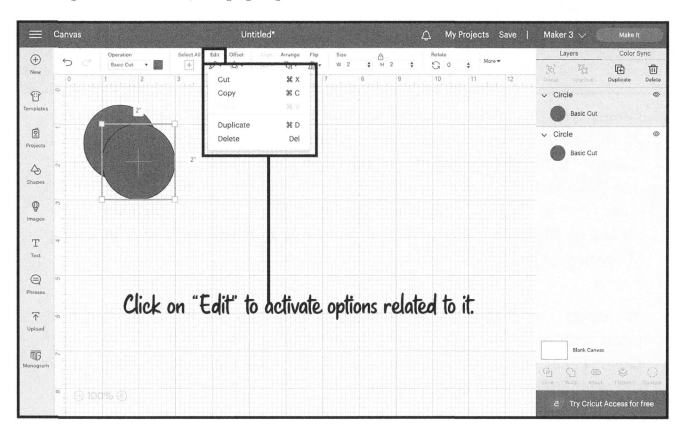

Click on "Edit" to activate options related to it.

To apply the Edit functions to design elements **directly on the Canvas**, simply right click on the selected element to see which options are available. Note that when you select a single element, many of the options will be grayed-out, as there is no use for them at that moment. We'll get to each of those other functions as we progress.

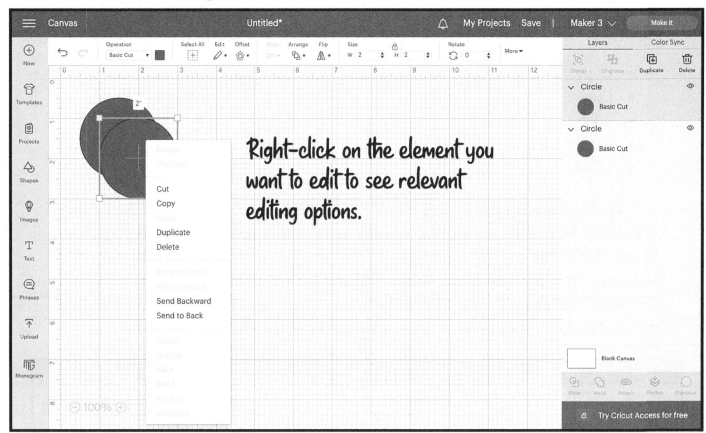

Finally, you can apply these actions via the **Layers Panel**, too. In the Layers Panel, select the layer you want to work with. In this case, we are working with the circle lying on top of the other circle in the Canvas, so it will be the very first one you see in the Layers Panel. Right-click on that top circle in the Layers Panel; this will bring up the same pop-up window you saw when you right-clicked on the circle directly in the Canvas area. (See the screenshot at the top of the next page.)

Pro Tip #1: Design Space gives you quick access to some actions you'll use most often at the top of the Layers Panel. If you look just above the first circle in your Layers Panel, you'll see four options: *Group*, *Ungroup*, *Duplicate*, and *Delete*. (See the second screenshot on the next page.)

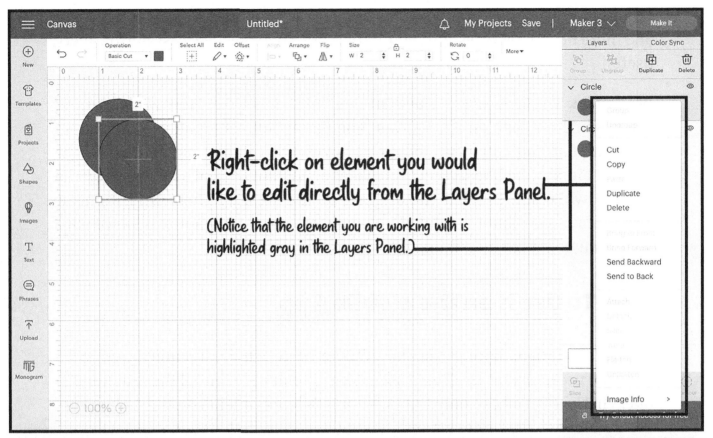

Right-click on element you would like to edit directly from the Layers Panel.

(Notice that the element you are working with is highlighted gray in the Layers Panel.)

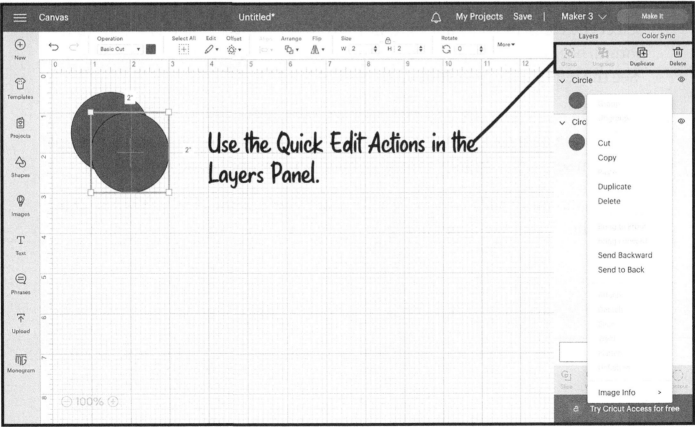

Use the Quick Edit Actions in the Layers Panel.

You'll recognize *Duplicate* and *Delete* as two Edit Functions. As you create more and more of your own designs, you'll find those two quick-access buttons very useful!

Pro Tip #2: The *Copy* action copies an element that you can *Paste* while keeping the original element on the Canvas. The *Cut* action also makes a copy of an element that you can *Paste*, but it removes the original element from the Canvas. Finally, the *Duplicate* action makes an instant copy of an element on the Canvas, while still keeping the original on the Canvas. There is no right or wrong way to go about it, as it all depends on what you want to achieve with your design. In time, you'll find what works best for you.

How To Use it on the Mobile App

On the mobile app, there are no Copy, Cut, or Paste actions. Technically, they're not even necessary, as the Duplicate action kind of contains all those actions in one. That's why you can only Duplicate and Delete elements on the mobile app. Let's start with the Delete action.

Select the element you want to remove from the Canvas, tap on Actions in the bottom bar, and then tap on the dustbin icon in the secondary bar that appears. (See the left-hand screenshot on the next page.)

Select the remaining circle and find the *Actions* function in the bar at the bottom of your Canvas screen. Tap on it to activate the *Actions* secondary bar, and swipe until you see *Duplicate*. (See the right-hand screenshot on the next page.)

Finally, tap on *Duplicate* to make an instant copy of the circle. (See the third screenshot on the next page.)

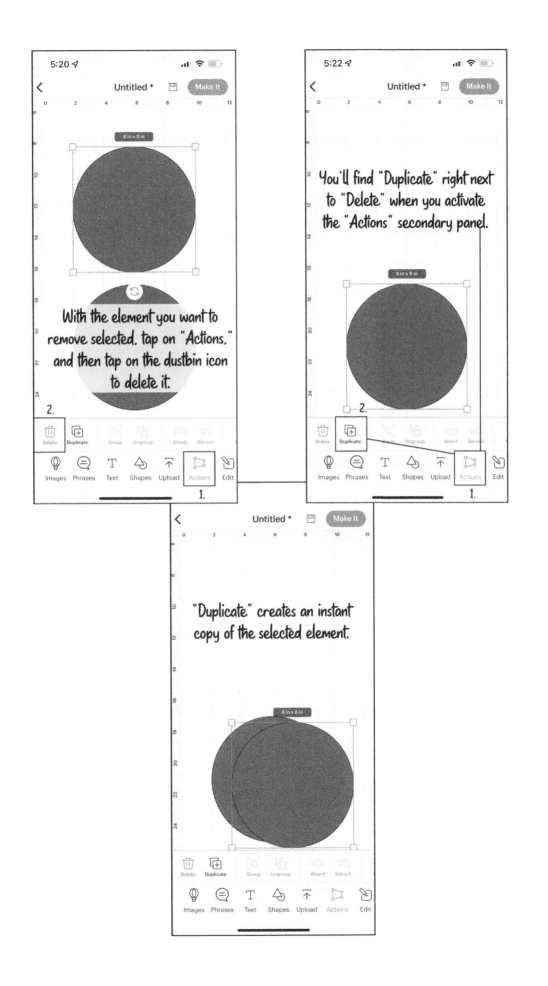

With the element you want to remove selected, tap on "Actions," and then tap on the dustbin icon to delete it.

You'll find "Duplicate" right next to "Delete" when you activate the "Actions" secondary panel.

"Duplicate" creates an instant copy of the selected element.

Edit Function Self-Assessment

True or False: I can use the Edit option on my mobile device to find the Duplicate action.

_____

What two actions do you have quick access to at the top of the desktop app's Layer Panel?

_____

Size

How To Use it on the Desktop App

You can resize any design element using the Edit Bar or the Canvas. You can also resize multiple elements at once, or adjust them individually. Let's continue with our circles.

First, we'll use the **Edit Bar** to make a size adjustment. On the Canvas, one circle is sitting on top of the other. For this example, I'm selecting the one at the bottom. The first step is to select the element by clicking on it. If you're following along (I hope you are!), you should now see something similar to the screenshot at the top of the next page.

Pro Tip: Don't confuse the Edit Bar's *Size* function with the Text element's *Font Size* function. The Edit Bar's *Size* function applies to all design elements, whereas the Text element's *Font Size* function helps you make only the text bigger or smaller.

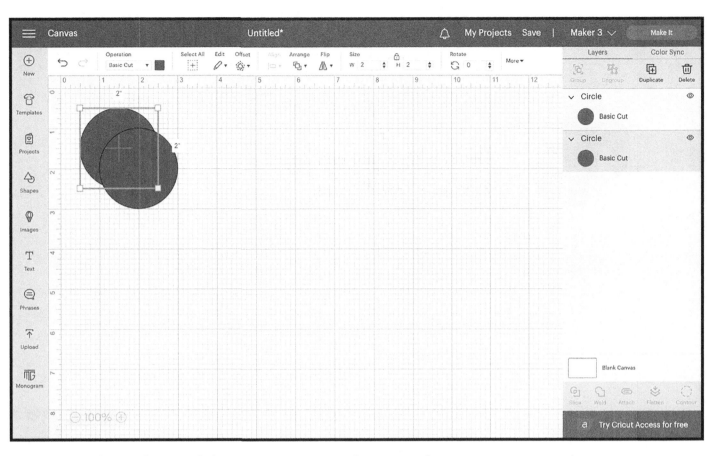

To adjust the circle's size, we can either use the step arrows to increase or decrease the size, or we can enter a value if we have something specific in mind, where we see the *Size* function in the Edit Bar. The numerical values you see when working with the *Size* function represent inches.

The "up" step arrow will increase the element's size and the "down" step arrow will decrease its size. Likewise, entering a larger number will make the element bigger, and entering a smaller number will make it smaller. Also, we can adjust the element's width (W), height (H), or both.

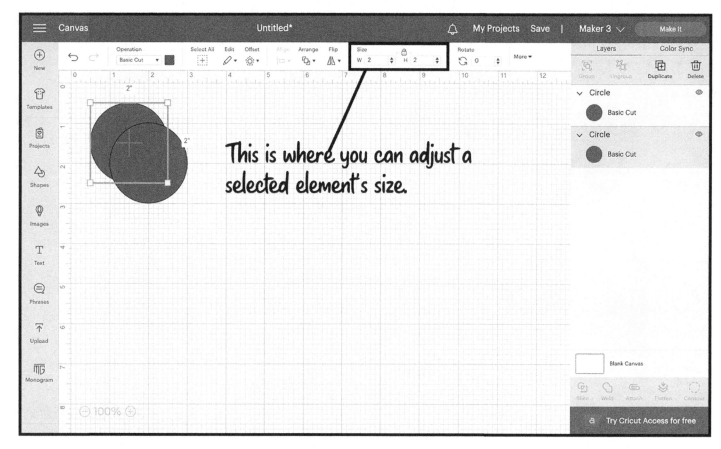

This is where you can adjust a selected element's size.

By default, all design elements' size settings are proportionally locked. This means that if you increase an element's width, the height will increase automatically to maintain the element's proportions. However, sometimes you want to tweak a shape even more, in which case you may want the width and height to increase or decrease independently of each other. To achieve that, you have to click on the little padlock you see above the width and height adjustment settings. When you click on the padlock, it will go from a locked position to an unlocked position. (See the screenshot at the top of the next page.)

For now, let's keep the padlock in the locked position. To see the size adjustments in action, I want to create some distance between the two circles on my Canvas. I'll select the top one and drag it to the side. (See the second screenshot on the next page.)

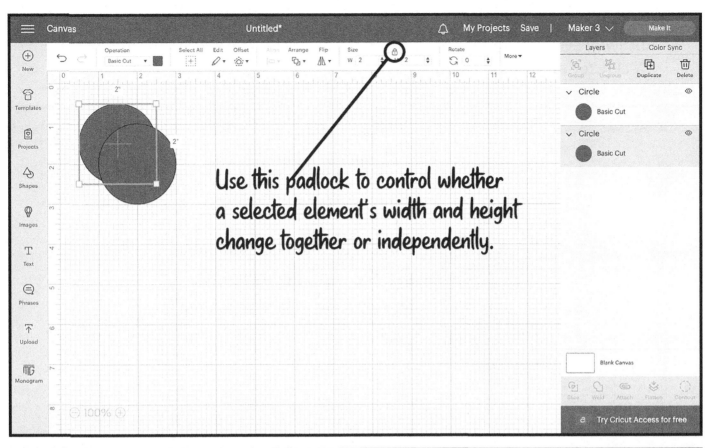

Use this padlock to control whether a selected element's width and height change together or independently.

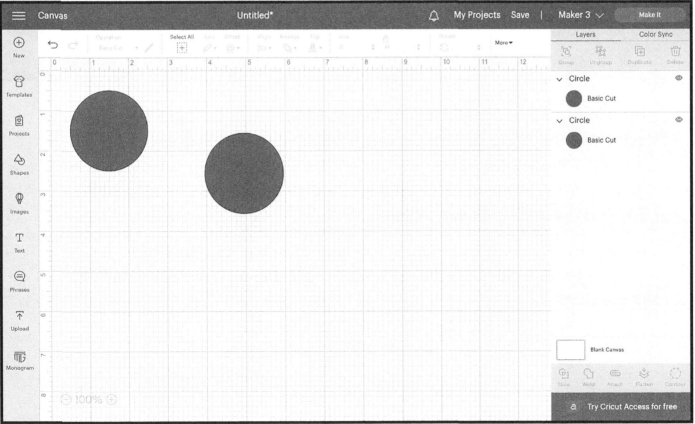

Let's increase its size to 5 inches. You can either click your "up" step arrow until you see "5," or you can enter the value inside the width box and hit the ENTER key on your keyboard.

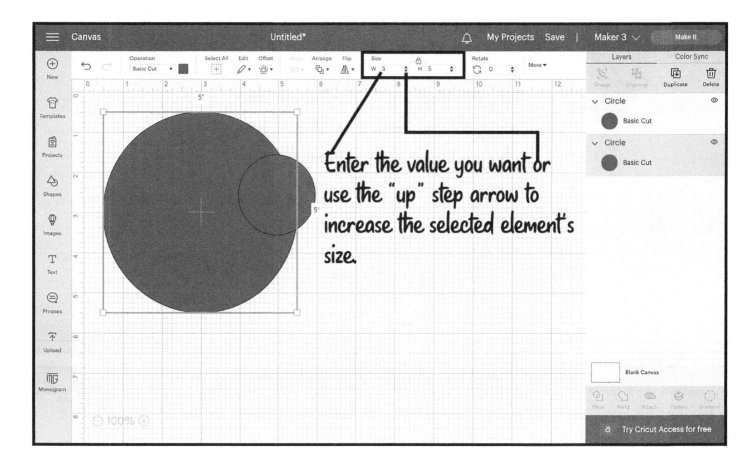

Pro Tip: If an element's width and height differ, it's normal practice to always adjust the width of a design element as opposed to the height when you know the size will increase or decrease proportionally. However, this is not a hard and fast rule. If you have a specific height in mind but not a specific width, go ahead and adjust the height instead.

If your two circles are overlapping like mine after you have increased the one's size, move the smaller one further away by clicking on it and dragging it more to the side.

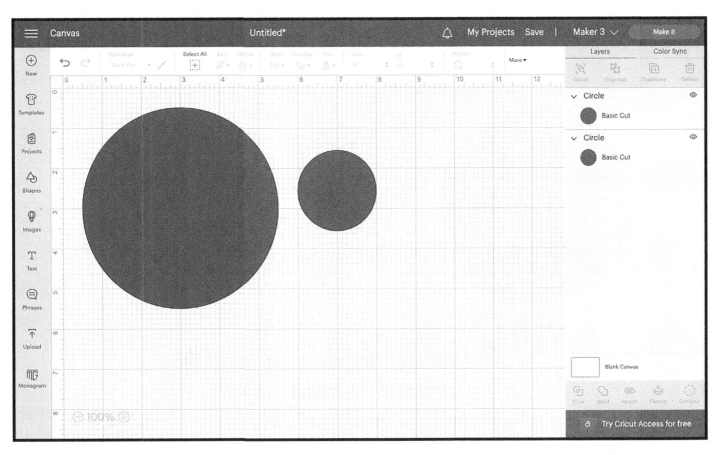

This time, let's adjust the smaller circle's size **directly in the Canvas Grid**. With the circle selected, hover over any of the four corners of the selection box until you see a straight diagonal arrow pointing both ways.

Pro Tip: If you are seeing a curved arrow pointing both ways, you are hovering too far away from the selection box and have instead activated the Rotate function, which we will talk about later. Bring your mouse a little closer to the selection box and see the arrow change from a curved one to a straight diagonal one.

To adjust the circle's size, click when you see that diagonal arrow and then drag your mouse away from the circle to increase its size or toward the circle to decrease its size.

The first screenshot on the next page shows what you'll see when you drag away from the circle, while the second screenshot shows what you'll see when you push toward the circle.

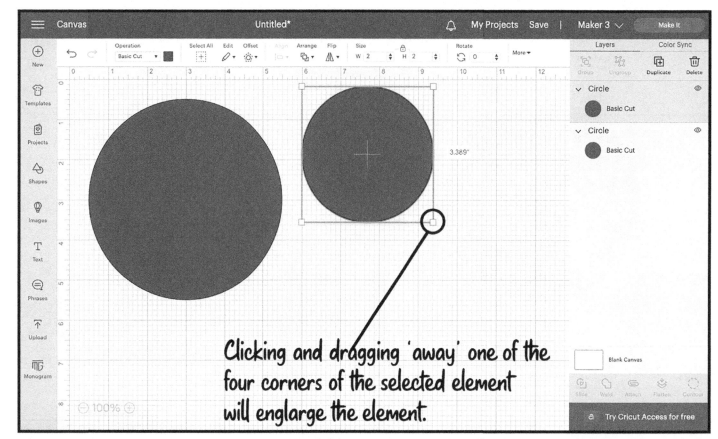

Clicking and dragging 'away' one of the four corners of the selected element will englarge the element.

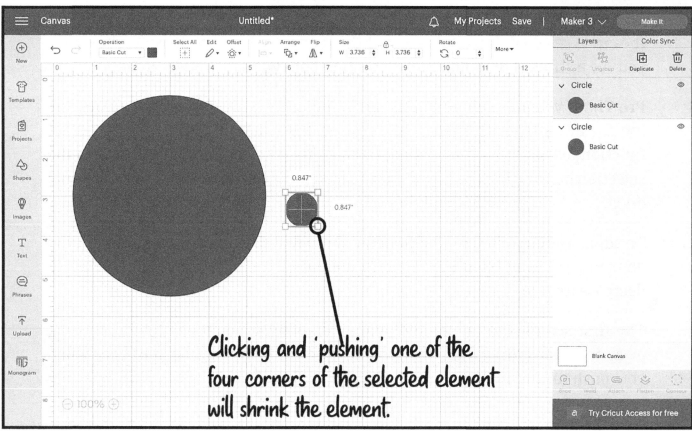

Clicking and 'pushing' one of the four corners of the selected element will shrink the element.

Let's say we want to change this circle into an oval shape. We'll first need to unlock the padlock I mentioned earlier. Make sure the circle is selected and then click on that padlock so it changes to the unlocked position. Let's adjust the circle's size again, using the selection box in the Canvas. See how you can change it into an oval now? This is more or less what you should see on your Canvas:

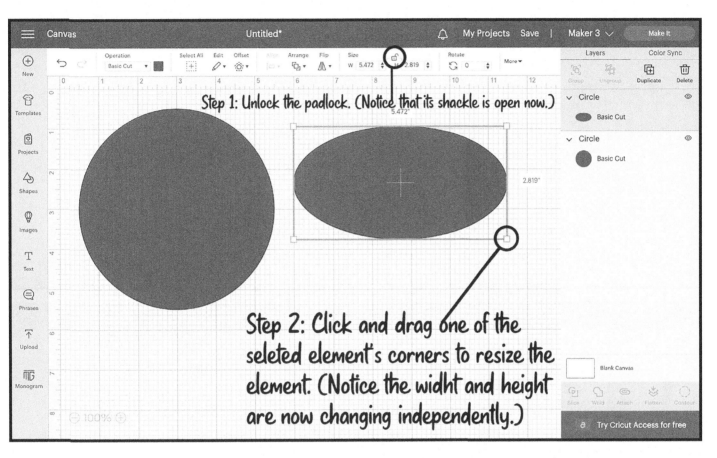

Let's play around with another shape. Select both circles using any method you learned in the *Select All* section and delete them using any method you learned in the *Edit Function* section. Right now, your Canvas should be blank again.

Pro Tip: You can quickly delete elements using your keyboard's BACKSPACE button.

Click on *Shapes* in the Design Panel and choose the heart. Unlock the padlock for the *Size* function in the Edit Bar and see how you can change its proportions by playing around with it on the Canvas. The screenshots on the next page shows what I came up with. Take your time to see how you can push and pull your shape out of proportion.

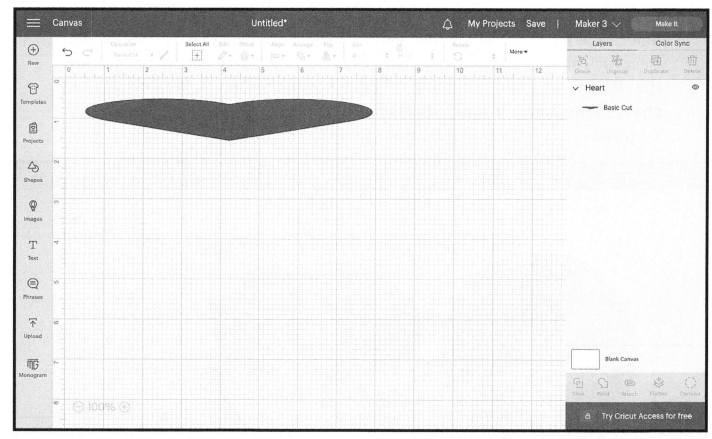

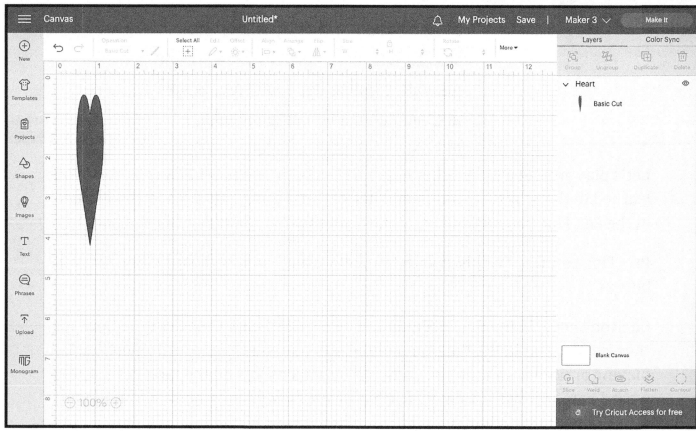

Right about now, you might be wondering if there is a way to fix a distorted shape or image if your playing around gets a little out of hand. Yep! You have a couple of options:

- Delete the shape or image and start from scratch.
- Click on the *Undo* icon in the far-left corner of the Edit Bar until you restore the shape or image to the way it was.

Pro Tip: If you ever start resizing an element and find yourself thinking, *"What the...!"* when it goes out of proportion, it's possible that Design Space is remembering that you had unlocked the *Size* function's padlock for a previous element. Also, it's easy to forget that you left the padlock unlocked for a specific element after you had adjusted its size. The best thing you can do to save your sanity is to get into the habit of always checking that little padlock's position before you tweak an element's size.

How To Use it on the Mobile App

As with the desktop app, you can adjust a design element's size proportionally, or you can unlock its proportional constraints to adjust its width and height independently. By default, elements' proportions are locked.

First, let's see how to resize an element under normal circumstances (that is, with the proportions locked in place).

Option 1

Select the element you want to tweak. Place your finger on the bottom-right corner and drag away from the element to increase its size, or push toward the element to decrease its size.

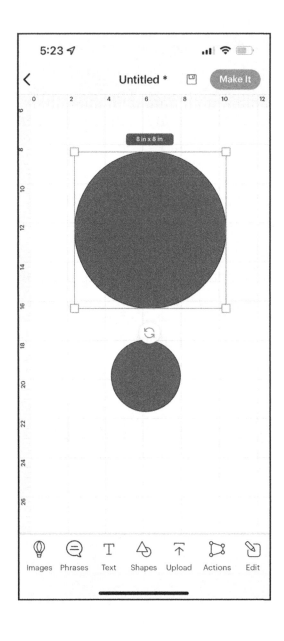

Option 2

If you prefer to enter a value to resize your element, tap on the *Edit* function in the bar at the bottom of your Canvas screen. This will bring up a secondary bar with different options, and one of those options says "Width" and "Height," with a padlock between them. (See the left-hand screenshot below.)

If you tap on the box above "Width," your app will let you enter the value you want. (See the right-hand screenshot below.)

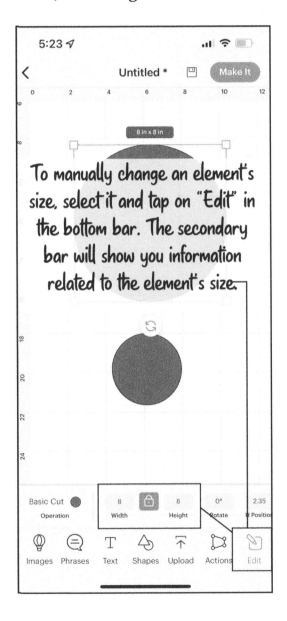

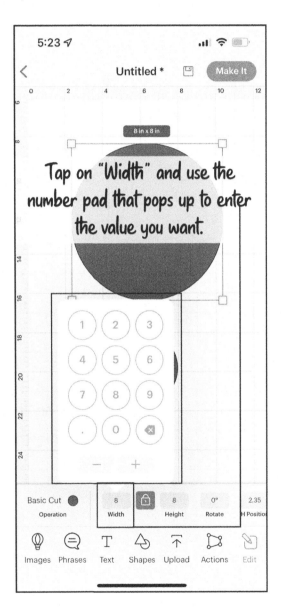

How to Unlock the Size Padlock

With the element selected, tap on *Edit* in the bar at the bottom of the screen to activate the *Edit* functions. Now you can tap on the little padlock you see in between the element's width and height settings.

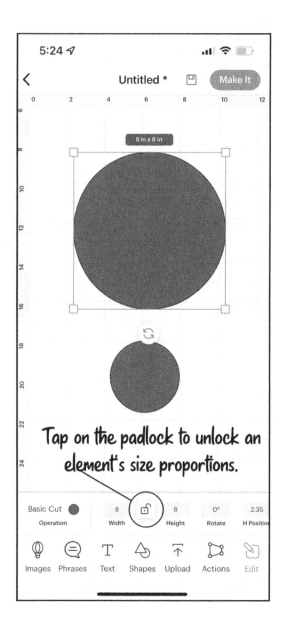

Size Function Self-Assessment

How would you explain the difference between adjusting an element's size when the Size function's padlock is locked vs. when it is unlocked?

_____

_____

_____

_____

_____

Rotate

How To Use it on the Desktop App

Before we continue, delete everything on the Canvas using any of the methods you learned in the *Edit* function section. After that, click on *Shapes* in the Design Panel and choose a heart.

The *Rotate* function lets you tilt design elements to the left or right as far as you want. To rotate an element using the **Edit Bar**, select the element first. Right next to the *Size* function, you'll see the *Rotate* function, and adjusting an element's amount of tilt works the same way as adjusting its size. Using the step arrows will tilt the element by one degree per click. Also, the "up" step arrow rotates the element to the right, while the "down" step arrow rotates it to the left. If you prefer entering a value, you can enter anything between 0 and 359, where the lower values represent tilts to the right and the higher values represent tilts to the left. Of course, degrees work in a circle, so if you go far enough to either side, you'll get the same results!

Let's turn the heart upside-down by entering a value of "180" into the *Rotate* value box. This is what you should see now:

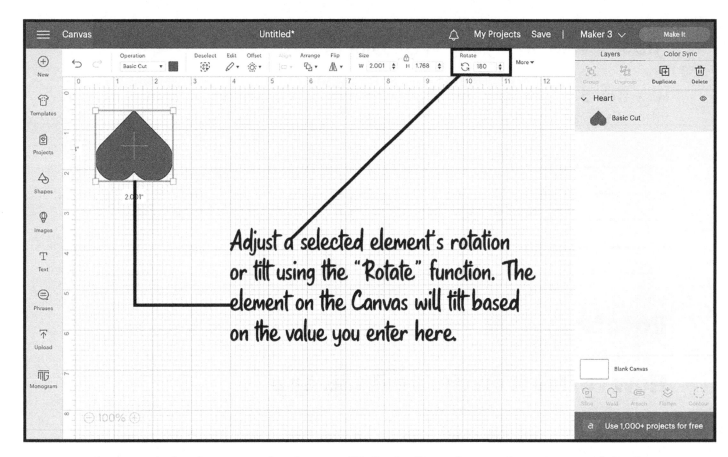

Adjust a selected element's rotation or tilt using the "Rotate" function. The element on the Canvas will tilt based on the value you enter here.

Let's rotate the heart again, but we'll do it **directly on the Canvas** this time. Remember when we adjusted the circles' sizes earlier and I told you if you see a curved arrow when hovering over the selection box, you're too far away and will rotate them instead of adjusting their size? Well, *now* I want you to hover a little further away from the selection box's corner until you see that curved arrow.

With the curved arrow visible, click and hold your mouse while dragging it to the left or right. While doing this, you should see the heart moving from side to side.

Pro Tip: It is very hard to rotate an element into an exact position directly on the Canvas. So, if you want an element rotated 90 degrees, it is better to enter that value into the Edit Bar, as opposed to trying to get it right by swinging the element around on the Canvas. However, if you're not exactly sure how much to rotate an element to make it look and feel right on the overall design, rotating it in the Canvas directly to test the best amount of tilt is the best option.

Before you move on to the next function, rotate your heart back to its original position by entering "0" into the *Rotate* function's box in the Edit Bar. Remember to hit the ENTER key on your keyboard to commit the change.

How To Use it on the Mobile App

If you still have the circles on your Canvas from our previous exercises, go ahead and delete them first. When you're done, add a heart to the Canvas.

There are two ways you can apply the *Rotate* function on your mobile app. We'll start with the easier option, as you already have access to it when you have an element selected on the Canvas.

Option 1

Select the shape and look for the rotate icon (two arrows forming a circle) underneath the selection box. Put your finger on the icon and drag your finger to the right or left. On the Android app, tap and hold the arrow turning toward itself at the upper-right corner of the selection box. While holding on, drag your finger to the right and to the left. You'll see the heart moving along with the motions of your finger.

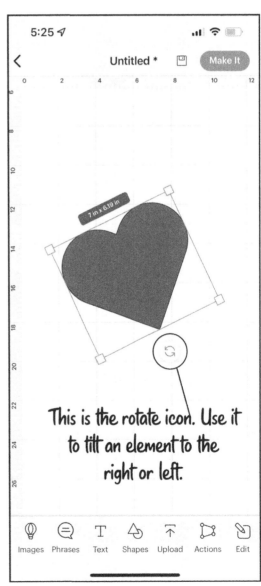

This is the rotate icon. Use it to tilt an element to the right or left.

Of course, doing this directly on the Canvas has the same drawback of doing it this way on the desktop app—it's very hard to get it in an exact position. Depending on what you're trying to achieve with your design, you might want to specify the degrees the element should tilt, instead.

Option 2

With the element selected, tap on *Edit* in the bar at the bottom of your screen. When the secondary bar pops up, swipe until you see the *Rotate* function. (See the left-hand screenshot below.) Tap on rotate to activate the numbers pad so you can enter a specific value (see the right-hand screenshot below).

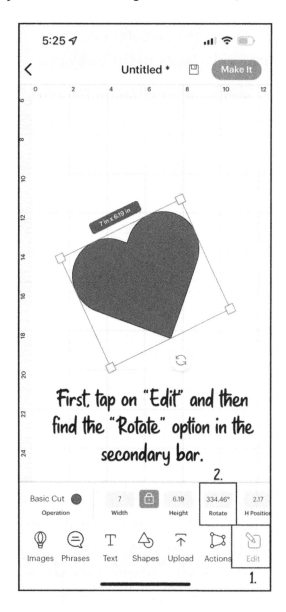

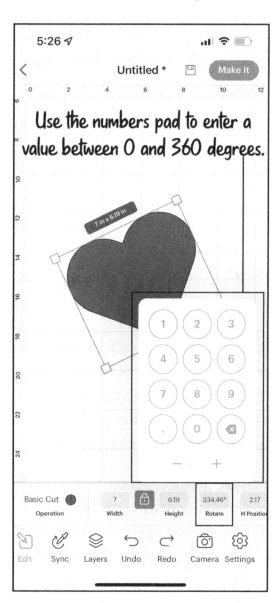

Let's tilt the heart back to its original position by entering "0" into the box above *Rotate*. When you return to the Canvas, you'll see the heart right-side up again, like you see in the screenshot on the next page.

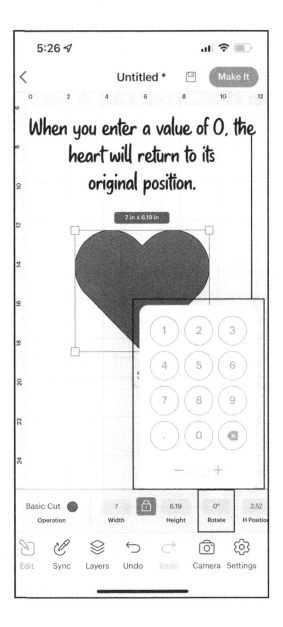

Rotate Function Self-Assessment

If someone asked you, "What's the purpose of the Rotate function in Design Space?" how would you answer?

_____

_____

_____

_____

_____

Position

How To Use it on the Desktop App

"Position" simply refers to the location of an element on the Canvas. You will rarely, if ever, use the *Position* function via the **Edit Bar**, the reason being that it moves an element around in tiny increments, so it ends up being a tedious task. That said, it might be just the thing you need when you need to nudge an element a teeny bit. Depending on the size of your computer or laptop screen, you will see this function next to the *Rotate* function. If not, you'll see *More* next to the *Rotate* function with a little downward arrow next to it. When you click on the arrow, the *Position* settings will appear.

- The "X" position moves an element to the right or left (the "up" step arrow moves it to the right and the "down" step arrow moves it to the left).

- The "Y" position moves an element up or down (the "up" step arrow moves it down and the "down" step arrow moves it up).

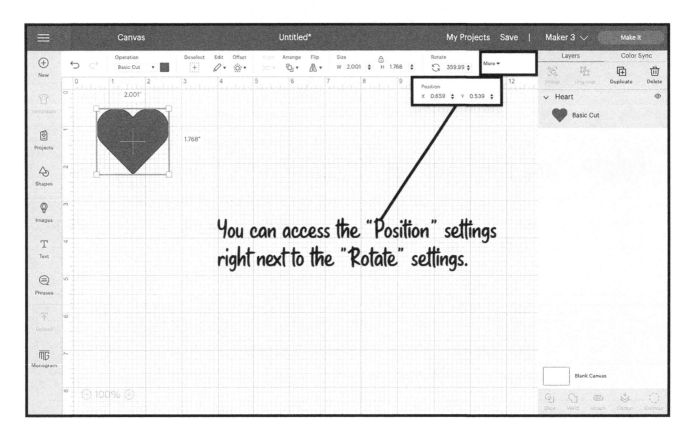

You can access the "Position" settings right next to the "Rotate" settings.

While it's good to know about the ability to adjust an element's position using the Edit Bar, you'll mostly just move things around **directly on the Canvas**. All you have to do is click on and drag an element to wherever you want it. It is also possible to move multiple elements (or all the elements) on the Canvas at once, using the selection methods we discussed in the *Select All* function section.

Play around by moving the heart on your Canvas to another position.

How To Use it on the Mobile App

As with the other functions we have discussed so far, you have two options if you want to move an element or multiple elements around.

Option 1

For simplicity's sake, this should really be your go-to option, as it is the easiest and quickest way. All you have to do is tap on the element (or elements) you'd like to move, press down, and drag it with your finger to the spot you'd like to place it.

Option 2

This option is similar to using the Edit Bar when working with the desktop app, and I don't recommend it unless you need to make precision adjustments to an element's position.

With the element selected, tap on *Edit* in the bar at the bottom of the screen and swipe until you see "H Position" and "V Position." (See the left-hand screenshot on the next page.)

Tap on either "H Position" or "V Position" to edit where the element should go on the Canvas. Unlike the Edit Bar on the desktop app, there are no step arrows here, so you'll have to enter a value. (See the right-hand screenshot on the next page.)

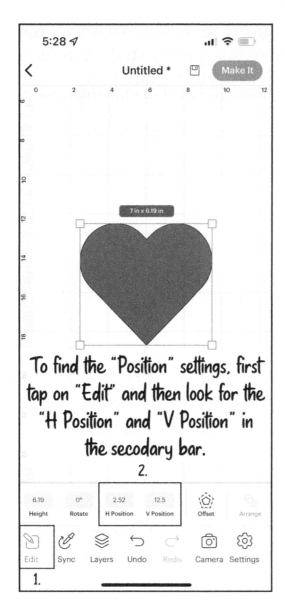

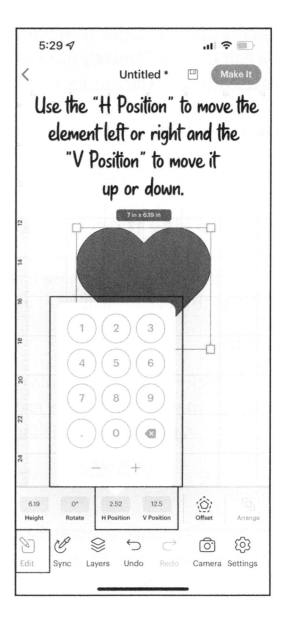

Pro Tip: For the "H Position," higher values will push the element to the right while lower values will push it to the left. And for the "V Position," higher values will push the element down while lower values will push it up.

Position Function Self-Assessment

What is the best method to move elements around on the Canvas when you don't need to make precision adjustments? Explain this for both the desktop and mobile apps.

_____

_____

_____

_____

_____

Arrange

Before we get started...

Take note that there is a difference between an element's *physical* position on the Canvas and its *hierarchical* position in relation to other elements on the Canvas.

If you have three elements on the Canvas, you may have them positioned next to each other, far away from each other, close to each other, or maybe on top of each other. Those are their physical positions on the Canvas, and it's the *Position* function that helps you move them around.

However, each one of those elements has a hierarchical position, too, and none of them can occupy the same position, kind of like how you get first, second, and third places in a race. In other words, one element is at the top, one is in the middle, and another one is at the bottom. And although they can't occupy the same positions, you can move them around. For example, you can move the bottom element so it takes up the top position and vice versa.

If you stack elements on your Canvas on top of each other (as you'll often do when designing your projects), this hierarchical order becomes apparent, and the *Arrange* function is the one that helps you determine your design elements' hierarchical positions on the Canvas.

How To Use it on the Desktop App

To better understand the *Arrange* function, we need more elements on the Canvas. Click on *Shapes* in the Design Panel and choose a square (it doesn't matter if you choose the one with the round or sharp edges). Next, let's *Duplicate* the heart twice, using any of the methods we talked about in the *Edit* function section. Finally, move your shapes around so there is some space between them. Apart from your shapes probably being in different positions than mine, this is what you should see now:

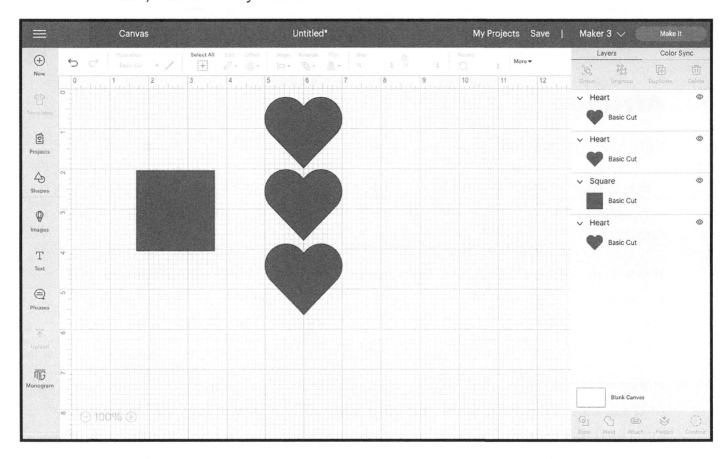

Increase the square's size so it is large enough for a heart to fit inside it (see the screenshot on the next page).

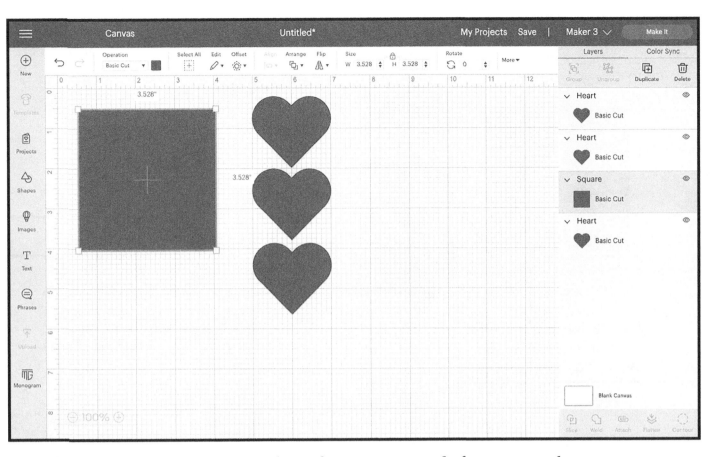

At this stage, when you look at the **Layers Panel**, from top to bottom, you should see:

- Heart
- Heart
- Square
- Heart

This information tells you that, if you were to drag the elements so they all overlap, they would be arranged in that exact order. Since the heart shape at the bottom of the list is smaller than the square above it, you will not actually see it once they are aligned. Let's see this in action.

Click on the last heart shape in the Layers Panel. This will help you identify which heart on the Canvas is the one at the bottom.

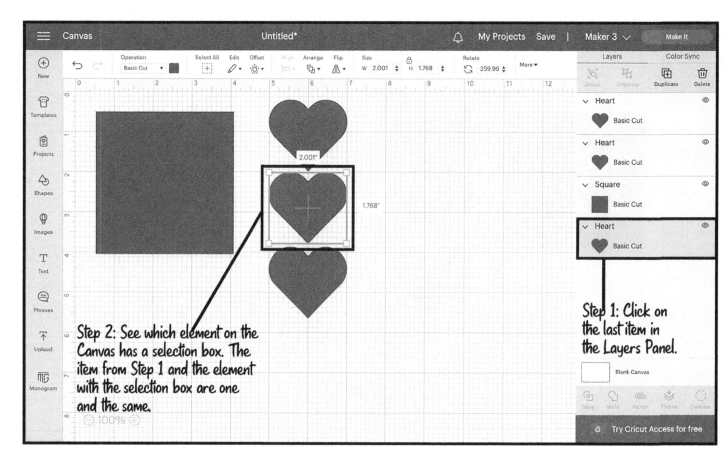

Now, **directly on the Canvas**, move the heart with the selection box around it toward the square shape and try to position it more or less in the center of the square. Note that, because the heart currently sits underneath the square (as you see in the Layers Panel), you will no longer see the heart, but you will see its selection box.

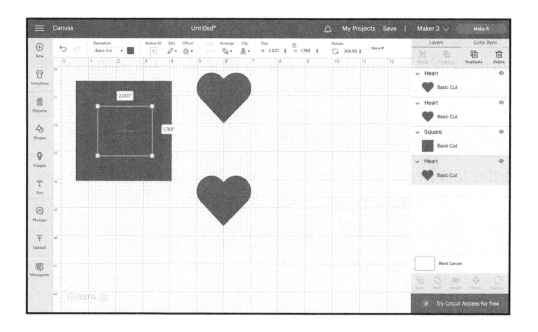

Next, we'll move this heart so it sits on top of the square using the **Edit Bar's** *Arrange* function. With the heart still selected, click on *Arrange* in the Edit Bar. If you have accidentally deselected the heart, simply click on the last item you see in the Layers Panel again and then follow the above step.

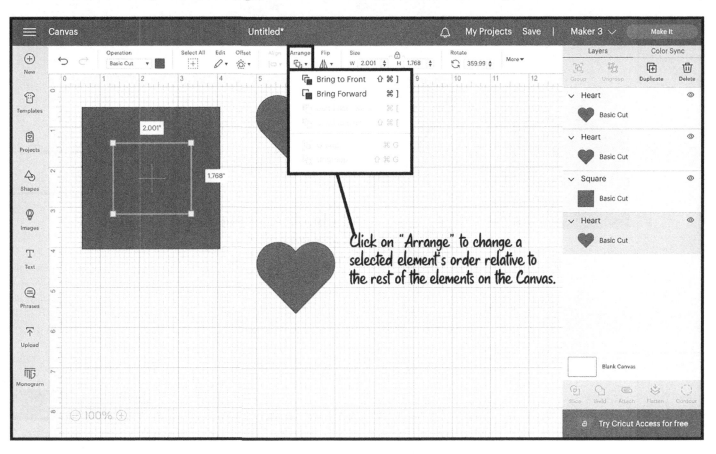

The two available options you see may confuse you, as they seem to be saying the same thing. However, *Bring to Front* means that you want to bring an element *all* the way to the front of the Canvas so it sits on top of everything else in the Canvas. *Bring Forward* means that you want to move the selected element one spot up so it sits on top of the element currently above it.

Pro Tip: If you ever get confused, look at the icons next to the descriptions of the *Arrange* function's options. One icon shows a black box sitting on top of all the other boxes, while the other icon shows a black box sitting on top of one other box.

For this exercise, we just want the heart to move one spot up so it can sit on top of the square, so let's click on *Bring Forward.* You should now see the heart shape sitting on top of the square, where you could not see it before.

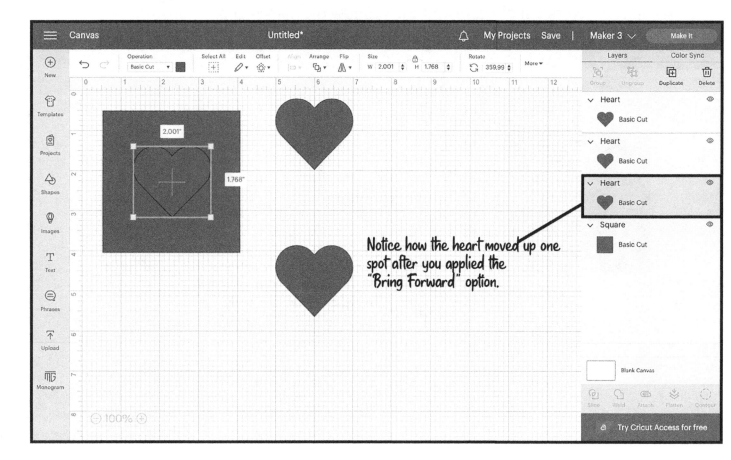

Look at the Layers Panel again. See how the order of the elements have changed? It should now look like this:

- Heart
- Heart
- Heart
- Square

The following two hearts are already in the correct order, so you need not actually do anything with them. However, if we were to use the *Arrange* function **directly on the Canvas**, we would right click on the selected element and then select the action we want to complete, like you see on the next page.

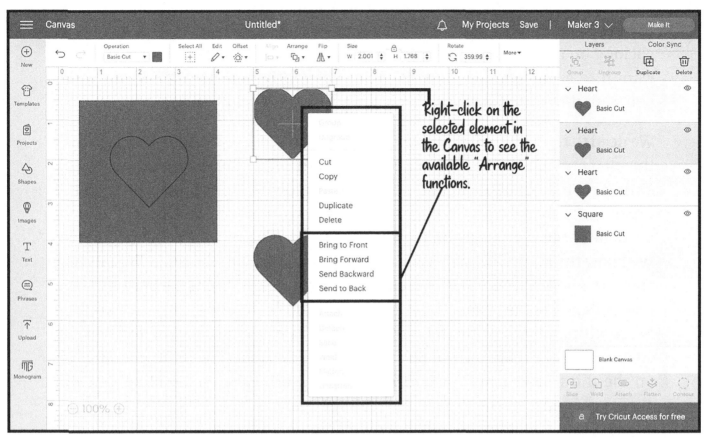

And if we were to use the *Arrange* function via the **Layers Panel**, we would select an element underneath another element, right click, and select the desired function, like this:

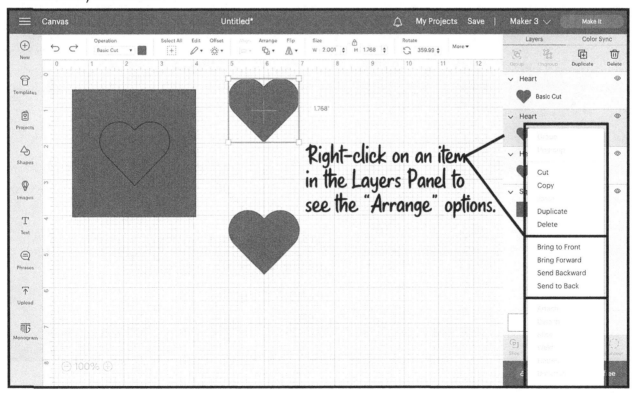

Pro Tip: A quick way to change the order of elements via the Layers Panel is by clicking on the element you want to move and then dragging it upward if you want it to move forward (so it sits on top of another element) or downward if you want it to move backward (so it sits underneath another element).

We need to resize the other two hearts so it will be easier to see them as we stack the elements on top of each other. Let's start with the one that is currently sitting on top of the heart we placed on the square (we're talking about the order of the shapes here, as opposed to their positions on the Canvas). To help us identify the right heart on the Canvas, we need help from the Layers Panel. We know the square lies at the bottom, and the heart we moved earlier sits just above it. All we have to do now is click on the third heart from the bottom in the Layers Panel, as the Layers Panel is telling us that's the one sitting on top of the heart sitting on top of the square (again, we're talking about the *order* of the shapes, and not their current positions on the Canvas). The moment you click on the third heart from the bottom in the Layers Panel, a selection box will appear around it on the Canvas, like you see below:

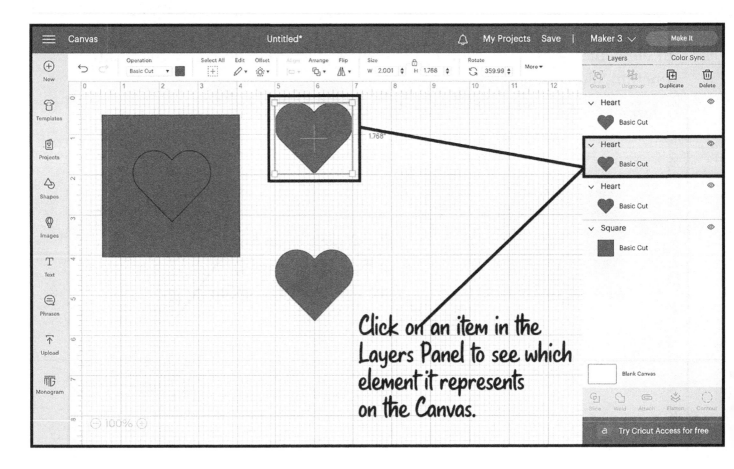

Click on an item in the Layers Panel to see which element it represents on the Canvas.

Once selected, adjust the heart's width to 1.5 inches and press the ENTER key on your keyboard. Since the adjustment padlock is in the locked position, the height will adjust automatically in proportion to the value you enter.

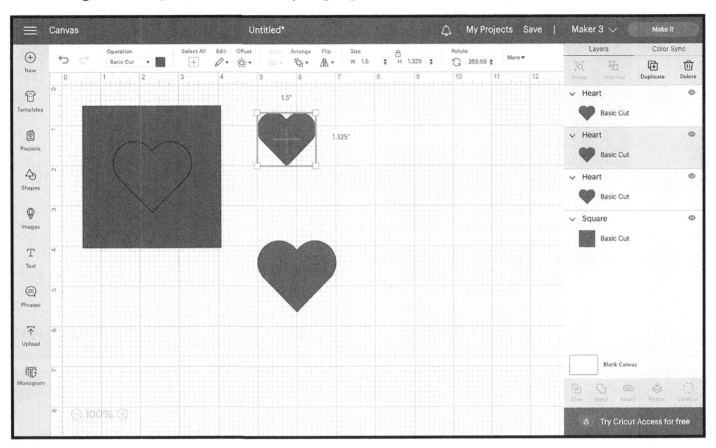

Now drag the heart over to the heart you placed on the square earlier and position it so it sits more or less center on that heart. (See the first screenshot on the next page.)

Since it's easy to identify the last heart we need to stack on the other shapes (it's the only 'odd one out' on the canvas now), you can just click on it in the Canvas area. Before we drag it over to the stacked elements, let's adjust its size to 1 inch. When you have moved the last heart over, your Canvas should look like the Canvas in the second screenshot on the next page.

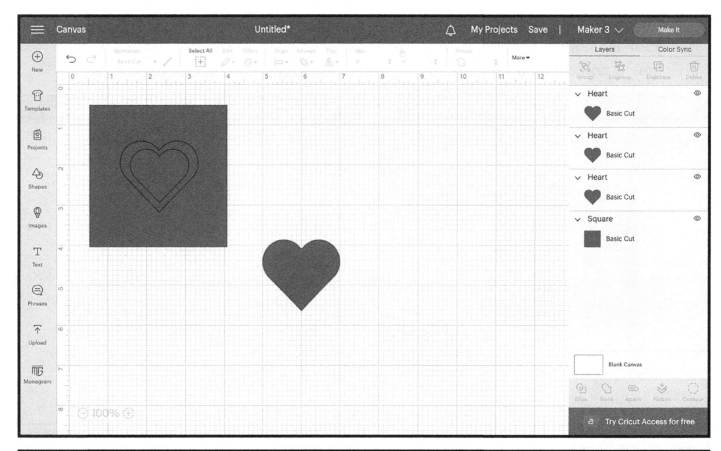

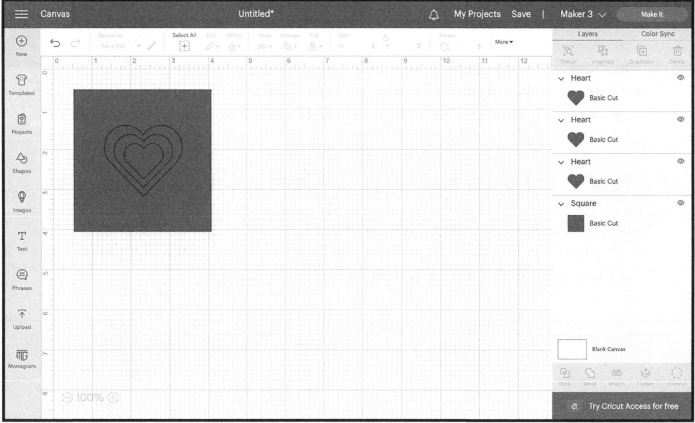

There are two more *Arrange* function options we have not yet explored: *Send Backward* and *Send to Back*. To see how they work, select the second heart from the top in the Layers Panel. Next, click on the *Arrange* function in the Edit Bar. Notice how all four arrangement options are now available.

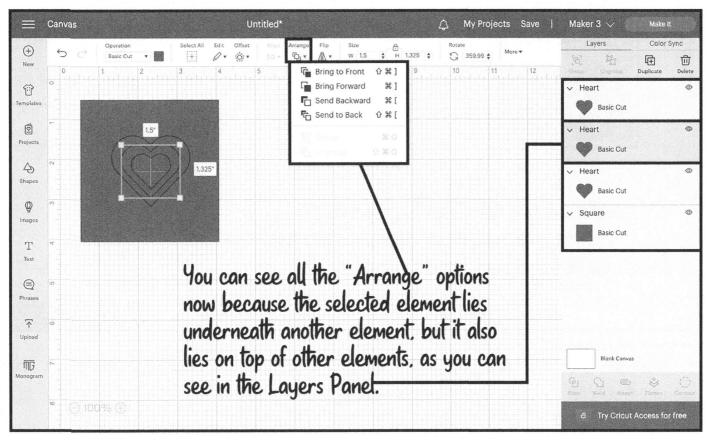

As with the *Bring to Front* and *Bring Forward* actions, the secret to understanding the *Send Backward* and *Send to Back* actions lie in the icons right next to the descriptions.

Send Backward pushes an element one spot down so it sits underneath the element it is currently sitting on top of, while *Send to Back* pushes an element *all* the way underneath everything else on the Canvas.

Play around by applying one of the new options you just learned about. I moved my heart (the one I had selected) all the way to the back, and you can see what it looks like on the next page.

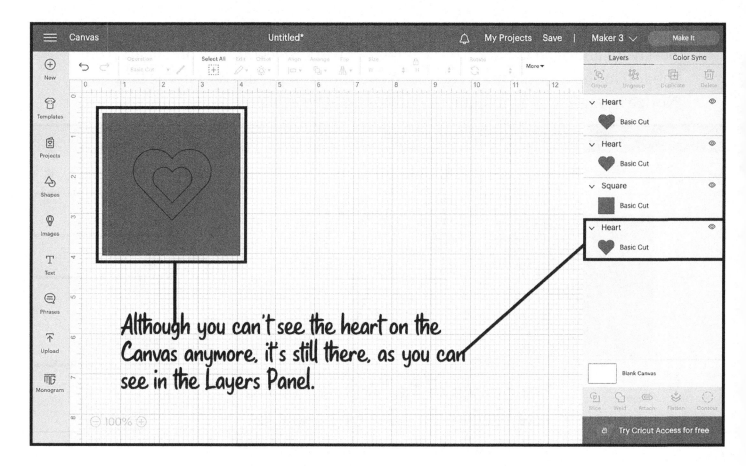

Although you can't see the heart on the Canvas anymore, it's still there, as you can see in the Layers Panel.

Granted, you can't actually see the heart anymore, but it's definitely there. The best way to confirm this is by looking at the Layers Panel. The square is no longer the one at the very bottom, but the heart I just moved is.

How To Use it on the Mobile App

The only way to arrange the order of elements on the mobile app is via the Edit function in the bar at the bottom of the Canvas screen. First, let's add a square to the Canvas and make it bigger; around 5 inches is fine. Next, *Duplicate* the heart you already have in the Canvas twice. Enlarge one a bit, but it should be small enough to fit inside the square, and then make the other two slightly smaller (each one should be a different size). Apart from your shapes being in different positions than mine, the screenshot on the next page shows what you should be seeing now.

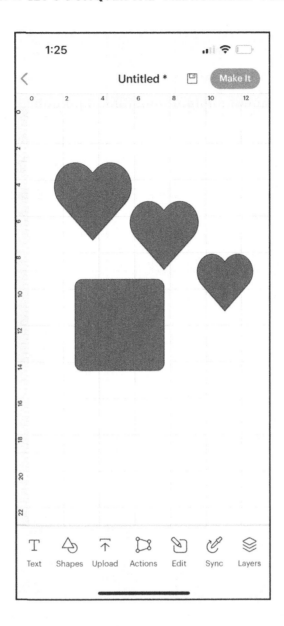

Pro Tip: If you don't have the desktop app and skipped ahead to this part, you missed some important information about the *Arrange* options that we're not going to repeat here. Unless you are familiar with the *Arrange* function, please take a moment to track back to the beginning of this section to read about it.

The idea with this exercise is to stack all the shapes in the Canvas on top of each other, from the largest shape to the smallest shape.

We'll start with the square, so go ahead and select it. Tap on *Edit* in the bottom bar and swipe the secondary bar until you see Arrange, like you see in the left-hand screenshot on the next page. Now tap on *Arrange* and then tap on *Send to Back*, like you see in the right-hand illustration on the next page.

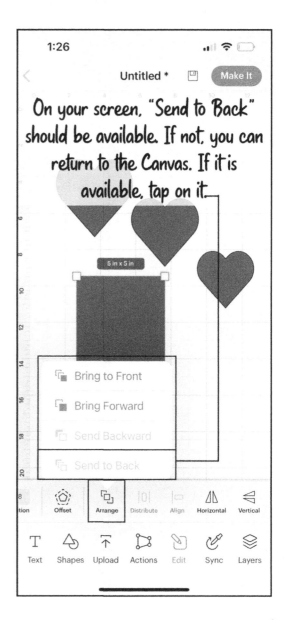

Next, select the biggest heart and drag it so it sits more or less in the square's center. (See the left-hand illustration on the next page.) Of the two hearts remaining outside the square, select the bigger one and drag it over to the square and heart you have already positioned on top of it. If you can see the outline of this heart as it comes in contact with the square and first heart, like you see in the right-hand screenshot on the next page, it means it's in the correct order and you don't have to do anything with the *Arrange* function for it.

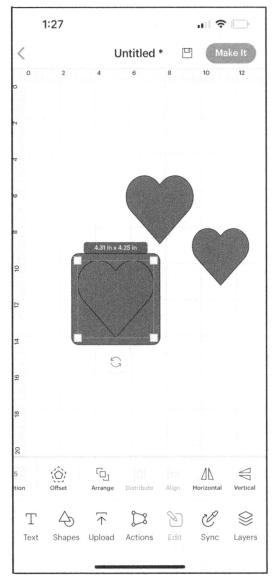

However, if its outline seems to disappear as it comes in contact with the heart sitting on top of the square, like you see in left-hand illustration on the next page, it means that it is sitting underneath that heart and needs to move up a position so it can sit on top of it. If that's the case, go to the *Arrange* function and choose the *Bring Forward* option. You should now see the heart's outline appear, and you're ready to position it on top of the bigger heart. Try to get it more or less in the center of the square and bigger heart (like you see in the right-hand illustration above), but don't aim for perfection.

Finally, you can move the smallest heart over so it sits on top of the other shapes, like you see in the right-hand screenshot on the next page. Again, if it looks like it's disappearing underneath the other hearts, use the *Arrange* function's *Bring Forward* or *Bring to Front* option to make it sit at the very top.

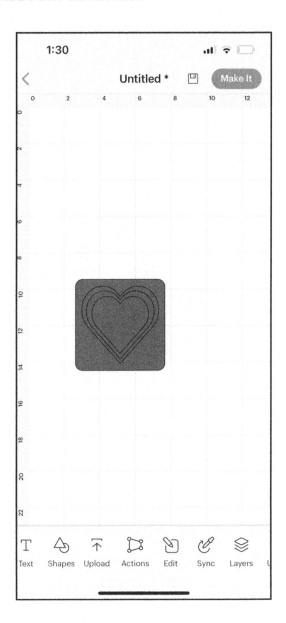

Pro Tip: Although you can see the arrangement of elements on your mobile app's Layers Panel when you open it, you can't actually do anything to change their order from there like you can on the desktop app.

Arrange Function Self-Assessment

How would you explain the difference between a design element's physical position and its hierarchical position on the Canvas?

_____

_____

_____

_____

_____

If you have five or more elements on your Canvas, how do you know which one is at the very bottom and which one is at the very top?

_____

_____

_____

_____

_____

How do you move an element in front of another element?

_____

_____

_____

_____

_____

How do you move an element underneath another element?

_____

_____

_____

_____

_____

If I want to move an element all the way to the front, what Arrange option should I choose?

_____

_____

If I want to move an element all the way to the back, what Arrange option should I choose?

_____

_____

True or False: It's possible to rearrange the order of design elements in the mobile app's Layers Panel.

_____

_____

Slice

How To Use it on the Desktop App

The *Slice* function is basically your digital cookie cutter, allowing you to use design elements to cut out parts of other design elements in unique ways. This function only works when you have two elements overlapping each other, and you can apply it via directly on the Canvas or from the Layers Panel.

Let's see this in action with the shapes we stacked on each other in the previous section. We'll start by selecting the square and the heart directly on top of it and moving it to the side, away from the other two hearts. This is the result you should see after moving them:

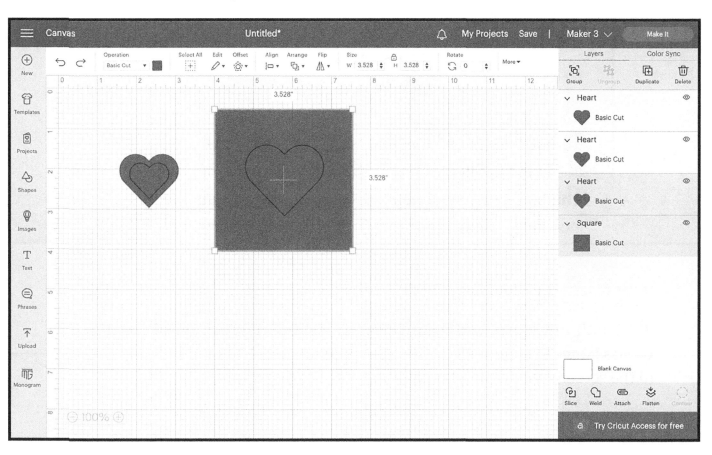

You can apply the *Slice* function with any of the following methods:

Option 1: On the Canvas

With both the square and heart selected, right click on them in the Canvas and choose *Slice* from the pop-up menu that appears.

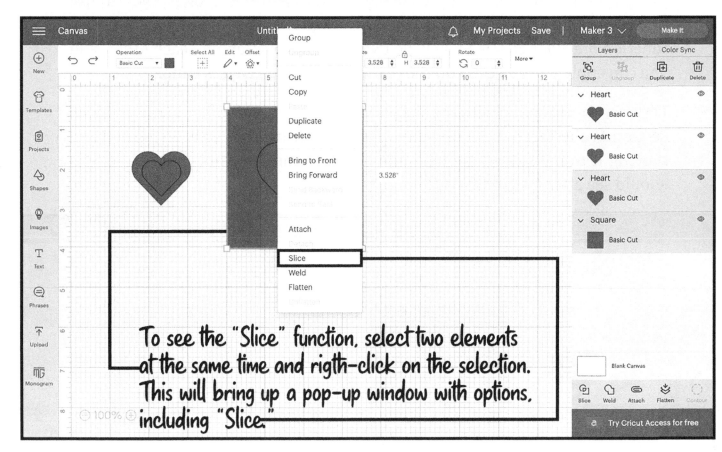

Option 2: In the Layers Panel

With both the square and heart selected, right click on either of them in the Layers Panel and choose *Slice* from the pop-up menu that appears, like you see in the screenshot on the next page.

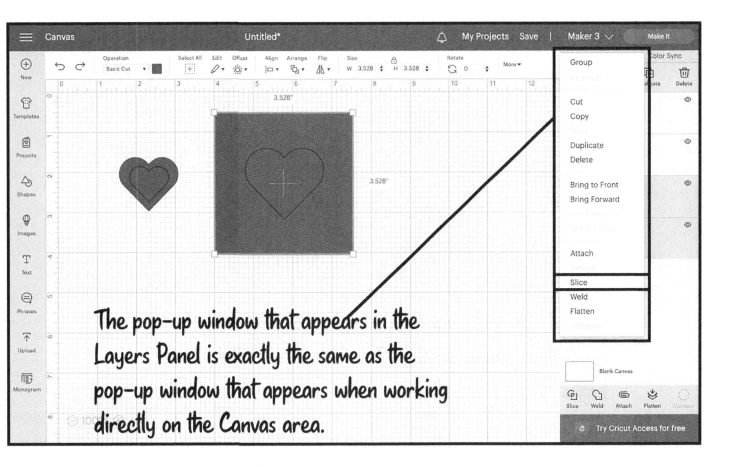

The pop-up window that appears in the Layers Panel is exactly the same as the pop-up window that appears when working directly on the Canvas area.

Option 3: Layers Panel Shortcut

With both the square and heart selected, a few shortcut actions will become active at the bottom of the Layers Panel. The first option from the left says *Slice*, and you can simply click on that icon instead of the other two methods. (See the first screenshot on the next page.)

Now it's your turn. Perform the Slice function using any of the above methods.

Uh-oh! As you can see, it looks like nothing has changed...

However, if you study your Layers Panel, you will see three new items, all named *Slice Result*. Let's see what they are. On the Canvas, click and drag the heart away from the square. According to the Layers Panel, we have just moved away one of the *Slice Result* layers. (See the second screenshot on the next page.)

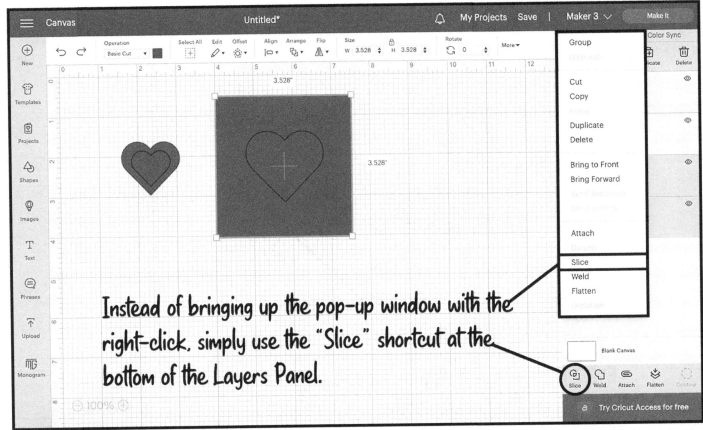

Instead of bringing up the pop-up window with the right-click, simply use the "Slice" shortcut at the bottom of the Layers Panel.

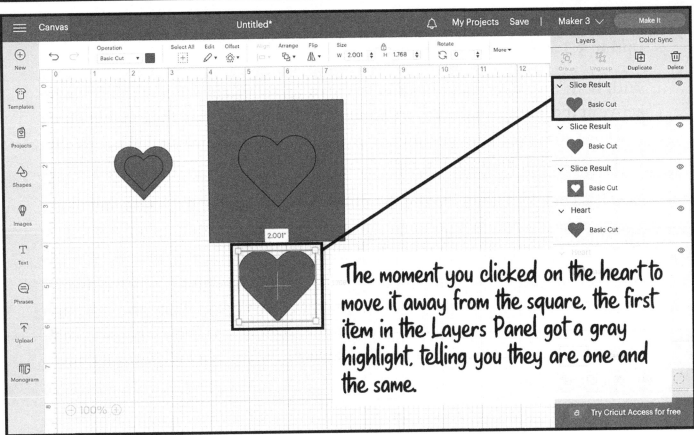

The moment you clicked on the heart to move it away from the square, the first item in the Layers Panel got a gray highlight, telling you they are one and the same.

Apart from the fact that there is now an extra heart on the Canvas, nothing seems different. Let's move the other heart, also called *Slice Result*, away from the square too. This time, the result of applying the Slice function is clear: there is a heart-shaped hole in the square!

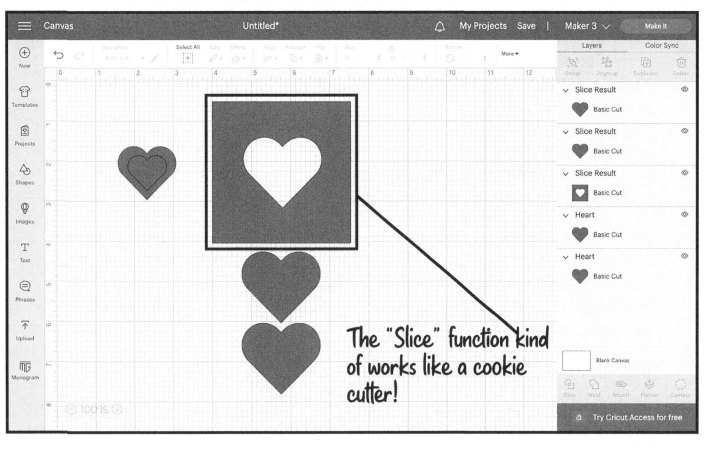

You can get very creative with this function and make all kinds of projects with cut-out effects. And its capabilities are not limited to shapes only. You can do this with letters, words, and even silhouettes of real-life objects like animals, household items, and whatever you can think of.

How To Use it on the Mobile App

We're still using the shapes from the previous section. Select the square and heart directly on top of it and move them to a clean space on the Canvas.

Pro Tip: Since the shapes are stacked, you might have some difficulty selecting both at once, so feel free to move them one at a time, put the heart back on the square, and then select both using the methods you learned in the *Select All* function section.

With the square and heart both selected, tap on *Actions* in the bar at the bottom of the screen. Swipe the secondary bar that appears until you see the Slice function, like you see in the left-hand screenshot on the next page.

Tap on *Slice* to apply the action. To see the result, select the heart on the square and drag it away. As you can see in the right-hand illustration on the next page, there is no hole in the square yet. Select the other heart on the square, too, and drag it away. This time, the heart-shaped hole in the square is clearly visible, like you see in the third screenshot on the next page.

But why did the *Slice* function make an extra heart?!

As mentioned at the start of this section, you need two elements for the *Slice* function to work. The action cuts out *every* contour of overlapping elements, so all the elements in that selection influence one another. In the case of our example, the extra heart was formed because the original heart lay perfectly in the middle of the square. However, if the original heart were off-center, like maybe sticking over the square's side, you would get a different result, like you see on page 190.

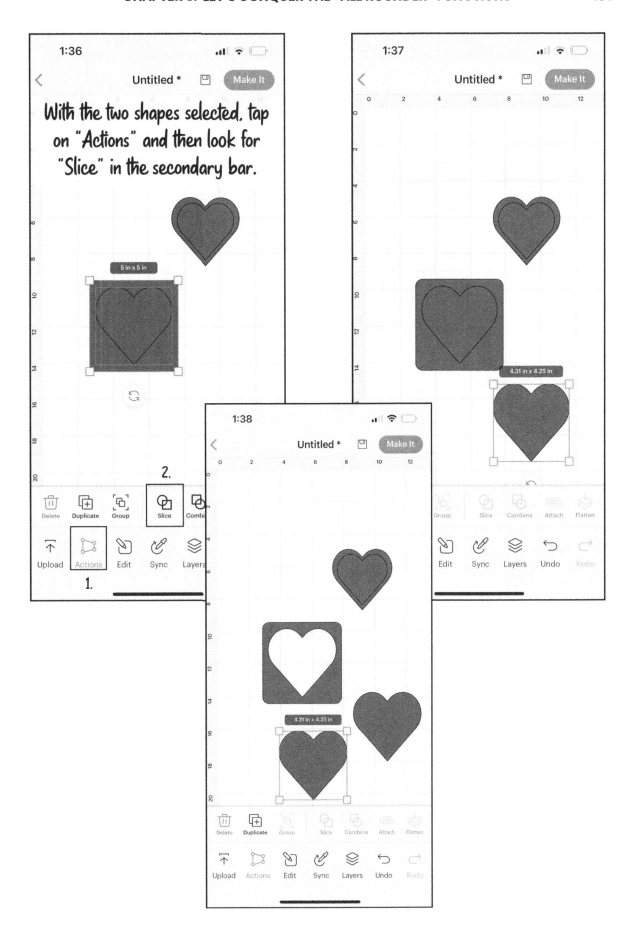

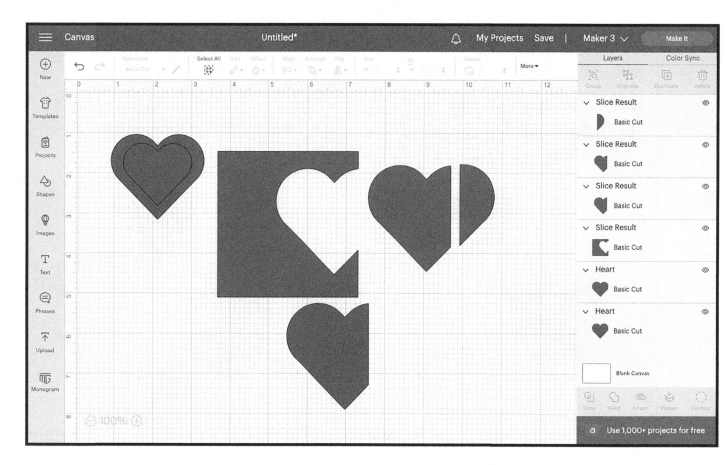

The above screenshot illustrates how the Slice Function can give you different results depending on where two elements overlap each other.

Slice Function Self-Assessment

In your own words, explain what the slice function does.

_____

_____

_____

_____

_____

Weld

How To Use it on the Desktop App

Good to know: While writing this book, Design Space had a major update that influenced the look of the Layers Panel. Note that your desktop app might look slightly different from the screenshots you see. You might see *Combine* instead of *Weld* next to *Slice* at the bottom of your Layers Panel. Simply click on *Combine* to access the *Weld* function and check out page 307 to learn more about the update that introduced the *Combine* function.

While the *Slice* function cuts out parts of shapes, the *Weld* function fuses them together. To see this in action, let's drag one of the heart shapes we moved away from the square back into place. Try to position it so it fits into the heart-shaped gap exactly. If you see white gaps, keep on tweaking the heart's position until the gaps are filled completely.

Pro Tip: This is one of those rare situations where using the Position function's step arrows in the Edit Bar might come in handy! By the way, you can also use your keyboard's arrow buttons instead of clicking on the step arrows.

To apply the *Weld* function, you can use the same three methods we discussed in the *Slice* function section that is, directly on the Canvas, via the Layers Panel, or with the Layers Panel shortcut). Of course, instead of *Slice*, you will choose *Weld* this time.

If you need a quick recap on those methods, refer back to the *Slice* function above.

Once you apply the *Weld* function, your result should look similar to the first screenshot on the next page. If you still see parts of the heart's outline after applying the *Weld* function, like in the second screenshot on the next page, you have two options to get rid of it.

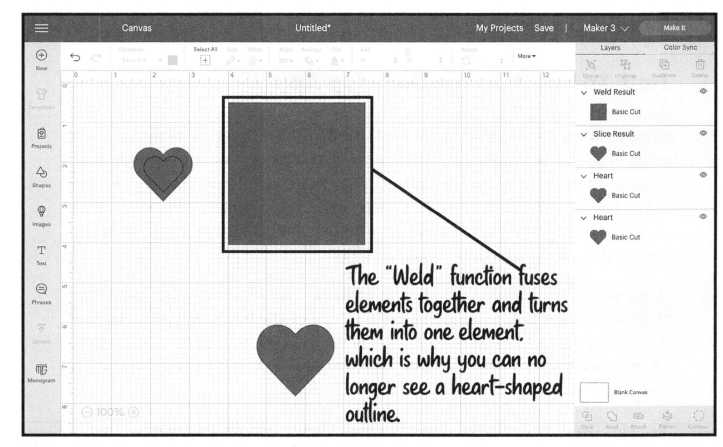

The "Weld" function fuses elements together and turns them into one element, which is why you can no longer see a heart-shaped outline.

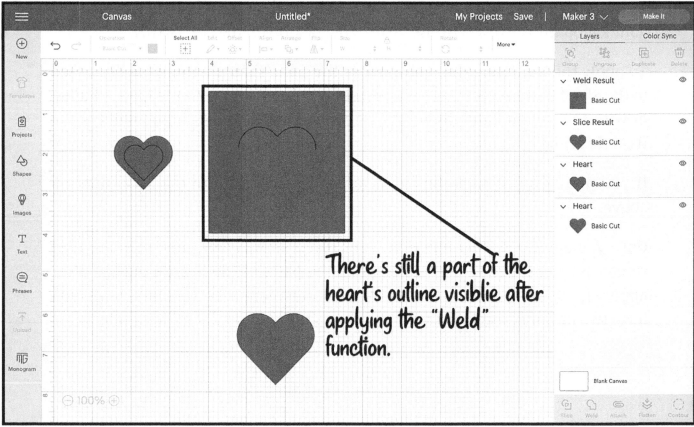

There's still a part of the heart's outline visiblie after applying the "Weld" function.

Option 1

Click on the *Undo* icon in the far-left corner of the Edit Bar to go back one step, then adjust the heart and apply the *Weld* function again. This may or may not work, and if you have a magical amount of patience in you, you can use the *Undo* function again, adjust the shape again, and apply the *Weld* function again. Of course, this process could repeat itself over and over (and over) until you get it right.

Option 2

Simply enlarge the heart shape so it goes over every edge of the gap and then use the *Weld* function. This will ensure that no outlines remain and you'll have a full square again.

But wait!

The *Weld* function offers you so much more than merely filling gaps. If you have a shape in mind that is not available in the Design Space Shapes library, you can use this function to create your own. Let's try out an example.

Before we make a new shape, let's stack the square and hearts on top of each other again. By now, the arrangement order of the shapes has changed from all of our tweaking, so the square is now on top of all the hearts. You can confirm this by looking at the Layers Panel; the square (now called *Weld Result*) is at the very top of the list in the Layers Panel, like you see in the first screenshot on the next page.

In the Layers Panel, click on the square and drag it all the way to the bottom of the list. Next, we need to arrange the heart that we initially moved with the square so it sits on top of it again. Click on that heart in the Canvas area. According to the Layers Panel, it is sitting on top of all the other shapes at the moment, as you can see in the second screenshot on the next page.

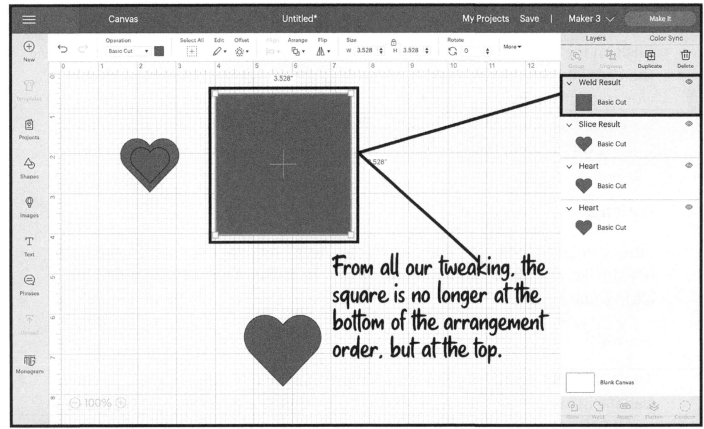

From all our tweaking, the square is no longer at the bottom of the arrangement order, but at the top.

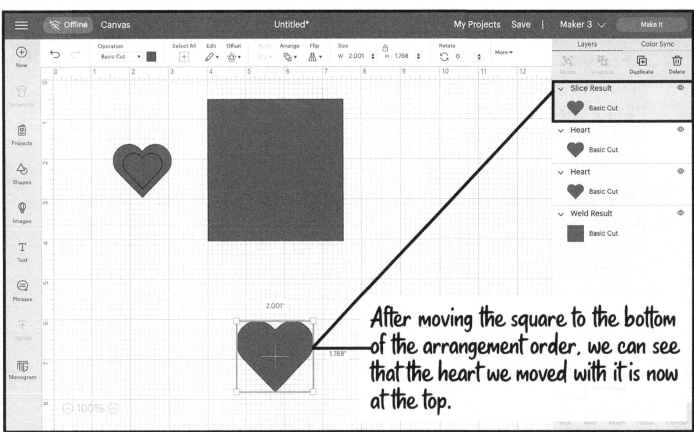

After moving the square to the bottom of the arrangement order, we can see that the heart we moved with it is now at the top.

Click on this heart in the Layers Panel and drag it toward the bottom of the list so it sits just above the square.

This is the order you should see in your Layers Panel now:

- Heart
- Heart
- Slice Result (previously called "Heart")
- Weld Result (previously called "Square")

Now we can stack everything in the Canvas area top of each other again. To start, move the heart that we dragged away from the square earlier back into position.

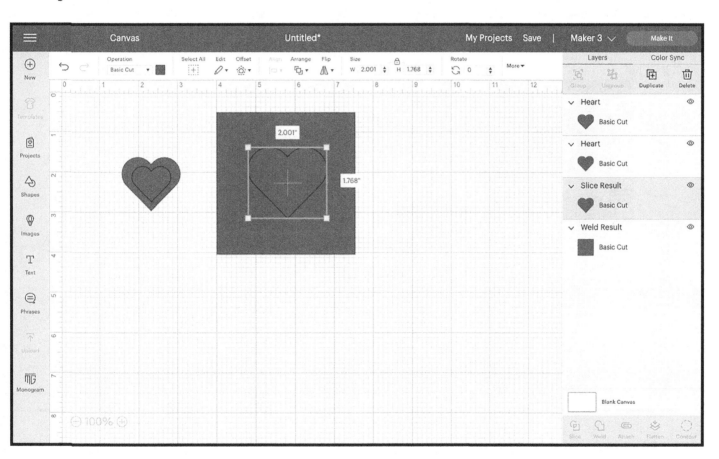

Next, select both the square and the heart on top of it and move them toward the other two hearts. Don't worry if everything does not line up perfectly. The most important thing you must see is that each shape is stacked in the correct order (from smallest to largest).

Now let's get back to the *Weld* function. Let's get some new shapes from the Shapes library in the Design Panel. Let's go with:

- A star
- A plus sign
- A heart

Pro Tip: You can't choose all the shapes at once, so you have to go back to the Shapes library every time to add a new shape to your Canvas.

Next, let's *Duplicate* the star. By now, this is what you should have on your Canvas:

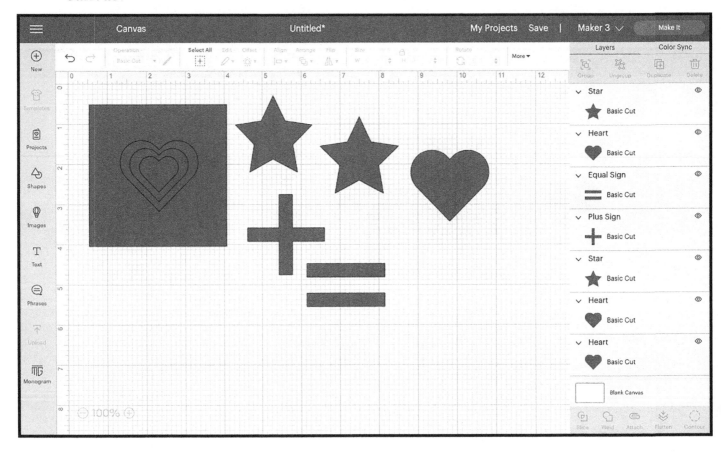

Play around with the extra shapes on your canvas by bringing them close to each other. See if you can create some kind of pattern you like. The most important part of this exercise is that the shapes should touch or overlap one another. The screenshot on the next page shows what I came up with.

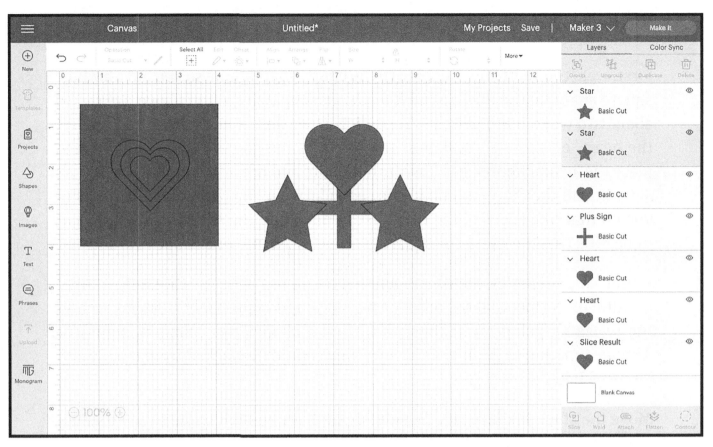

When you're happy with the arrangement of your shapes, apply the *Weld* function. You'll know it was applied successfully when the outlines of the individual shapes have disappeared and you have a single shape, like this:

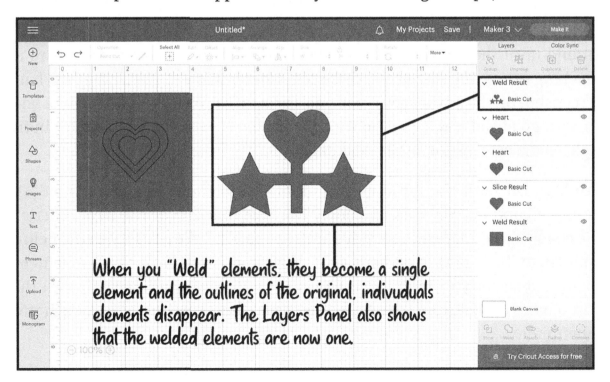

When you "Weld" elements, they become a single element and the outlines of the original, indivuduals elements disappear. The Layers Panel also shows that the welded elements are now one.

How To Use it on the Mobile App

First, weld the heart and square with the heart-shaped hole so you have a whole square again. In the *How To Use it on the Desktop App* section above, we talked about two ways to achieve this. The quickest, easiest way is option 2. So, select the heart, enlarge its edges past the edges of the gap inside the square, and place the heart over the gap. Select the square and the heart on top of it, tap on *Actions*, and then tap on *Weld* in the secondary bar that appears. The moment you do that, the edges of the heart in the middle of the square will disappear, indicating that the heart and square are now fused into one shape (the square).

With that done, stack the square and hearts on top of each other again, being mindful of the fact that the order of the shapes have probably changed with all the tweaking going on. If the order of your shapes has changed, apply the *Arrange* function to get it right again (they should be stacked from smallest to largest when you're done).

Move the stacked shapes to the side so you have enough space to see the new shapes you'll be adding to the Canvas.

Pro Tip: If your screen is getting too small for everything, zoom out of the Canvas to give yourself more working space.

Go to your Shapes library and add any four shapes you like. Move these shapes around until they form an arrangement you like, but make sure they're all touching or overlapping each other somewhere, like you see in the left-hand screenshot on the next page. When you're happy with the arrangement of your shapes, go ahead and apply the *Weld* function. See what I came up with in the right-hand screenshot on the next page.

Pro Tip: On **both the desktop and mobile app**, there are no "unweld" or "unslice" options. So, once you apply the *Slice* function or the *Weld* function, the change is permanent. The only way to go back from there is with the help of your trusty *Undo* button on both apps. However, if you *Weld* or *Slice* elements today and decide you don't like the results tomorrow, you'll have to start that part of your design from scratch, as your *Undo* function cannot go back in time indefinitely.

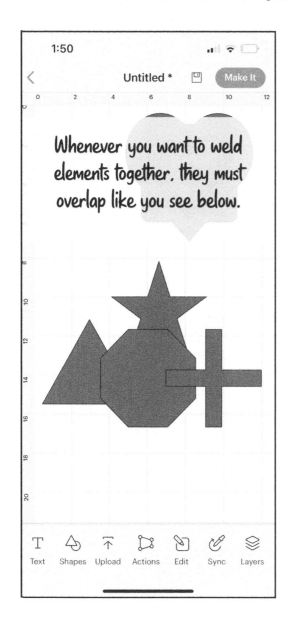

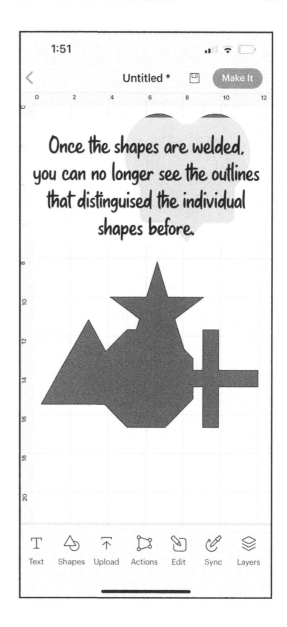

Weld Function Self-Assessment

In your own words, explain the difference between the Slice and Weld functions.

_____

_____

_____

_____

_____

True or False: If I use the Weld function to create a new shape, I can "unweld" it later.

_____

_____

Group/Ungroup

How To Use it on the Desktop App

When you group elements, you are essentially creating a way to bulk-select that group of elements whenever you click on just one of the elements within the group.

Before we practice this function, let's delete the welded shape we created in the *Weld* function section. Once deleted, you should only see the stacked shapes we have been working with all along.

At the moment, if you click on any individual shape within that stack and drag your mouse, you will take the selected shape away from its current position without affecting the positions of the rest of the shapes.

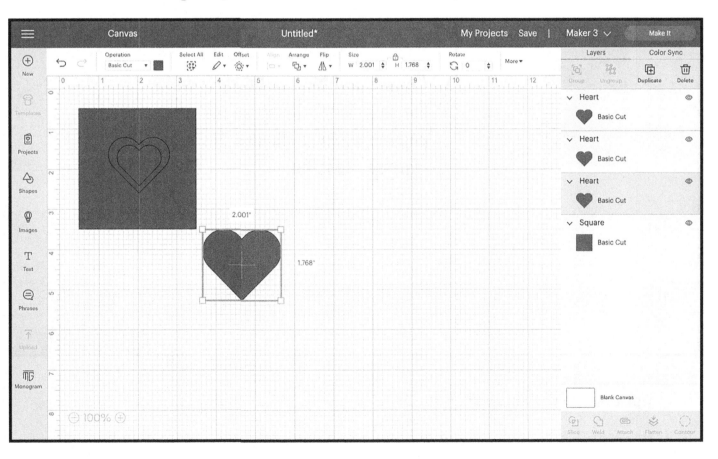

Let's say we want Design Space to treat those shapes as a unit. In other words, if we click on any one of the shapes within the stack, we want to select *all* of them at the same time. This is useful when, for example, you have in mind to move a group of elements from one spot to another spot on the Canvas.

Select all the shapes on the Canvas. Next, apply the *Group* function using any of the following methods:

Option 1: On the Canvas

Right click on the selection box around the shapes directly on the Canvas and click on *Group* when the pop-up menu appears.

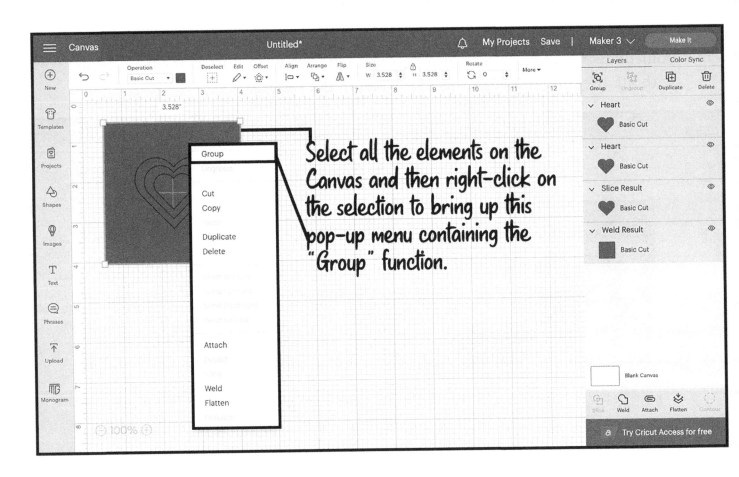

Option 2: In the Edit Bar

With all the shapes selected, click on the *Arrange* function in the Edit Bar and click on *Group*. (See the screenshot on the next page.)

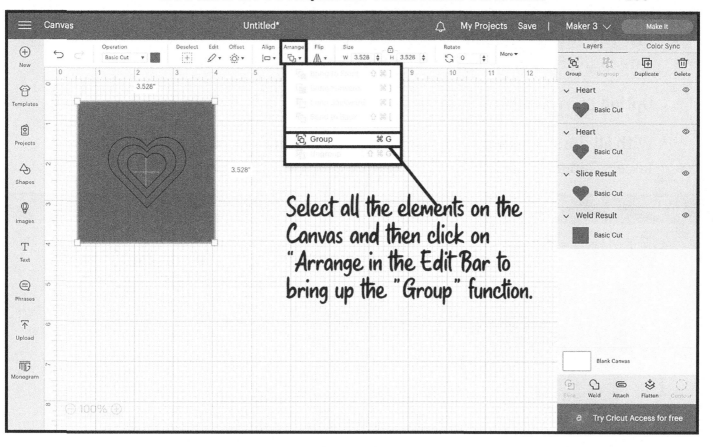

Select all the elements on the Canvas and then click on "Arrange in the Edit Bar to bring up the "Group" function.

Option 3: In the Layers Panel

With all the shapes selected, right click on any of them in the Layers Panel and click on *Group* when the pop-up menu appears.

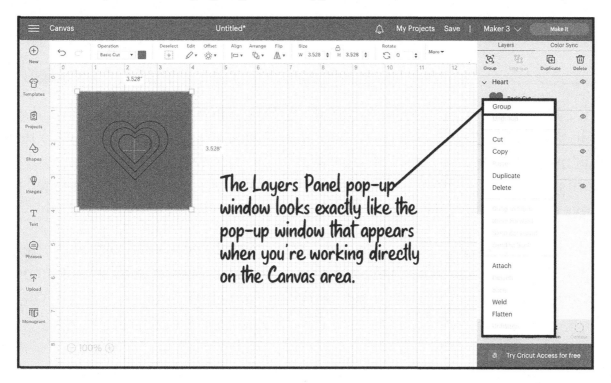

The Layers Panel pop-up window looks exactly like the pop-up window that appears when you're working directly on the Canvas area.

Pro Tip: If you accidentally left click, you will lose the entire selection, so be sure to select them all again when you give it another go.

Option 4: Layers Panel Shortcut

With all the shapes selected, click on the *Group* shortcut button at the top of the Layers Panel.

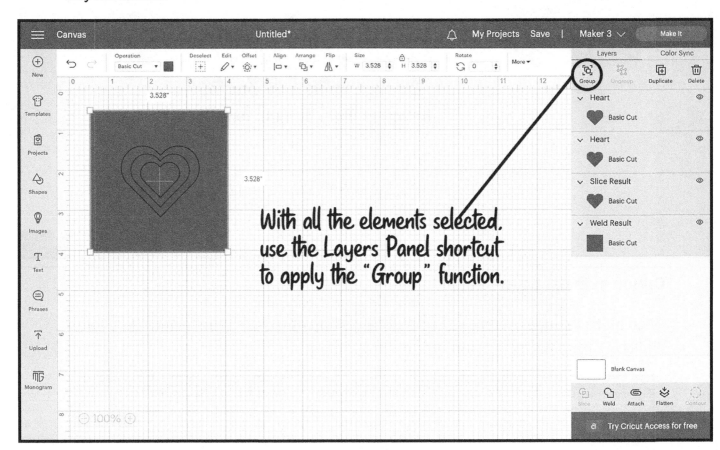

Once you have applied the *Group* function, the stacked shapes will behave like a unit. When you click on one, you will automatically select all of them. To test this out, click on the selection and drag your mouse so the selection moves from its current position to another one. As you can see, you have managed to move all the stacked elements instead of just one element within the stack.

Pro Tip #1: If you look at your Layers Panel, you will now see *Group* at the very top of the list, followed by the list of shapes. This tells you that all of the shapes are now part of the unit you created with the *Group* function.

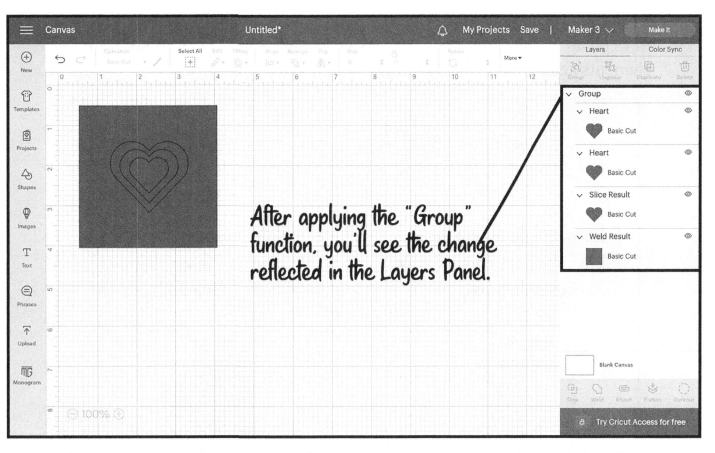

When you group elements together, you can no longer resize or move them individually. To do that, you need to use the *Ungroup* function first. This will break up the unit and Design Space will treat each element individually again.

The *Ungroup* function can be completed using the same options we talked about above. Of course, instead of *Group*, you will click on *Ungroup*. Use any of the methods you learned above to ungroup the stacked shapes. The *Group* should disappear from the Layers Panel and you should be able to tweak each shape individually again.

How To Use it on the Mobile App

Select all the stacked shapes, tap on *Actions*, and then look for the Group function, like you see in the screenshot on the left side of the next page. Tap on *Group* to make your stacked shapes behave like a unit. From now on, if you tap on any one of those stacked shapes, you'll be able to move all of them at once without affecting their positions relative to each other.

Do you see how the *Group* in the bar at the bottom of your screen has changed to *Ungroup* in the right-hand screenshot below? If you need to separate the elements again, that is the option you will choose.

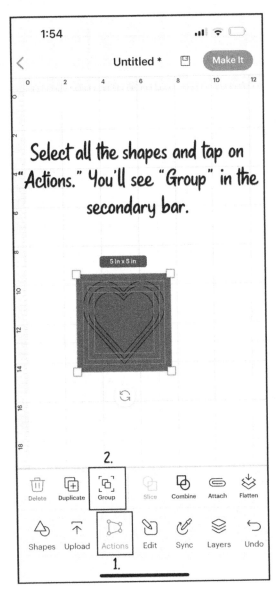 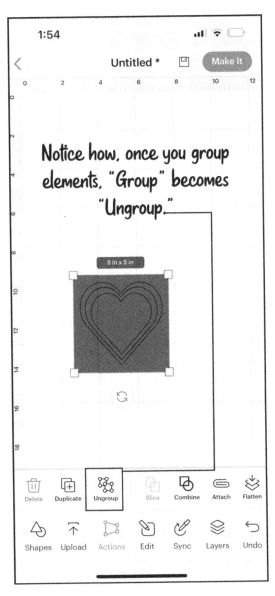

Pro Tip: As long as your elements are grouped, you can't edit them individually. So, if you want to adjust the size, all of their sizes will change at the same time (while maintaining their relative proportions as long as the *Size* function's padlock is locked). Or, if you change the color, all the elements' colors within that group will change together. If you want to make changes to individual elements within a group, you'll have to use the *Ungroup* function to separate them first.

Group/Ungroup Function Self-Assessment

In your own words, explain why the Group function is useful.

_____

_____

_____

_____

_____

True or False: If I realize I made a mistake with a design element after grouping it with a few other design elements, I can separate the group to tweak that element.

_____

_____

Attach

How To Use it on the Desktop App

At face value, the *Attach* function seems to work exactly like the *Group* function in the sense that the *Attach* function also makes a unit out of individual design elements, allowing you to move them all at once.

However, the *Attach* function is very important for another reason, and that has to do with the cutting process. If you don't use the *Attach* function when you have completed your design and move on to the Make It screen, Design Space will arrange your design elements all over the cutting mat's surface in any way it thinks will best save space. While this is really cool for the sake of saving material, it is also really impractical and will leave you feeling discouraged as you try to figure out which parts went where on the overall design after your machine has cut out the individual parts.

This is what our stacked shapes will look like on the Make It screen if we do *not* use the *Attach* function before starting the cutting process:

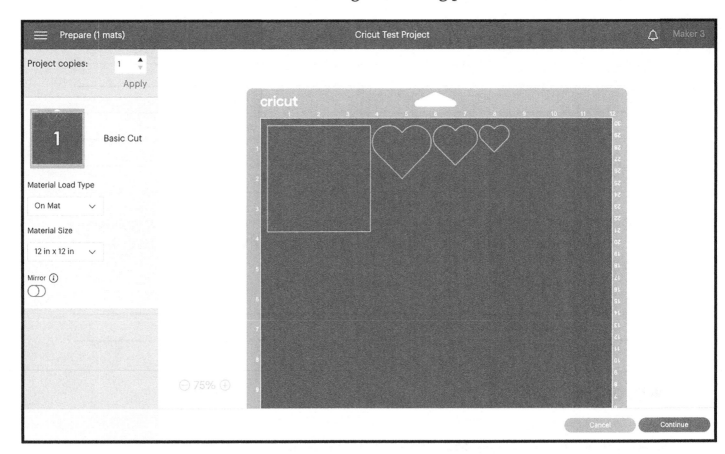

Of course, you might not *want* to use the *Attach* function at all—depending on what you are planning with your design. For the most part, though, you'll probably use it. It is your go-to function when you want the elements on your Design Space Canvas to be cut out exactly as you see them on the screen. To activate the *Attach* function, you have the following options:

Option 1: On the Canvas

With all the elements you want to attach selected, right-click on the selection area directly on the Canvas and choose A*ttach* from the pop-up menu. (See the first screenshot on the next page.)

Option 2: In the Layers Panel

Select all the elements you want to attach, right click on any one of them in the Layers Panel, and click on *Attach* when the pop-up menu appears. (See the second illustration on the next page.)

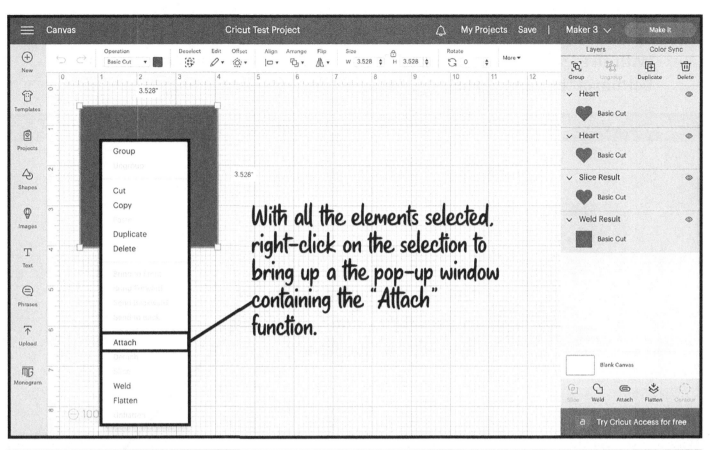

With all the elements selected, right-click on the selection to bring up a the pop-up window containing the "Attach" function.

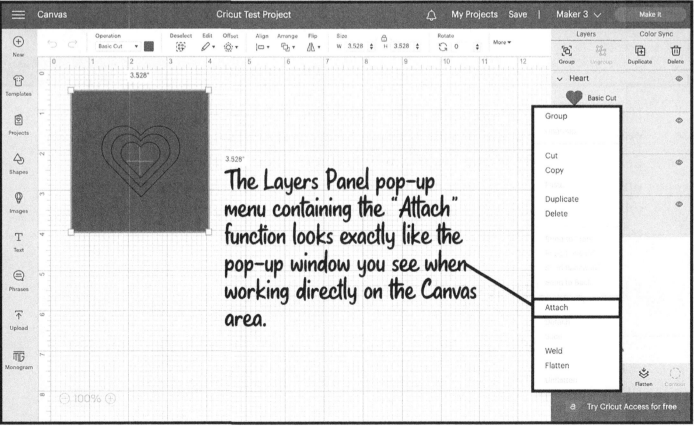

The Layers Panel pop-up menu containing the "Attach" function looks exactly like the pop-up window you see when working directly on the Canvas area.

Option 3: Layers Panel Shortcut

With all the elements you want to attach selected, click on the *Attach* icon at the bottom of the Layers Panel.

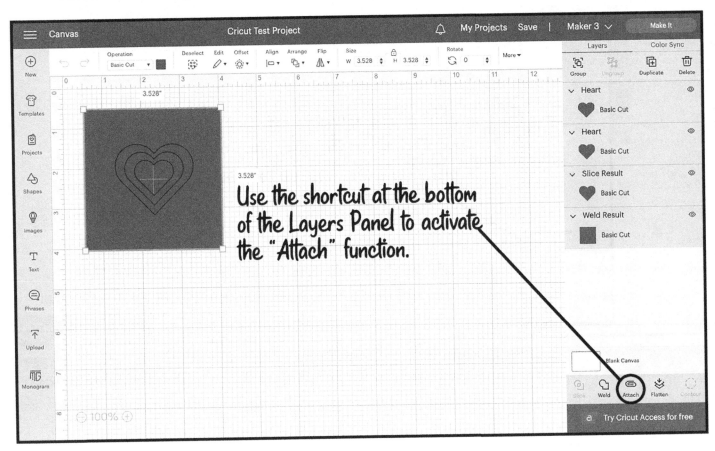

If, after attaching elements, you realize one still needs an additional tweak, you'll have to use the *Detach* function before you can make the change. You can detach elements in the exact way you *Attach* them. If they are attached, the option will automatically change from *Attach* to *Detach*. When you're happy with your tweaks, be sure to apply the *Attach* function again before proceeding to the cutting process.

How To Use it on the Mobile App

Select the elements you want to attach (the stacked shapes in this case), tap on *Actions* in the bar at the bottom of your Canvas screen, and look for the *Attach* function.

Tap on *Attach*. If *Attach* grays out and *Detach* becomes active at the bottom of the screen, you're good to go.

When NOT to use the Attach function

If your design is made up of elements with different colors, don't attach the different colors together. For example, if there are blue, yellow, and red design elements, you don't want them together. If you attach those, Design Space will think you want to use a single piece of material for the *entire* design.

Another scenario in which you don't want to attach elements is when you want to cut out full shapes, even though they're the same color and you have stacked them on top of each other in the Canvas.

For example, sticking with the stacked shapes we've been working with, if we want to create a vinyl cut-out of each shape and stick them on top if each other on a mug, we can't use the *Attach* function, because we want the machine to understand that it needs to cut out the individual, solid shapes. If we keep them attached, the machine will just cut those shapes as it sees it on the preview screen, and this will create the same cookie-cutter effect you would otherwise get with the Slice function. Once you remove the vinyl from the cutting mat after the cutting process, you'll sit with incomplete shapes; that is, shapes with holes in them that represent the other shapes.

Pro Tip: If you can't cut out a design with the *Attach* function activated, keep the original design open on your computer or mobile device's screen as a reference you can refer back to when assembling your project after the cutting process. You can even make a printout of the original design if you prefer. Whatever your method, *always* have a copy of your original design handy.

Attach/Detach Function Self-Assessment

True or False: The Attach function does the same thing as the Group function.

_____

_____

True or False: You should *always* use the Attach function on a design before moving on to the cutting process.

_____

_____

Flatten/Unflatten

This is a feature you'll use whenever you do *Print Then Cut* projects. For these, you want to tell Design Space to merge all the individual elements on the Canvas into a single element, essentially turning it into a printable image. After printing out the image, Design Space will only cut around that image's borders. So, if you want to make stickers (as an example), this would be the way to go.

How To Use it on the Desktop App

Let's flatten our stacked shapes using any one of the following methods:

Option 1: On the Canvas

First, to cut out any confusion, let's remove our previous settings. Select the stacked elements and apply the *Detach* function. After that, select them again and apply the *Ungroup* function. Note, though, that you *can* apply the *Flatten* function even if elements are grouped or attached, or both. The only reason we're removing those previous settings is to keep the learning process as simple as possible. Now, with all the elements selected, right click on the selection box around them directly on the Canvas and click on *Flatten* when the pop-up menu appears.

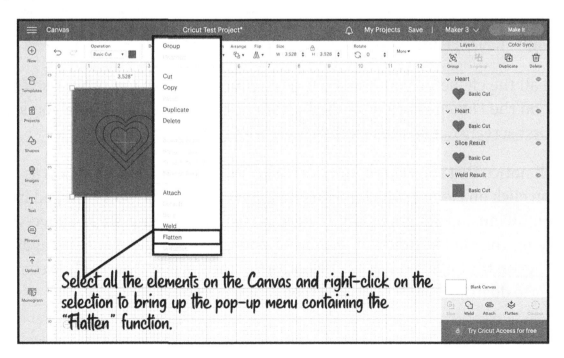

Select all the elements on the Canvas and right-click on the selection to bring up the pop-up menu containing the "Flatten" function.

Option 2: In the Layers Panel

Select all the elements you want to use for the *Print Then Cut* project, right click on one of them in the Layers Panel, and then choose *Flatten* from the pop-up menu.

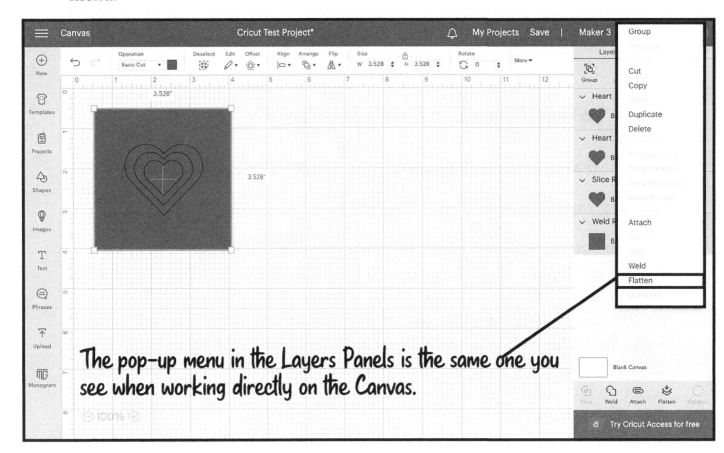

Option 3: Layers Panel Shortcut

With all the elements you want to use for your *Print Then Cut* project selected, click on the *Flatten* shortcut at the bottom of the Layers Panel, like you see in the first screenshot on the next page.

You'll notice that the *Flatten* function turns into the *Unflatten* function as soon as you click on *Flatten*, which means that you can turn the now-merged image into individual elements again, if needed, using the same steps above. After applying the *Flatten* function, go ahead and unflatten the elements again by clicking on the *Unflatten* icon at the bottom of the Layers Panel (or however you prefer to do it!). (See the second screenshot on the next page.)

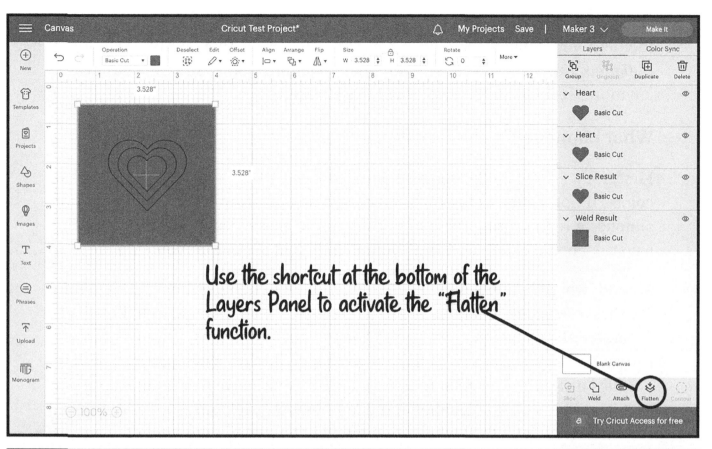

Use the shortcut at the bottom of the Layers Panel to activate the "Flatten" function.

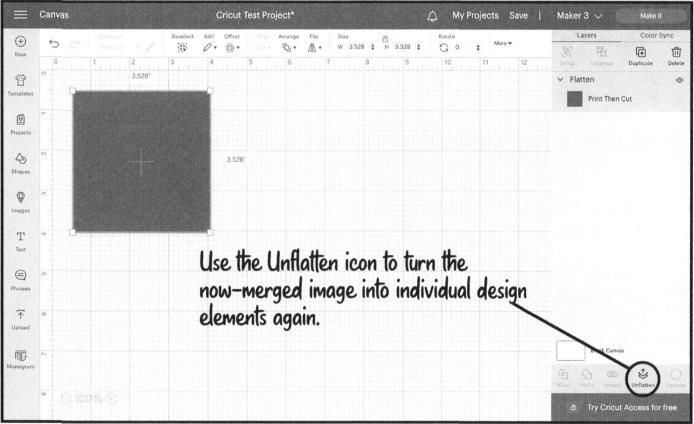

Use the Unflatten icon to turn the now-merged image into individual design elements again.

Of course, you might have noticed the hearts disappearing altogether the moment you applied the *Flatten* function. On top of that, despite using the *Unflatten* function, there are no lines separating the square and hearts anymore—everything looks like a single square.

What happened?

First, for a *Print Then Cut* image to work, stacked elements need to be different colors. If not, applying the *Flatten* function will just turn it into a single-color silhouette representing the outer edges of the entire design (in this case, the square), and that silhouette is all your printer will put out for you.

Second, when we applied the *Flatten* function, we changed the elements from *Cut* files to *Print then Cut* files, and that setting stayed the same, even though we separated the elements again (using the *Unflatten* function). If we want to see the separating lines again, we'll have to change the elements' settings back to *Cut* files using the *Operation* function, a setting exclusive to the desktop app's Edit Bar, which we'll talk about in the next chapter, right after we have a quick look at how to apply the *Flatten* function with the mobile app.

How To Use it on the Mobile App

As we did at the beginning of the desktop app exercise, let's first apply the *Detach* and *Ungroup* functions to the stacked shapes on the Canvas, using the methods we talked about in the *Group/Ungroup* and *Attach/Detach* sections.

When you're done, select all the shapes, tap on *Actions*, and swipe the secondary bar at the bottom of the screen until you see the *Flatten* function, as in the left-hand screenshot on the next page.

Tap on *Flatten*, and notice how it grays out while *Unflatten* next to it becomes active, as you see in the right-hand screenshot on the next page. Seeing this tells you that you applied the *Flatten* function successfully.

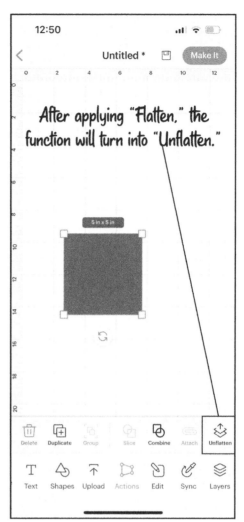

On the Android app, applying *Flatten* does not turn the shapes on the Canvas into a single gray square. But this does not mean that their settings have stayed the same. They, like the shapes on the desktop and iOS apps, have now turned into *Print Then Cut* files instead of *Cut* files. Before we move on to Chapter 4 to talk about Design Space's *Operation* settings, which determine what your Cricut machine will do once you move on to the *Make It* process, separate your shapes again by applying the *Unflatten* function.

Flatten/Unflatten Function Self-Assessment

When should you apply the Flatten function?

_____

_____

Chapter 3 Notes

Use this space to jot down the best take-aways you learned from Chapter 2. Use these notes as your personal quick-reference guide whenever you want to refresh your memory ons something specific.

_____

_____

_____

_____

_____

_____

_____

_____

_____

_____

_____

_____

_____

_____

_____

_____

_____

_____

_____

_____

_____

_____

_____

_____

Chapter 4
Let's Conquer the Edit Bar

Most Design Space functions can be completed from various parts of the Canvas interface, like you learned in Chapter 3. Some functions, however, are exclusive to either the Edit Bar or the Layers Panel. This means you'll find no corresponding options for them anywhere else on the desktop app's Canvas interface, like you do with the "all-rounder" functions.

In this chapter, we'll explore the functions you can only complete via the Edit Bar.

Before we jump in, though...

Do you realize how far you've come already?! Seriously, give yourself a pat on the back. If I told you to close your eyes and tell me what you see when I say, "Design Panel," or if I asked you to help me understand the difference between a ready-to-make project and an image, or if I asked you to help me change the space between my text element's individual letters, you'd know exactly what to say and do.

I remember feeling all warm and fuzzy inside the first time I actually *knew* what the heck people were talking about when throwing Design Space terms around on social media platforms. And being able to help another struggling Newbie by answering her question? Ah... pure bliss! You're well on your way to being able to share your knowledge with other Newbies, too!

In the meantime, if you believe this book has contributed to you feeling less intimidated by Cricut Design Space, there's someone else out there who will feel exactly the same way if they get a chance to read it, too. Problem is, they don't know about this book. But you can help them.

All it will take from you to change a fellow Newbie's life is two to five minutes of your time. They may never meet you, and you may never know who you helped, but that's the beauty of paying it forward in life. And, I know you know this is true—good things return to us when we selflessly give without expecting something in return. If that resonates with you, I'd really appreciate your input in helping me spread this book all over the world to Cricut Newbies who are really struggling to conquer Design Space.

Please head over to Amazon right now and share your honest feedback on the *Design Space Handbook for Newbies.* Your voice will give others an unbiased perspective of what they can achieve when applying everything they learn here.

From the bottom of my heart, I really appreciate your time and willingness to help.

Thank you.

Now let's conquer the Edit Bar!

Operation

With the operation function, you tell Design Space what you want your Cricut machine to do with the design when you move on to the *Make It* process.

How To Use it on the Desktop App

Let's track back to our stacked shapes. When we left them in Chapter 3, the *Flatten* function had turned them into a single *Print Then Cut* file, and while using the *Unflatten* function separated each shape into an individual element again, it did nothing to change those elements back into *Cut* files.

Pro Tip: The fact that Design Space does not revert elements' settings back to *Cut* files when you use the *Unflatten* function is *not* a flaw in the program's programming. It just doesn't know your intentions—you might just as well have the desire to make a quick tweak and continue with a *Print Then Cut* project, or you might not. The choice, then, is yours, and that's why you have to make the change manually if you want to change those elements back into *Cut* files.

To change elements' *Operation* settings, you first have to select the elements you'd like to make the changes for. In the case of our shapes, we'd like to apply the *Operation* setting to all the elements on the Canvas, so go ahead and select everything. Next, click on *Operation* in the Edit Bar. This will bring up a list of options, like you see in the screenshot on the next page.

In the pop-up menu, there are four categories of operations to choose from:

- Cut (with Basic, Wavy, and Perforate as options)
- Draw (with Pen, Foil, Score, Deboss, and Engrave as options)
- Print Then Cut
- Guide

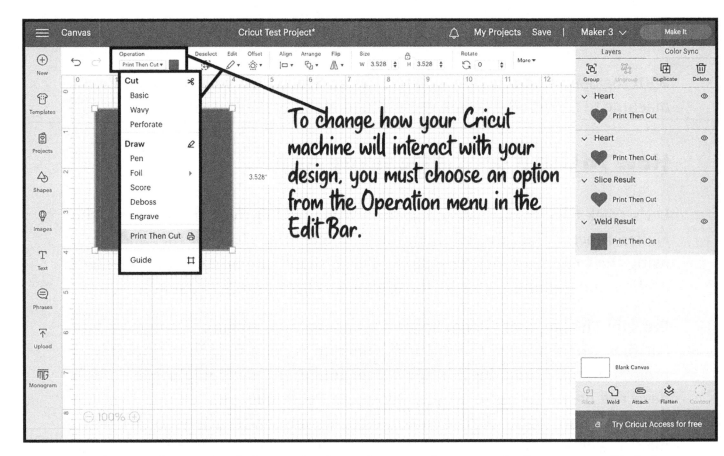

To change how your Cricut machine will interact with your design, you must choose an option from the Operation menu in the Edit Bar.

To change the stacked shapes back to the way they were before we applied the *Unflatten* function, click on the first option, *Basic Cut*. Once you do that, the outline of each shape will return.

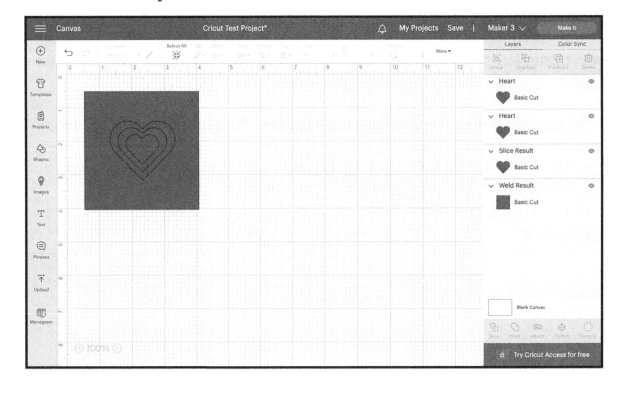

Pro Tip: Those outlines you see are the guidelines your Cricut machine will use when cutting out your design. You won't actually see any outlines once the cutting process is over, unless you intentionally create some sort of outline while creating a design.

If you're ever unsure of a design element's *Operation* settings, just look at the information in the little box underneath *Operation* in the Edit Bar. It's current setting will be visible there without having to open the *Operation* menu. The Layers Panel also contains an element's *Operation* settings information, and it will always be identical to what you see in the Edit Bar. For example, the first item in your Layers Panel at the moment says, "Heart," followed by a heart thumbnail and "Basic Cut" next to the thumbnail. If you click on that first heart, you'll see "Basic Cut" in the Edit Bar, too.

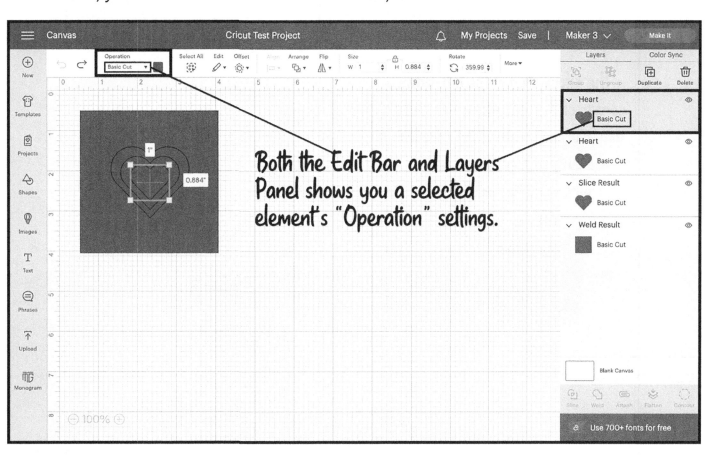

How To Use it on the Mobile App

Select the elements for which you want to change the *Operation* settings. For this example, we're still working with the stacked shapes, and since we want to change all of them, we need to select the whole bunch. When you've got them all, tap on *Edit* in the bar at the bottom of the screen. The secondary bar's very first option says *Print Then Cut*, followed by *Operation*. Tap on it. (See the left-hand screenshot below.) When you tap on *Print Then Cut*, the *Operation* menu will appear. If you're using the Android app, your screen will open a window with two options. Choose *Type*; this will open the *Operation* menu you see in the right-hand illustration below.

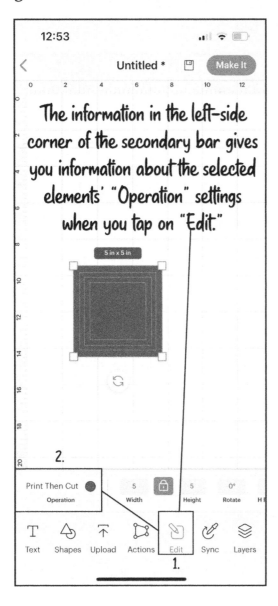
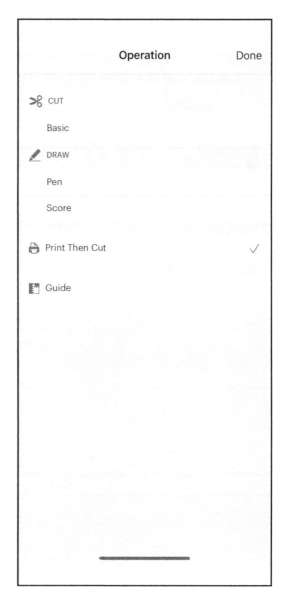

Next, choose *Basic Cut.* Back on the Canvas, you'll now see "Basic Cut," followed by "Operation" in that secondary bar at the bottom of your Canvas.

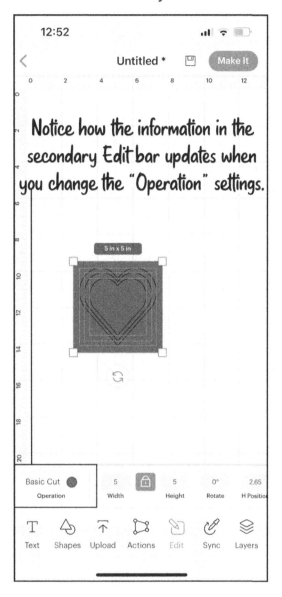

A Quick Look at what Each Operation Setting Means

As a Newbie, you'll be working with the *Basic Cut*, *Pen Draw*, and *Print Then Cut* options for the most part. The more experience you gain and the more Cricut tools you get, the more you'll venture into the other options.

Apart from the *Print Then Cut* and *Guide* options, each *Operation* option can be completed with Cricut's range of specialized tools, such as the Fine-Point

Blade, Wavy Blade, Scoring Wheel or Scoring Stylus, Engraving Tip, and so on. I talk about these tools, and which tools can be used with each Cricut model, extensively in *Cricut for Newbies*.

Cut

Basic: Unless you're using a Wavy Blade or Perforation Blade, this is the option you'll use to cut out anything from paper to wood. The tools you'll use here are the Fine-Point Blade, the Knife Blade, or the Rotary Blade. Which one gets used depends on the material you want to cut and your Cricut model, but Design Space will always guide you to choose the right one.

Wavy: This is a specialized cut you can achieve with Cricut's Wavy Blade if you want decorative edges for your design.

Perforate: Another specialized cut you can achieve using Cricut's Perforation blade. This one will create evenly-spaced, deep cut lines for easily tearing pieces of material apart. Think puzzles or raffle tickets.

Draw

Pen: Use this option whenever you want your Cricut to draw or write something with a Cricut Pen.

Foil: A specialized effect you can create using Cricut's Foil Transfer Tool. With this tool, you can easily and quickly create shiny foil embellishments or accents on designs.

Score: Create accurate fold lines on papercraft projects using the Cricut Scoring Stylus or Scoring Wheel.

Deboss: Create permanent imprints in material using Cricut's Debossing Tip.

Engrave: Engrave designs into various materials using Cricut's Engraving Tip.

Pro Tip: Different design elements on your Canvas can have different *Operation* settings, and some settings can even be part of the same project. For example, you can create a greeting card that your Cricut can draw or write on *and* cut out.

All you have to do is specify what you want and follow the instructions on the Make It screen; Design Space and your Cricut machine will make the magic happen.

Print Then Cut

This is the option you'll use for all the designs you want to print out with your home printer before your Cricut goes on to cut them. It's the perfect option for designs that contain a lot of color, or for custom stickers or button designs or maybe printable vinyl projects (and more!).

Guide

This option was added to the *Operation* menu in early 2022. It turns any element on the Canvas into a guide for your actual design, much like a template. And like the templates from the desktop app's Template library, your machine will not recognize a guide as an element that needs to be cut or drawn at all.

Let's see how it works.

For now, we'll ignore the stacked shapes on the Canvas. Let's imagine you want to create a set of hand-written labels for the kitchen using your Cricut Pens. You know the size of the labels, so all you need is to make sure the descriptions you create will fit on the labels. To make your work easier, you can use a shape to serve as a guide to help you get the descriptions just right.

Let's say you have a few labels that are 4 inches wide and 1.5 inches high and a few others that are 2 inches wide and 3 inches high. The first step is to choose two rectangular or square shapes to use as the guides. Starting with either one, unlock its size using any method you learned earlier and change it to 4 inches by 1.5 inches. Unlock the other rectangle's size and change it to 2 inches by 3 inches. (You can move the two rectangles away from the stacked shapes if they're overlapping.) The screenshot on the following page illustrates more or less what you should see now.

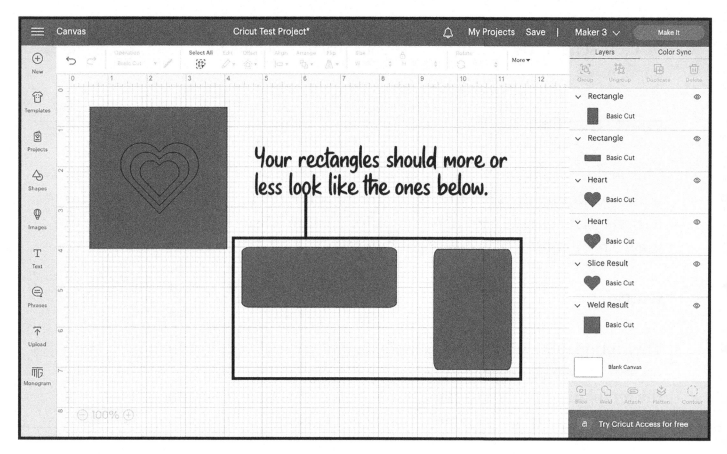

Select both the rectangles, click on *Operation* in the Edit Bar, and choose *Guide* from the pop-up menu.

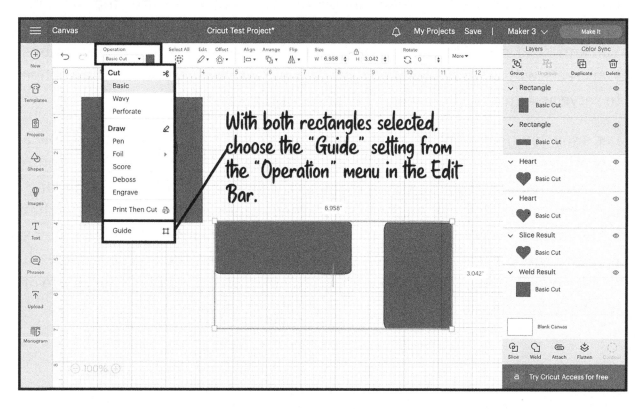

Doing so will turn your rectangles into outlines.

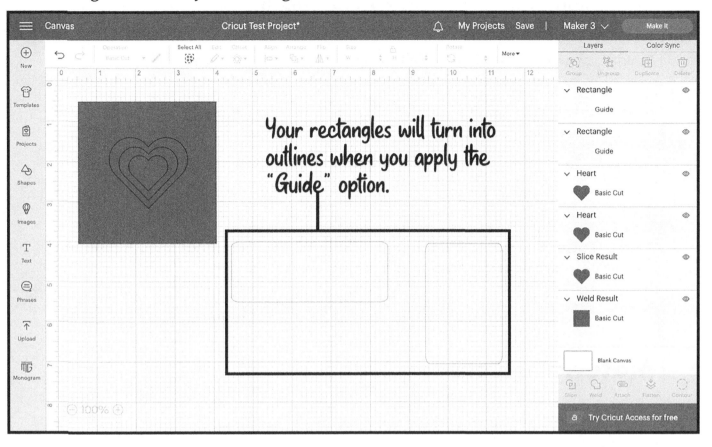

Now you can use those outlines to represent the actual label stickers you are going to have your Cricut machine write on. The goal is to create your text inside the rectangles (or guides) to get the spacing and size of your words perfect. When you're happy to start the *Make It* process, there is no need to delete the guides, as your Cricut will not do anything with them. In fact, it might be best to keep them for later reference, should you decide to make new labels.

Before we move on to the next function, you can delete the guides we just created.

Pro Tip: The Guide option is only available on the desktop app.

Operation Function Self-Assessment

In your own words, explain what the Operation function does.

_____

_____

_____

_____

_____

True or False: It's impossible to have different Operation functions for different elements when working on a single project idea.

_____

Material Colors

Until now, we have been working with a single color. However, when preparing a design for an actual project, you will probably use different colors, especially if your design comprises different elements. This function helps you to visualize what your design will look like once your Cricut machine has done its cutting magic. The illustrations in the book are black, white, and shades of gray, but you should use the colors you want to have in your projects as you continue with the exercises.

How To Use It on the Desktop App

Let's continue to use our stacked shapes to see this function in action.

First, select the square. Remember, you can make this selection on the Canvas or in the Layers Panel. Once selected, click on the gray box next to the *Operation* function. You will see a pop-up window appear with color options, as shown in the screenshot on the next page.

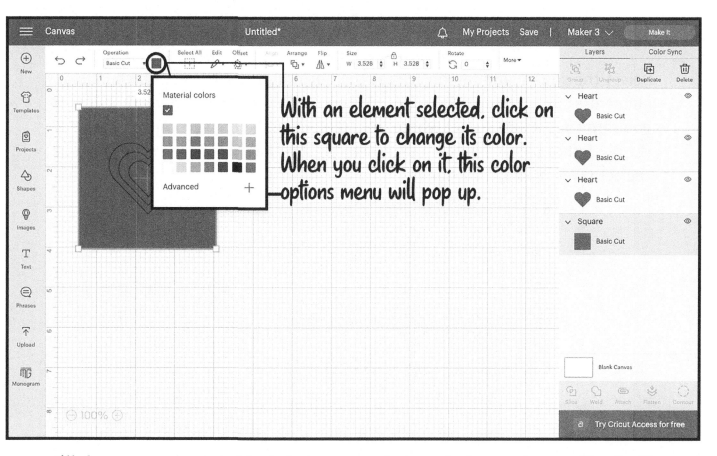

I'll change my square to black, but you can choose whatever color you like. I will keep the heart sitting directly on the square the same color and move on to the heart on top of *it* to change it to a lighter shade of gray. Finally, I'll change the very top heart to an even lighter shade of gray. When your elements are different colors, this is more or less what you'll see on your canvas:

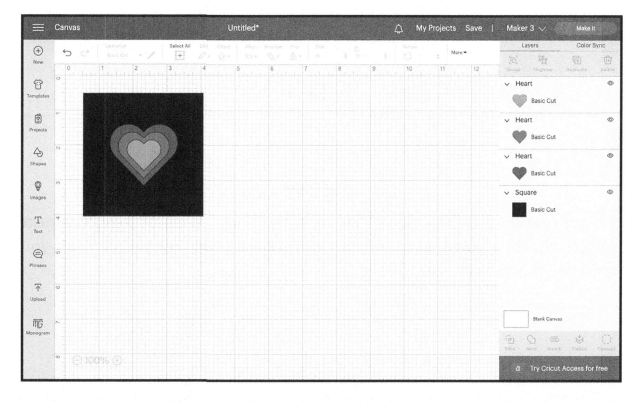

How To Use It on the Mobile App

Select the square and tap on *Edit* at the bottom of the screen. To change an element's color on the mobile app, you have to tap on the *Operation* function. If you think you might forget where to find elements' color settings, just look at the dot left of the current operation setting. It will always be the same color as the actual element on the Canvas.

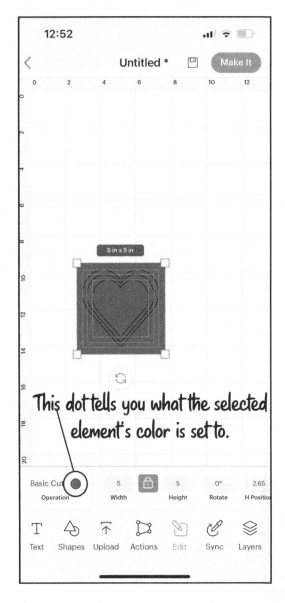

Tap on *Operation*. On the menu that appears, choose *Material Color*. The next screen will show you a bunch of colors to choose from. Tap on the color you want and return to the Canvas.

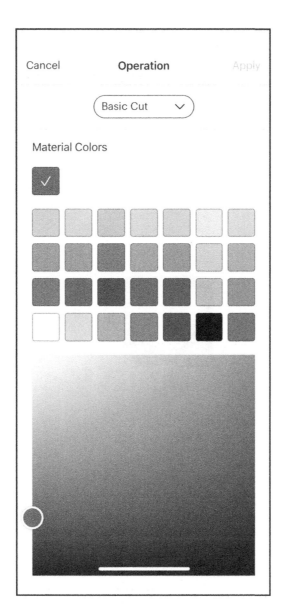

Pro Tip: Until you're more familiar with Design Space, only choose colors from the pre-defined palette you see at the top of the screen. In fact, even pros rarely use the color picker at the bottom!

I'll choose black for my square, but you can choose any color.

Like the example I showed for the desktop app, I'll keep the heart sitting directly on the square the same color, change the one on top of *it* to a lighter shade of gray, and change the very top heart to an even lighter shade of gray. Go ahead and change the shapes on your Canvas to whatever colors you'd like. You can see my result on the next page.

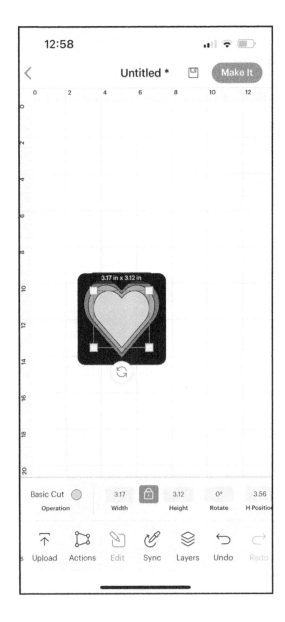

Pro Tip: There is no need to get too specific with your color choices in Design Space. If your red vinyl is a different shade of red than what you see on the screen, it doesn't matter. The idea is to use Design Space to visualize the final design to get a 'more-or-less' idea of what it will look like after you have assembled and applied the design onto its intended surface. On-screen colors are not identical to physical colors, because your screen has the ability to display literally endless color options, whereas printers and the materials you use for your craft projects are limited in that regard.

Material Colors Function Self-Assessment

In your own words, explain where I can find an element's color settings on the mobile app.

_____

_____

_____

_____

_____

True or False: The color you choose for an element in Design Space must be 100% the same as the color of the material you'll use for your project.

_____

Offset

The *Offset* function helps you make a design more dynamic by creating a proportionally smaller or larger layer of the design. The new layer acts like a decorative shadow of sorts. Depending on the type of designs you will create as your crafting journey progresses, you might never use this function. However, if you're into things like stickers and cake toppers, the *Offset* function will come in handy. If you're interested in learning more about this feature, check out this informative post from Cricut: https://cricut.com/blog/offset-design-space/.

How To Use it on the Desktop App

To play around with the *Offset* function, let's select the little heart in the very front of our stack of shapes and move it away from the stack. Next, click on *Offset* in the Edit Bar (see the screenshot at the top if the next page).

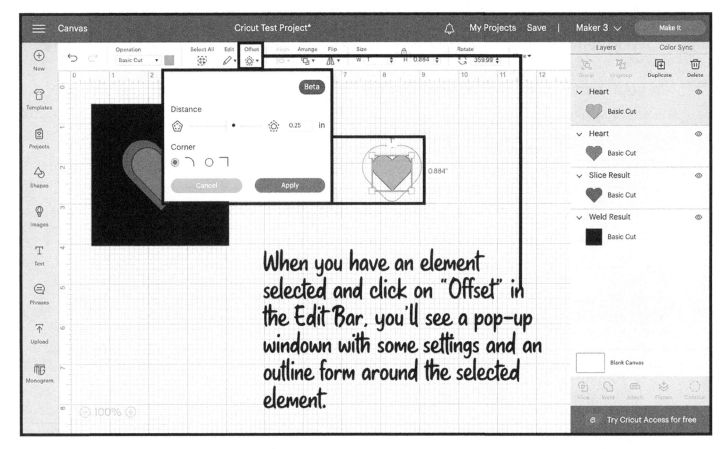

When you have an element selected and click on "Offset" in the Edit Bar, you'll see a pop-up window with some settings and an outline form around the selected element.

The pop-up box you see will help you adjust the offset layer. You can adjust its size by using the slider bar under *Distance* or by entering a value in the box next to the slider. If you move the slider to the left, the offset layer will shrink proportionally to the design; if you move the slider to the right, the offset layer will grow proportionally to the design. Let's see what it looks like in action.

At the moment, you should see a thin, blue line outside the heart's edges on the Canvas. It's a guide that shows you how much bigger the offset layer will be than the original heart. Slide the dot on the bar to the left until it's just past the halfway marker. Notice the thin, blue line is now inside your heart, which means the offset layer will be that much smaller than the original heart (see the first screenshot on the next page. The second illustration on the next page shows you what will happen if you click the *Accept* button.

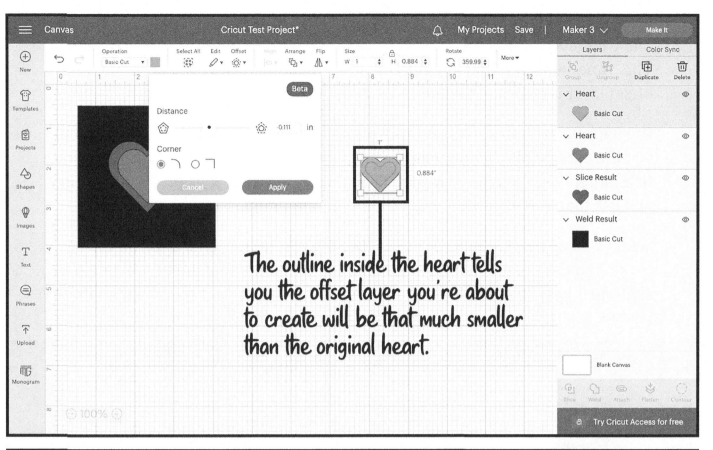

The outline inside the heart tells you the offset layer you're about to create will be that much smaller than the original heart.

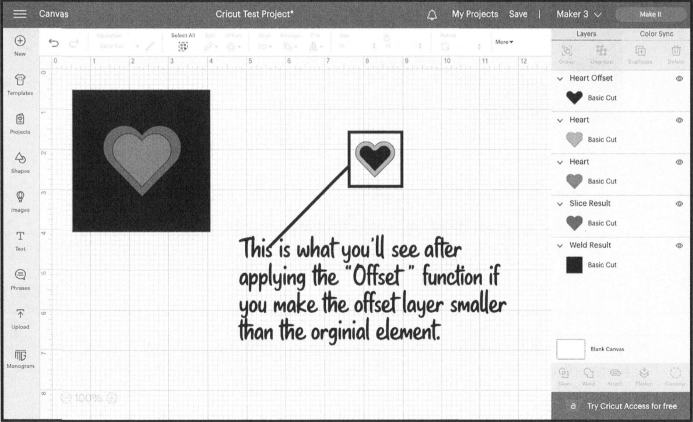

This is what you'll see after applying the "Offset" function if you make the offset layer smaller than the orginial element.

Let's take another heart from the stacked shapes and move it underneath the one we moved earlier. Be sure to leave enough space between the two hearts. This time, we're going to select the *Offset* function again, but we'll make the offset layer larger than the original heart.

Pro Tip: By default, an offset layer is slightly larger than the design element you are applying it to. However, if you have already applied the *Offset* function to another design element, Design Space will remember your previous settings and use that as the starting point for the next element.

With the new heart selected, click on the *Offset* function again. As you can see, the dot on the slider is still sitting to the left of the midline. Move it over to the right, just past the midline, so you can see the blue outline around the heart go past its edges.

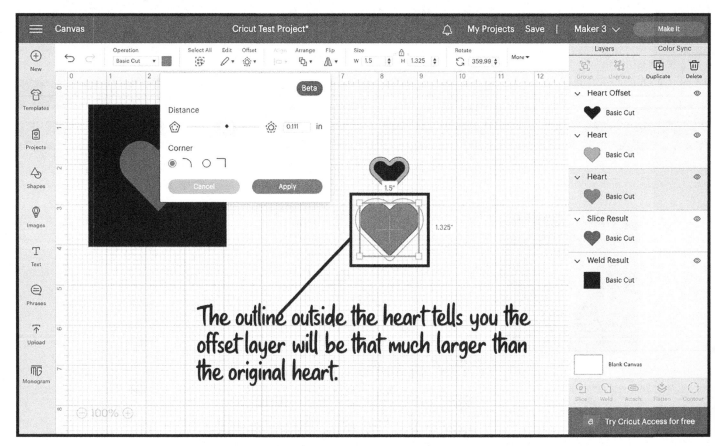

The outline outside the heart tells you the offset layer will be that much larger than the original heart.

When you're happy with the outline's position, click on the *Apply* button. The screenshot on the next page shows you more or less what you should see on your canvas now.

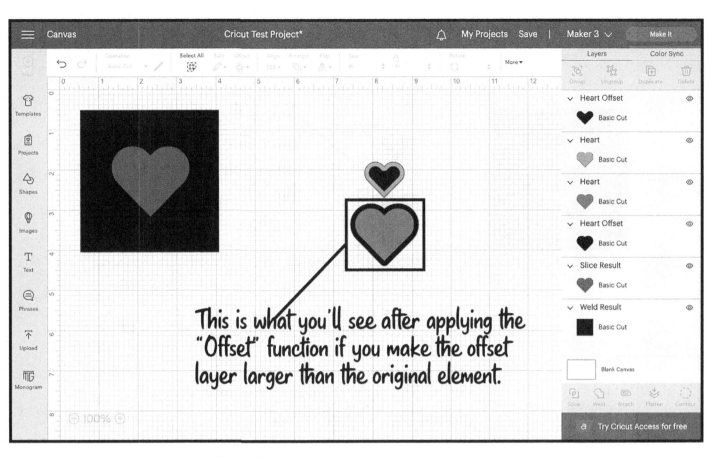

As you can see, a smaller offset layer goes on top of the original design, whereas a larger offset layer goes behind the original design. To better understand this, let's move the smaller, gray circle, which is the original, away from the offset layer behind it. The screenshot at the top of the next page shows what you'll see when you move the original heart away.

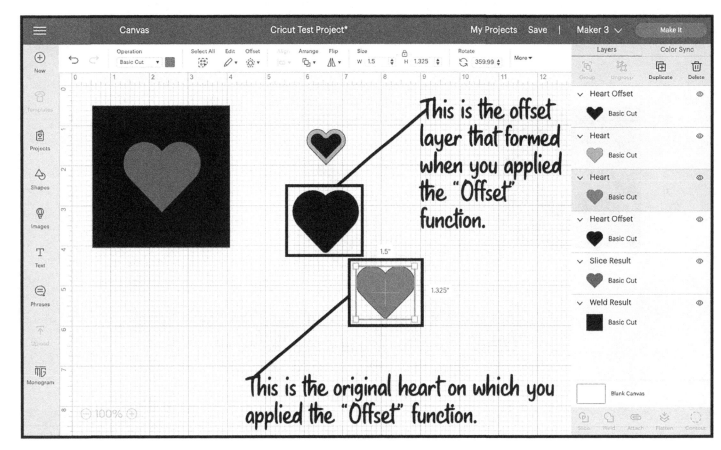

How To Use it on the Mobile App

If you have an Android device, this feature is not yet available for you.

On your iOS device, select the heart in the very front of the stacked shapes and drag it to the side. While you have it selected, tap on *Edit* in the bar at the bottom of the screen and swipe until you see *Offset*, as you can see in the left-hand screenshot on the next page. Tap on *Offset* and use the slider that appears to control the size of the offset layer you want to create. Slide it to the right to create a proportionally larger offset layer or to the left to create a proportionally smaller layer. If you want to enter a specific value instead, you can do so in the little box provided above the slider. For the example, I'll go with a larger offset layer by simply moving the slider. The outline around the design element tells you where the offset layer's edges will be, as you can see in the right-hand screenshot on the next page.

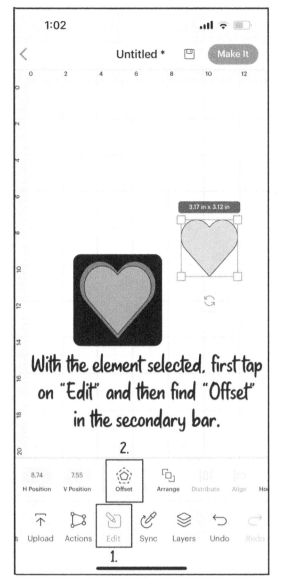

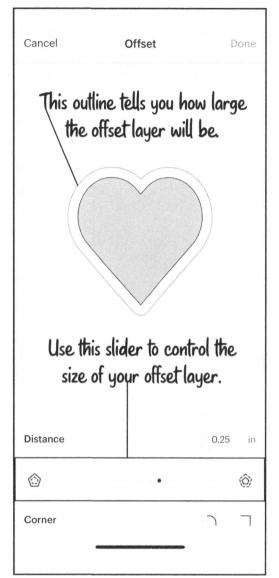

When you're ready to create your offset layer, tap on *Done*. Back on the Canvas, you'll see a new outline behind the heart, like you see in the screenshot on the next page.

Pro Tip #1: With both the desktop and iOS apps, you can specify whether the offset layer should have sharp or rounded corners. What you choose will always depend on the characteristics of the element you are applying the offset layer to.

Pro Tip #2: With the iOS app, you can specify whether the original element and its offset layer should be welded together. If you toggle this option to the "on" position, you will not be able to move the two away from each other at all. This option is also available on the desktop app, but only when working with a text element or with multiple elements.

Pro Tip #3: You can apply multiple offset layers to a single element to make the design pop even more.

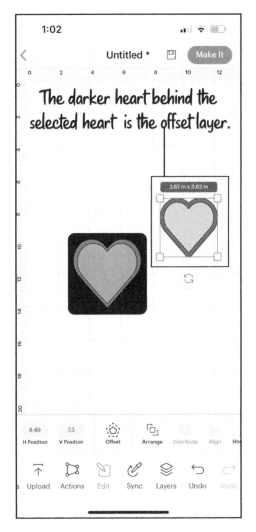

Offset Function Self-Assessment

In your own words, explain what the Offset function does.

_____

_____

_____

_____

_____

Align

This function aligns design elements relative to each other. It's a quick and easy way to make accurate adjustments so you can be sure everything lines up perfectly. We'll use the *Align* function to stack our shapes again, instead of doing it manually this time.

How To Use it on the Desktop App

First, delete the offset layers we created in the previous section. Second, move the last heart away from the square and place it on any open spot you see on the Canvas. Right now, your shapes should be more or less all over the place, like mine:

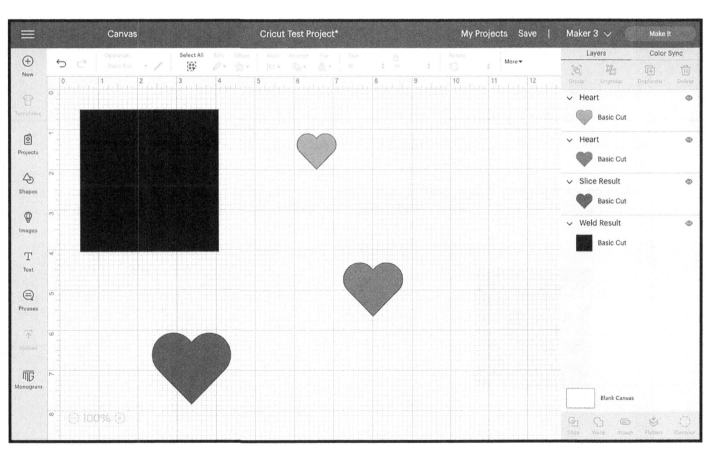

Select all the shapes on the Canvas and click on *Align* in the Edit Bar.

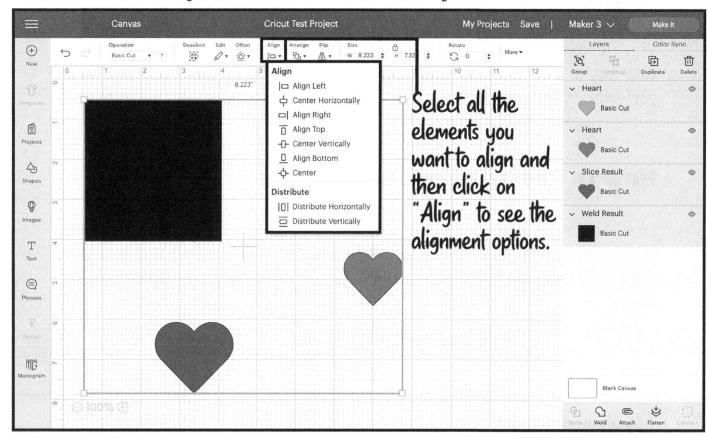

Align Left will push all the elements in the selection so their left-side edges line up.

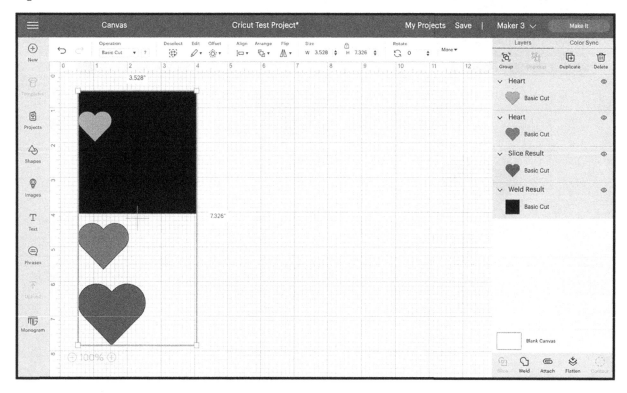

Align Right will push all the elements in the selection so their right-side edges line up.

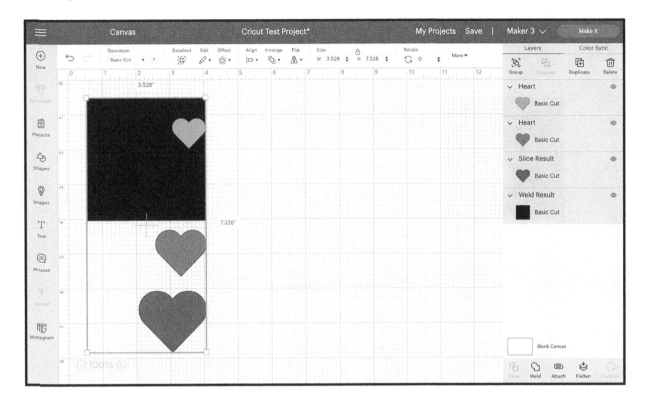

Align Top will push all the elements in the selection so their top edges line up.

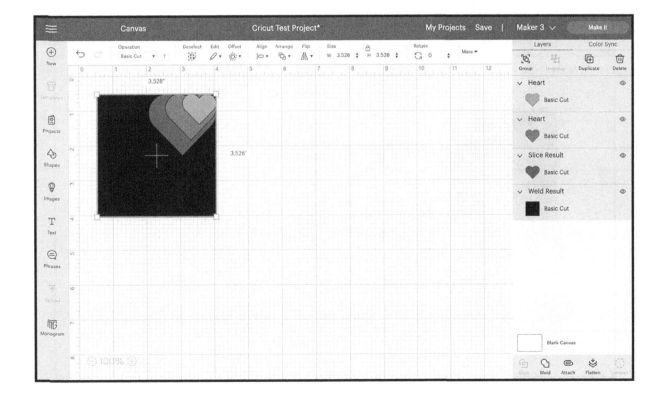

Align Bottom will push all the elements in the selection so their bottom edges line up.

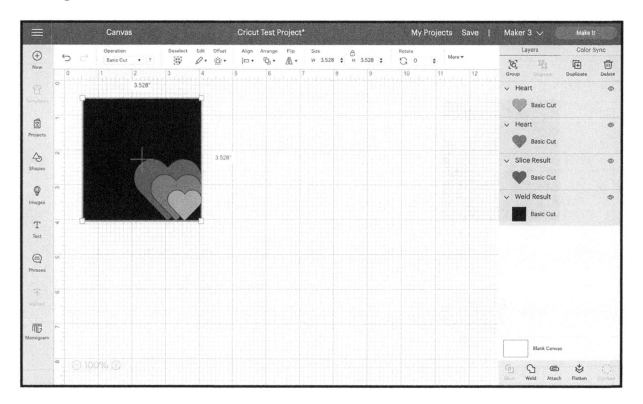

Center Horizontally will line up all the elements in the selection to an imaginary top-to-bottom straight line dividing the elements in equal left and right halves.

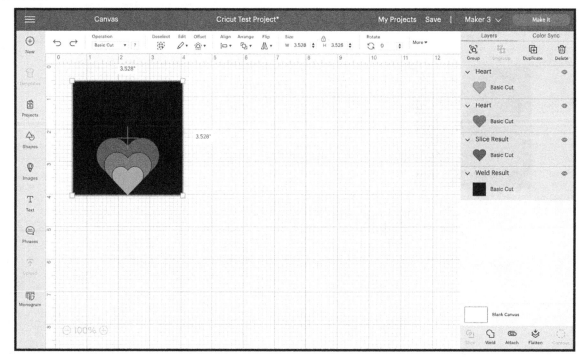

Center Vertically will line up all the elements in the selection to an imaginary left-to-right straight line dividing the elements in equal top and bottom halves.

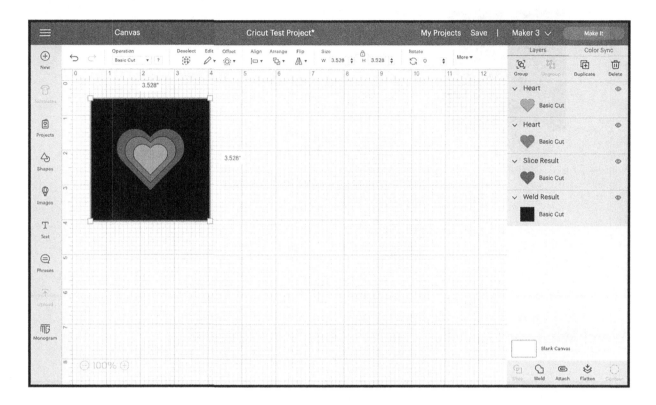

Finally, *Center* will line up all the shapes so they lie in the center of two imaginary straight lines crossing each other. Now, because of the sequence we followed in aligning our stacked shapes, they are actually already center-aligned. So, if we were to apply the *Center* setting, nothing would change. However, if the elements were still all over the show and we applied the *Center* setting, everything would line up as you saw in the last illustration.

But... Why did *Center Vertically* have the same effect as *Center*?

Remember how I said the sequence we followed made sure the shapes were already center-aligned? Let me show you what *Center Vertically* looks like if you *don't* apply *Center Horizontally* beforehand. First, let me scatter my shapes over the Canvas again (see the screenshot on the next page).

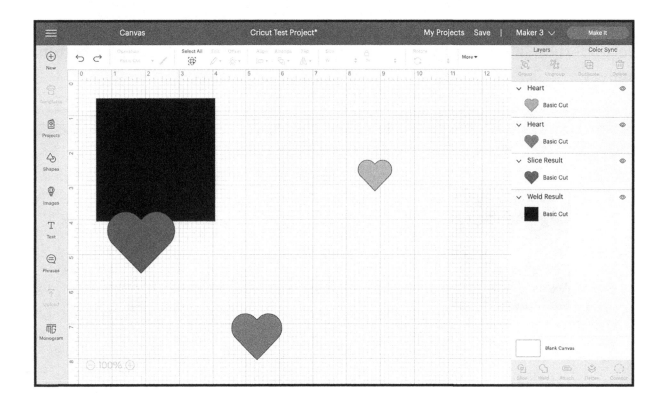

Watch what happens when I click on *Center Vertically* now:

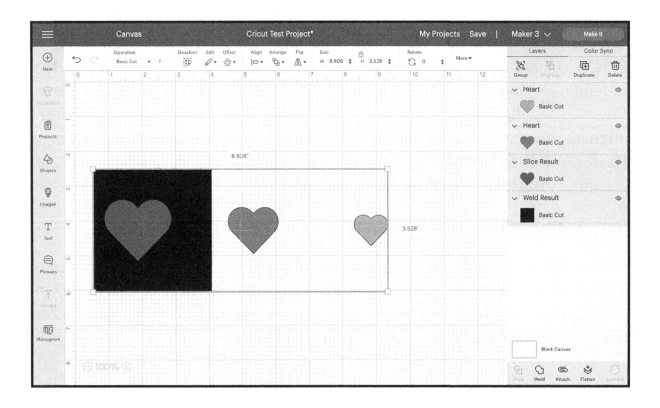

Now, if I go and click on *Center Horizontally*, it would have the same effect as before; that is, all the shapes would line up as if I had applied the *Center* function.

Case in point: Applying *Center* is the same as applying *Center Horizontally* first and *Center Vertically* second, and vice versa. It's like a 'do it all in one go' button.

How To Use it on the Mobile App

For this exercise, we won't go through every alignment option again. Instead, I'll show you how to access the *Alignment* function and we'll apply the *Center* option immediately.

First, delete the offset layer you created earlier and then scatter your shapes all over the Canvas by moving them around like you see in the left-hand screenshot on the next page. (You don't *have* to do this, but it is easier to help you better understand the *Align* function's usefulness.)

With all the shapes on the Canvas selected, tap on *Edit* in the bottom toolbar and swipe until you see *Align* (see the right-hand illustration on the next page). When you tap on *Align*, a pop-up will appear to show you all the alignment options. Choose *Center*. Back in the Canvas, you should see everything lined up perfectly again (see the third screenshot on the next page).

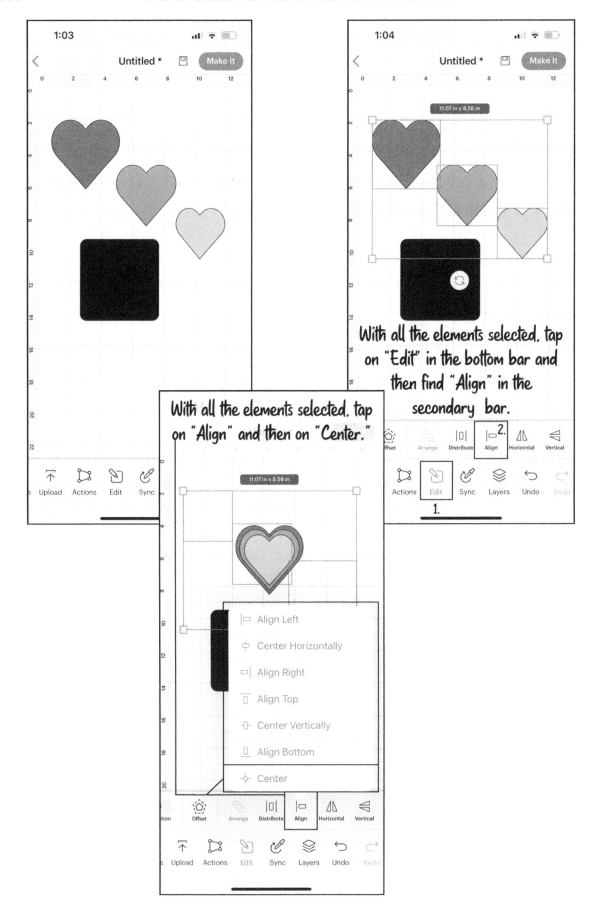

With all the elements selected, tap on "Edit" in the bottom bar and then find "Align" in the secondary bar.

With all the elements selected, tap on "Align" and then on "Center."

Align Left

Center Horizontally

Align Right

Align Top

Center Vertically

Align Bottom

Center

The Distribute Options

This is a way to evenly space out your design elements. *Distribute Horizontally* will use the elements to the farthest right and left sides as the starting points to space out all the elements in the selection. *Distribute Vertically* will use the elements that are way at the top and way at the bottom of the selection to space out everything in that selection. The *Distribute* options are available on the desktop and mobile apps.

Align Function Self-Assessment

If I want to align design elements on my Canvas horizontally and vertically in one go, which option should I choose?

Flip

The *Flip* function creates an instant mirror image on a design element. It is useful for creating interesting symmetrical designs with shapes and images and for mirroring designs before cutting them out for Iron-On projects.

Iron-On is a heat transfer vinyl, perfect for putting fabrics like canvas shoes, t-shirts, tote bags, and so on. It can also be applied to other base materials like mugs. Whenever you work with heat transfer materials, you have to mirror your designs before starting the cutting process, as it needs to be cut upside-down.

How to Use it on the Desktop App

Let's find a phrase from the Phrases library for this example. Go to *Phrases*, activate the *Free* filter and choose anything you like. I'll go with the one you see on the next page.

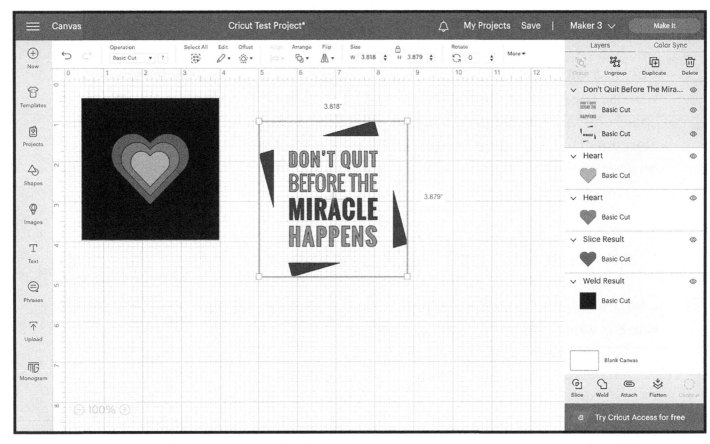

With the image selected, click on *Flip* in the Edit Bar.

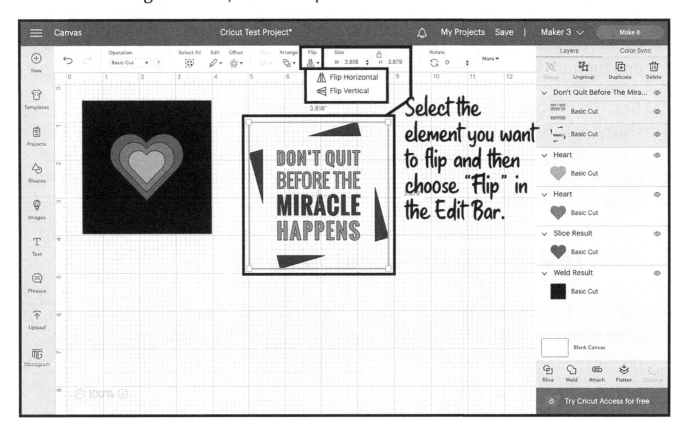

The first option, *Flip Horizontal*, basically reverses the image's left and right sides while keeping the image right-side-up.

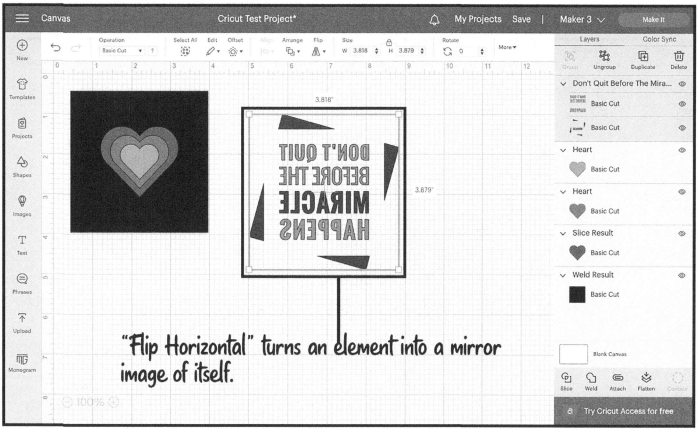

If you're following along and you just applied the *Flip Horizontal* action, go ahead and apply it again to get the image the way it was before. The second option, *Flip Vertical*, flips the image upside-down.

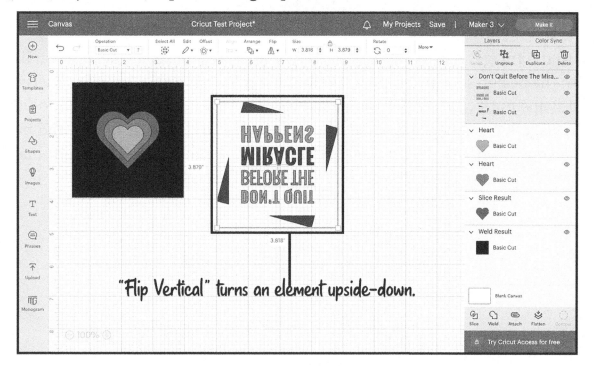

The *Flip* function can be applied to shapes, too. For example, with a combination of the *Flip* and *Rotate* functions, you can create something like this with simple heart shapes:

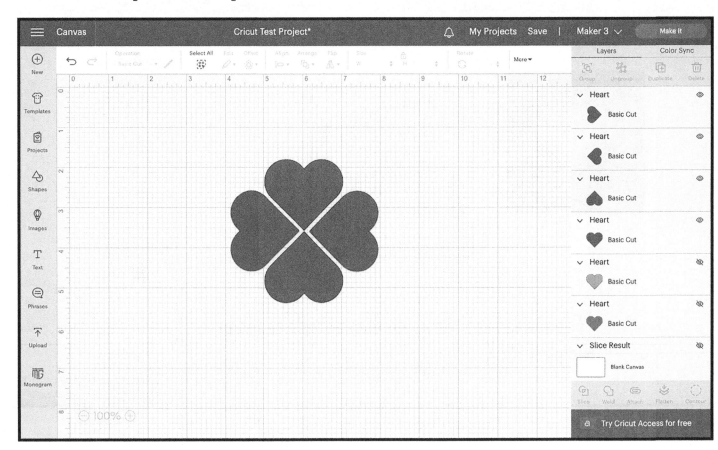

How to Use it on the Mobile App

Go to the Images library, apply the *Free* filter, and choose any design you like. With the design selected, tap on *Edit* in the toolbar at the bottom of the screen, and swipe until you see *Horizontal* and *Vertical*. (See the top screenshot on the next page.) The left-hand screenshot below the first screenshot on the next page shows what the *Horizontal* setting will look like, while the right-hand screenshot shows what the *Vertical* setting will look like.

To find the "Flip" settings, first select an element, tap on "Edit" in the bottom bar, and then locate "Flip" in the secodary bar.

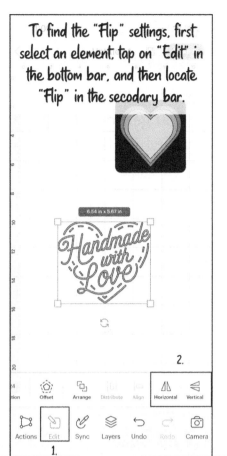

2.

1.

"Flip Horizontal" turns an element into a mirror image of itself.

"Flip Vertical" turns an element upside down.

2.

1.

2.

1.

Pro Tip #1: When working with Iron-On projects, you'll always choose the *Flip Horizontally* option before starting the cutting process.

Pro Tip #2: No worries if you forget to apply the *Flip* function to an Iron-On project on the Canvas. When you get to the Make It screen, you can apply the *Mirror* setting to flip the design, which is essentially the same thing.

Flip Function Self-Assessment

What does the Flip Horizontal action do?

_____

_____

_____

_____

_____

What does the Flip Vertical action do?

_____

_____

_____

_____

_____

Chapter 4 Notes

Use this space to jot down the best take-aways you learned from Chapter 2.
Use these notes as your personal quick-reference guide whenever you want
to refresh your memory ons something specific.

_____

_____

_____

_____

_____

_____

_____

_____

_____

_____

_____

_____

_____

_____

_____

_____

_____

_____

_____

_____

_____

_____

_____

_____

_____

_____

_____

Chapter 5
Let's Conquer Layers and the Layers Panel

OK... I have a confession to make.

We've been working with layers since the very beginning of this book.

And if you've been following along with your computer, laptop, tablet, or cell phone, you're now officially a Newbie who knows how to work with layers in Design Space.

I see that smile. And you know what? You deserve it. You've really been putting in everything to conquer this Design Space beast, and look at everything you've achieved so far!

But why didn't I tell you...?

Well, I wanted you to go through the learning curve without feeling stressed or thinking you wouldn't be able to understand the terms and explanations. Now that you are comfortable with words like "design elements" and "arrangement" and "position," we can bring all of them together to define and understand layers better. So, without further ado, let's conquer layers once and for all.

What are Layers?

In Design Space, a single design is made up of different design elements. Each element on the Canvas comes together with the other elements on the Canvas to form the whole picture, and each of those elements can be tweaked individually without affecting the rest of the elements. And, yes, you've already guessed it—another term for what we've been referring to as "design elements" this entire time is "layers."

Pro Tip: Design Space is unique compared to other design programs. It automatically turns anything you add to the Canvas into its own layer, and you have no control over this process. In most other design programs, you have control over how many elements go onto a single layer. For example, if you have six stars and six circles, each shape can be on a separate layer (so, there will be 12 layers), or the six stars can go together on one layer while the six circles go together on another layer (so, there will be 2 layers, each with six shapes). However, even when working in other design programs, the unwritten rule is to add one design element per layer.

What is Layering?

You might have heard this term before and scratched your head over it. "Layering" is simply the process of building a design made up of layers from scratch, whether digital or physical. For example, if you're making a shaker card, you're actually applying the principles of building one layer on top of the other to make up a complete design or craft project (so, you're layering).

Still, if you hear someone using the term, chances are she's referring to layering in a digital design program and she's probably familiar with graphic design and design programs other than Design Space, as it's not really a term we use much in Cricut crafting or crafting in general.

Why Layers?

Edit One Little Bit a Time

Imagine creating a stunning, one-of-a-kind, irreplaceable drawing and... it has an eyesore. It's tiny, but it's ruining *everything*. And there's nothing you can do about it. If you want to fix it, you'll have to do the entire thing from scratch. And you *know* you can't recreate it, even if you give it your best shot.

Yeah.

Doesn't make you feel good, does it?

I felt my stomach turn just writing that paragraph.

Lucky for us, we'll never have that issue when creating in Design Space. When you build a digital design using layers, each layer can be edited individually. Should a blunder pop up (and they *do*!), you can fix it hassle free *and* keep your pretty design intact. It's a win-win all the way.

Layers are the Lifeline of Most Cut Projects

When first starting out, you'll probably work with single-color, single-layer projects. That is, you'll mostly go for simple window decals, a decal for your Cricut machine, maybe something to show your passion for a cause on the back of your car, or a hilarious coffee mug for your friend who's always spilling its contents when working at a desk.

However, you'll soon outgrow simple designs and move on to ones with different colors and elements, which all require you to understand layers. There is no escaping working with layers, so you have to embrace them. Besides, you've been working with layers all along in this book, and you've been doing wonderfully!

Total Design Freedom

The fact that layers work in hierarchical levels means you can play around with literally endless possibilities to come up with unique designs that each contain a little piece of your love and personality. It's also thanks to layers that you can create new shapes using functions like *Weld* and *Slice*. With simple actions like *Duplicate* and *Delete* you can mold a design into something totally different, all without having to start over every time you think, *"Oh! What if I try this..."* or *"Ooo! That might make things interesting!"*

Once you get to know them a little better, layers are pretty freakin' magical to work with.

How Do Layers Work?

The Design Panel is a lot like a staircase, which is made up of levels of steps to get you from the bottom to the top and vice versa. Without those steps, the staircase wouldn't exist and you'd never be able to get from point A to point B. Likewise, without layers, your design can't exist. Imagine that the Layers Panel is a staircase, and each layer that makes up your design is a step in that staircase. The bottom layer represents the very first step at the bottom, while the top layer represents the very last step at the top; all the layers in between represent the other steps as you move up or down the staircase.

However, unlike a conventional staircase, your Layers Panel is dynamic. You can change the order of the elements any way you like. When we practiced using the *Arrange* function in Chapter 3, we were really practicing the art of re-arranging the order of the layers.

Every time you add a layer (or design element) to the Canvas, Design Space will automatically place it on top of the layer you added before it. So, if you don't rearrange the layers manually using the *Arrange* function, the normal hierarchical order of your layers will be that whatever you add first will lie at the bottom and whatever you add last will lie at the top.

Another unique aspect about layers is the ability to turn a selection of layers into a unit that functions as though the layers are one. It's also possible to bulk-edit these selections, giving you a convenient way to make immediate changes to all the layers within a selection at once. That's where the *Group* function comes in, which we talked about in Chapter 3.

Finally, not all designs' layers get stacked on top of each other like we've been practicing with the shapes. Some designs may consist of layers that overlap each other in some areas but for the most part, each one occupies its own little space on the Canvas. Even so, there is *still* a hierarchy at play.

Let's do a design together so you can see what I mean.

How to Work with Layers

As I walk you through this tutorial, you're going to apply a lot of what you learned in the previous chapters. Apart from telling you what to add to the Canvas and what to do with it, this tutorial will not give you step-by-step instructions on *how* to apply the tweaks, but it will give you clues to help you remember. This is the perfect opportunity to test your new knowledge. If you get stuck at any step along the way, track back to the relevant part in the book that explains how to apply the function and come back to continue with the tutorial. It may sound tedious, but this book is all about practical application and making the information you learn stick, and the best way to make it stick is through practice and double-checking what you've already learned. Trust me, you'll be a Design Space ninja in no time with this learning method. Also note, for the same reasons mentioned above, we will only use screenshots for the desktop app in this chapter. If you get stuck while following along with your mobile app, head back to the previous chapters for a refresher.

While learning the "all-rounder" functions in Chapter 3, you worked quite a bit with the Layers Panel, so nothing here will feel strange. In fact, this will actually be a recap that offers more details on what you've already learned.

The Layers Panel is your bird's eye view of *everything* on the Canvas. More importantly, it shows you the hierarchical order of each element (or layer). It also gives you specific information on each element (or layer) like the type of layer, the layer's operation settings, and whether the layer is currently visible or hidden on the Canvas.

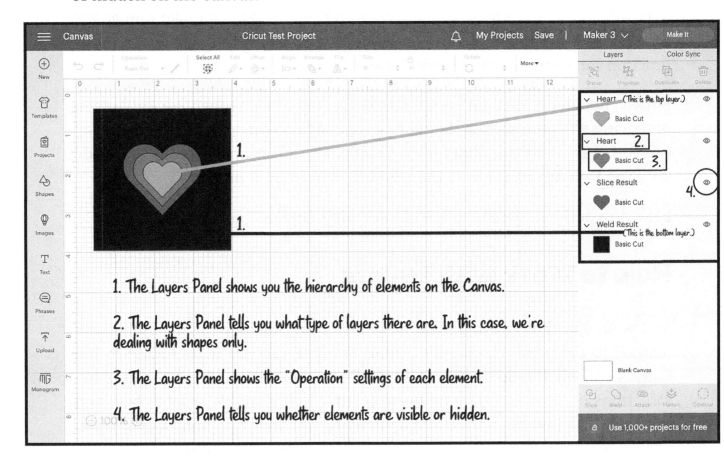

1. The Layers Panel shows you the hierarchy of elements on the Canvas.

2. The Layers Panel tells you what type of layers there are. In this case, we're dealing with shapes only.

3. The Layers Panel shows the "Operation" settings of each element.

4. The Layers Panel tells you whether elements are visible or hidden.

You already know what the operation settings entail (*Cut*, *Draw*, and *Print Then Cut*), and you are already familiar with the various types of layers you can work with in Design Space:

- Shapes
- Images
- Text
- Phrases
- Uploaded PNGs and JPGs
- Uploaded SVGs
- Projects (which may contain any one or a combination of the above types of layers)

But what about visible and hidden layers? Let's say you add something to the Canvas and you kind of like it but you kind of don't, and you're really not sure whether it should stay or go. Do you delete it and hope you remember what it was if you change your mind within the next few creative sessions? Do you move it to the side and hope it won't distract you while working on the rest of the design?

Luckily, you don't have to compromise on your creativity with any of that. All you have to do is click on the little eye icon you see to the right of each layer in the Layers Panel to temporarily hide the layers you're not too sure of at the moment. If the eye is open, it means the layer is visible; if the eye has a diagonal strikethrough, it means the layer is hidden.

Pro Tip #1: Your Cricut machine can't see a hidden layer, so it won't cut or draw it at all. Likewise, if you're doing a *Print Then Cut* project, the printer won't see any hidden layers and therefore won't print them out.

Pro Tip #2: You can make *Guide* layers visible and hidden, too. Although your Cricut can't see *Guide* layers, they can distract you sometimes while working. Since you may still need those guides later, it makes more sense to hide them as opposed to deleting them.

Let's hide the shapes we've been working with until now by clicking on each one's eyeball icon in the Layers Panel. Your Canvas should now appear empty.

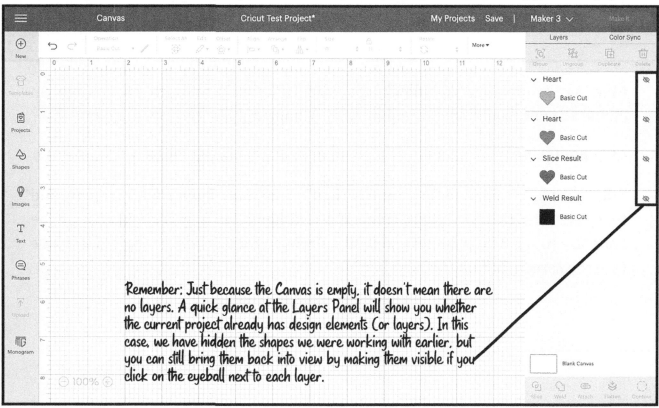

Remember: Just because the Canvas is empty, it doesn't mean there are no layers. A quick glance at the Layers Panel will show you whether the current project already has design elements (or layers). In this case, we have hidden the shapes we were working with earlier, but you can still bring them back into view by making them visible if you click on the eyeball next to each layer.

We'll start a new design by creating a rectangular guide. That way, we can be sure the design will fit nicely on a standard size canvas or blank artboard. Add a square to the Canvas and change its size to 8 inches wide by 12 inches high and change its *Operation* settings to *Guide.*

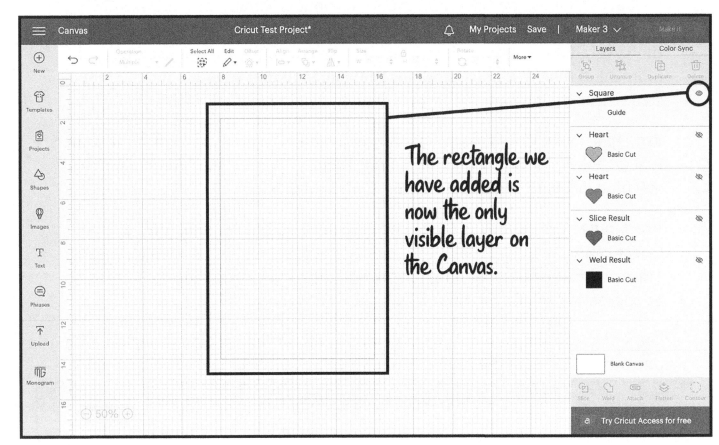

Clue #1: Remember to unlock the *Size* function's padlock to change an element's width and height individually (Chapter 3).

Clue #2: *Operation* is a function you can only apply via the *Edit Bar* (Chapter 4).

Add a text layer, change the font to Cricut's free font, *Trade Gothic Display*, and type "IN THIS HOUSE." Next, rotate the text layer 270 degrees and change the *Font Size* to 94. Move the text so it sits almost against the rectangle's left side (see the screenshot on the next page).

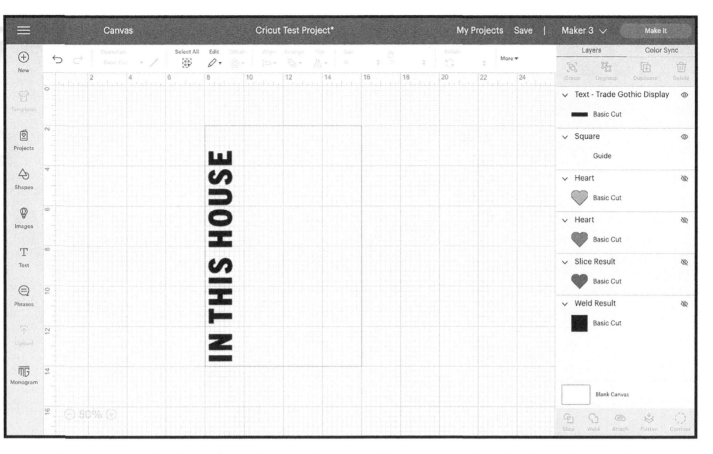

Clue #1: Use the font menu's search bar or filters to quickly find the font you're looking for (Chapter 2).

Clue #2: The quickest way to rotate an element if you know the exact angle you want is via the Edit Bar (Chapter 3.)

Add another text layer to the Canvas. The font should already be set to *Trade Gothic Display*. If not, go ahead and apply it again. Change the *Font Size* to 40, change the words to "WE ARE," and place the element in the upper left corner of the rectangular guide (see the first screenshot on the next page).

Let's add another text layer. This time, change the font to *Karley* (another free Cricut Font), and change the *Font Size* to 96. Now change the word to "FAMILY" and position it next to "WE ARE." (See the second screenshot on the next page.)

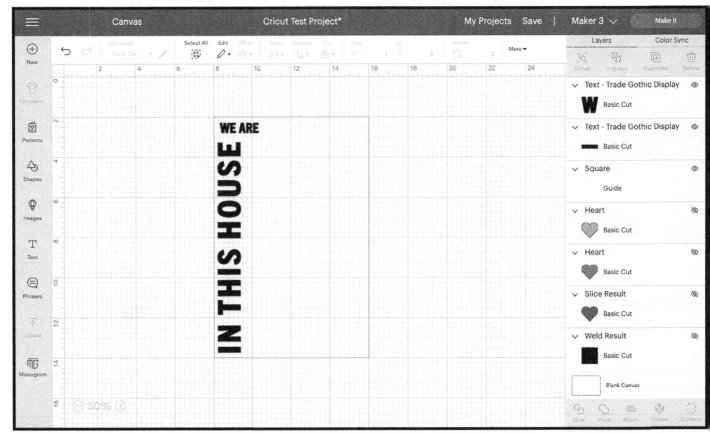

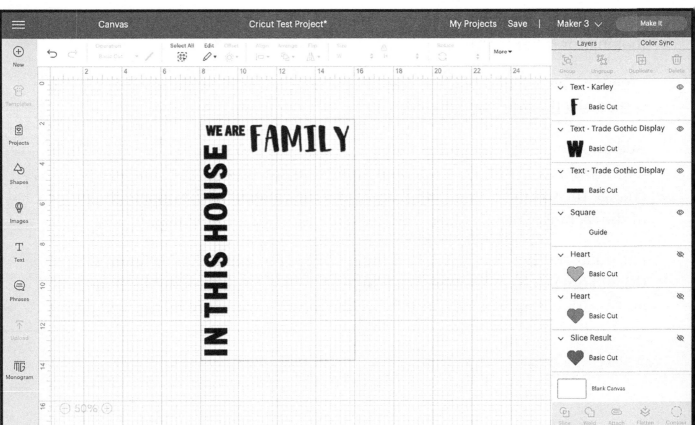

Let's pause for a moment to examine the Layers Panel to see the hierarchy of the layers we've been adding to the Canvas. The layers at the bottom of the Layers Panel are the shapes we stacked in the previous chapter. Since we hid them earlier, we can't actually see them on the Canvas.

The first *visible* layer, when looking from the top downward, is the last text element we added ("FAMILY"). Remember how I said earlier that every new element you add to the Canvas automatically goes on top of the other layers? Keep this in mind as you continue building this design, as it will help you understand the Layers Panel even better.

When we don't stack design elements on top of each other, as is the case with this design, it's easy to forget that their positions on the Canvas is not necessarily representative of their hierarchical order in the Layers Panel. We'll see this unfold as we continue adding text layers to the current design. It's not technically necessary to be concerned with the order of the layers when working on designs like the one we're doing now, as their order cannot affect the outcome. However, because the human brain likes logical order, it will serve you well to get into the habit of rearranging the order of layers you create to correspond with the positions you place them in on the Canvas. Apart from helping you make more sense of layers, getting into the habit of rearranging their order will help you feel more comfortable and familiar with the interface when dealing with designs that have not been arranged logically.

Let's move the "IN THIS HOUSE" to the top of the Layers Panel, since it's the first part we would naturally read when looking at the design. Keeping our staircase analogy in mind, we're starting at the top of the staircase and walking down. The quickest way to rearrange layers is directly in the Layers Panel. So, in the Layers Panel, click and drag the "IN THIS HOUSE" layer to the top of the panel. (See the screenshot at the top of the next page.)

Pro Tip: In the Layers Panel, each layer has a thumbnail to help you identify it more easily. For text layers, the thumbnail is the first letter of the first word. In the instance of "IN THIS HOUSE," the thumbnail is an "I." Note, though, that the "I" looks like a horizontal line in this case, the reason being that we rotated the element earlier.

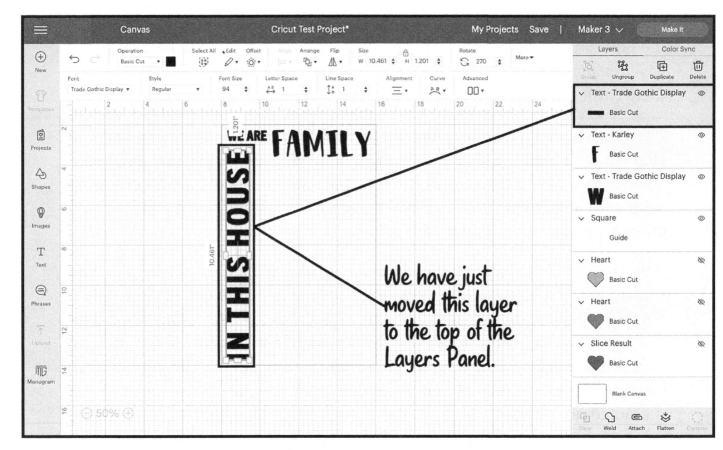

Let's rearrange the order of "WE ARE" too, so it sits directly below "IN THIS HOUSE."

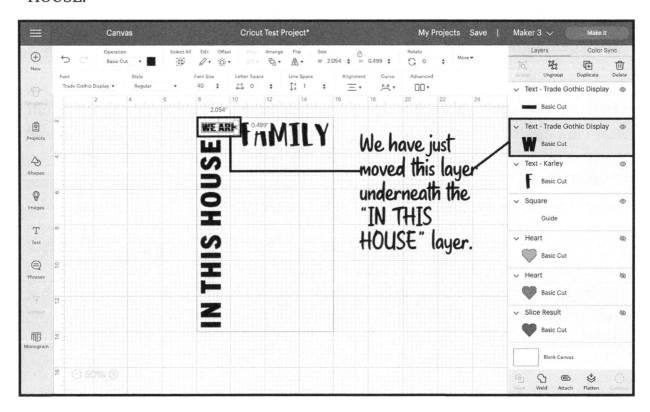

The "FAMILY" layer does not need to move, as it is already in the right order.

Moving on, let's duplicate "WE ARE." Move the copy down so it sits more or less in the middle below "WE ARE FAMILY," and change the wording to "WE DO."

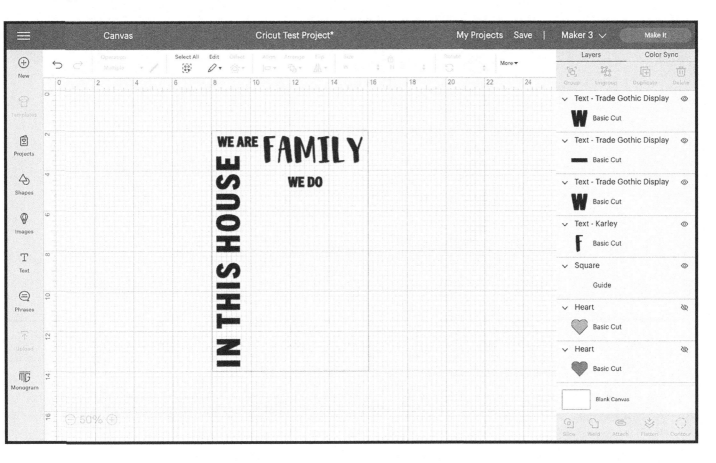

Duplicate "FAMILY," change the copy's wording to "REAL," move it down so it sits below "WE DO," and change its *Font Size* to 60. (See the first screenshot on the next page.)

As we build the design, let's continue rearranging the layers to adhere to a logical order. The second layer, which has a "W" thumbnail, should move in below the "FAMILY" layer, which has a "F" thumbnail. Click and drag it into the right order. Next, move the layer you see at the very top (the one with the "R" thumbnail) so it sits below the layer with the "W" thumbnail you just moved.

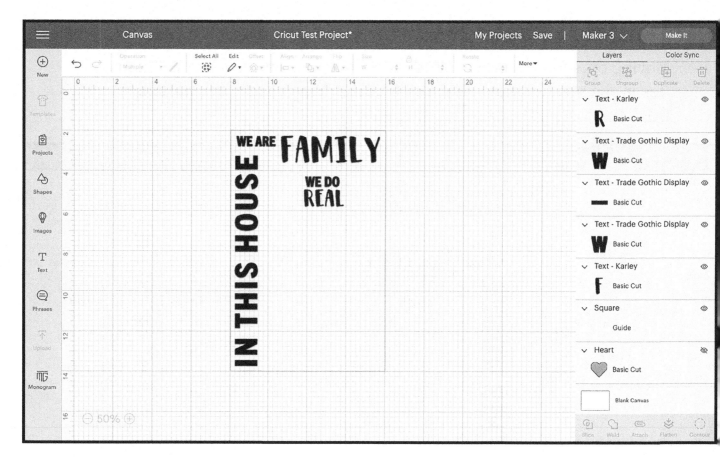

Let's duplicate the "WE DO," move the copy downward, and change it so it says "WE MAKE."

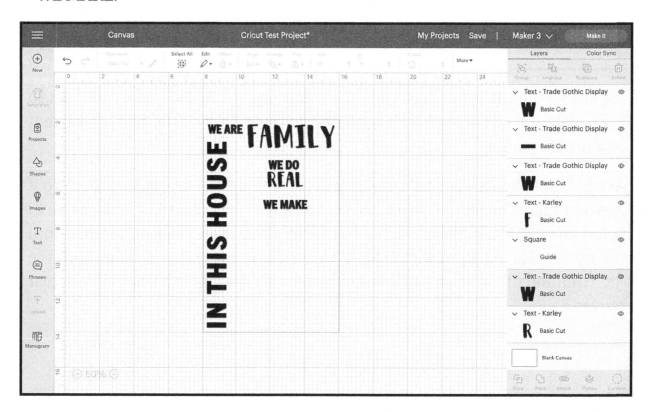

Next, let's duplicate "REAL" and move the copy below "WE MAKE." Change the wording to "MISTAKES."

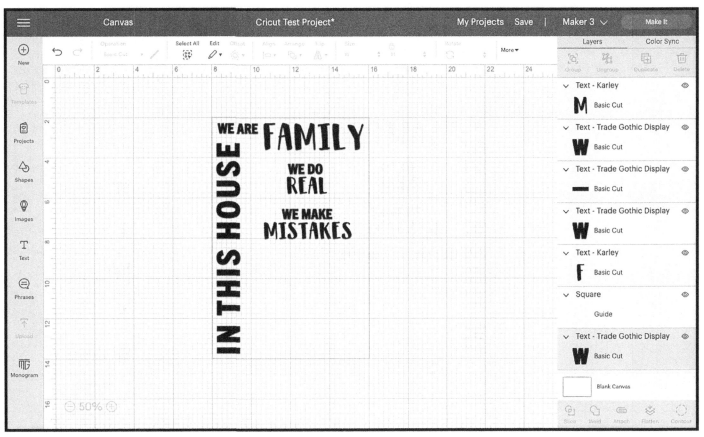

As with the previous layers, rearrange the order of the layers you have just added so they flow logically. The "WE MAKE" layer should follow the "REAL" layer, and the "MISTAKES" layer should follow the "WE MAKE" layer.

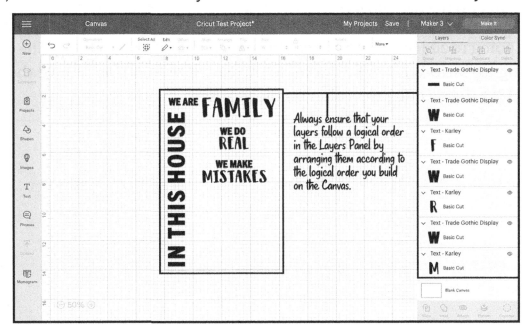

Duplicate the "WE MAKE" layer, move the copy down, and change its words to "WE FORGIVE AND GIVE."

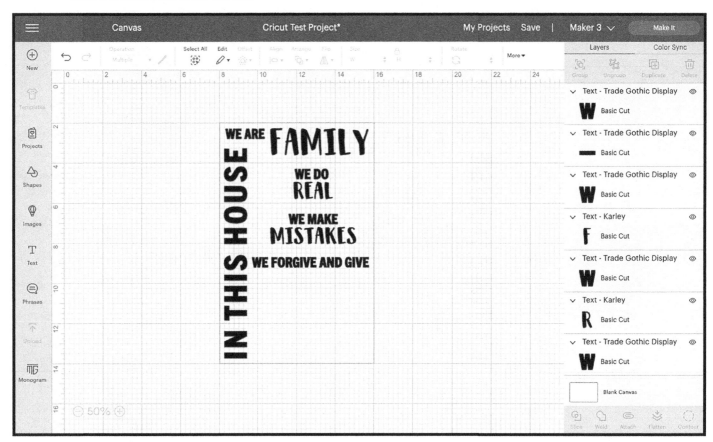

Duplicate the "MISTAKES" layer, move the copy down, and change its wording to "SECOND CHANCES." Also change this layer's *Font Size* to 50. (See the first screenshot on the next page.)

We're going to add one more phrase. Duplicate "WE MAKE," change the copy's wording to "AND WE LOVE," increase the *Font Size* to 60, and move the layer down. (See the second screenshot on the next page.)

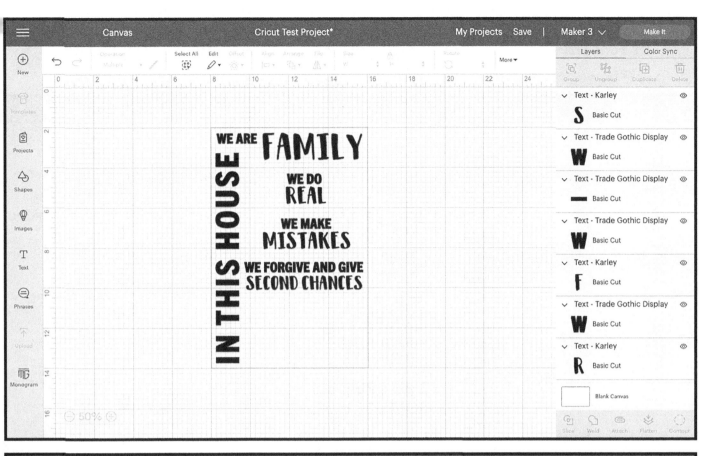

Duplicate "SECOND CHANCES," change the copy to "ABUNDANTLY," increase its *Font Size* to 65, and move it into position underneath the "AND WE LOVE" layer.

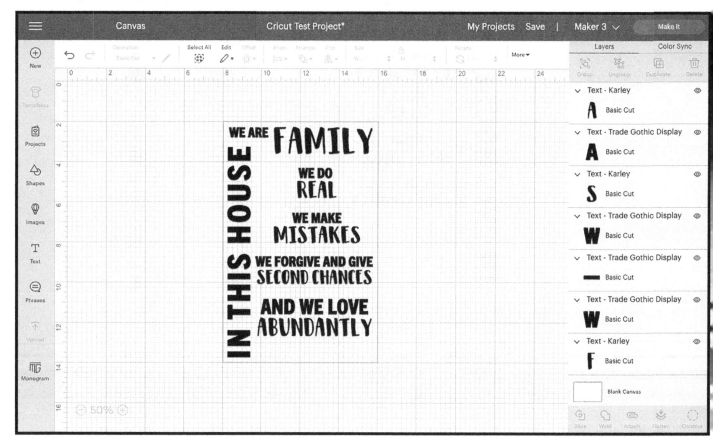

One last time, let's rearrange the layers we just added so the Layers Panel gives us a logical flow. When you're done, your Layers Panel should show your thumbnails in the following order:

- I (turned on its side; "IN THIS HOSE")
- W ("WE ARE")
- F ("FAMILY")
- W ("WE DO")
- R ("REAL")
- W ("WE MAKE")
- M ("MISTAKES")
- W ("WE FORGIVE AND GIVE")
- S ("SECOND CHANCES")
- A ("AND WE LOVE")
- A ("ABUNDANTLY")

Let's ask Design Space to help us align the above text elements in the middle of the rectangular guide. Select the relevant text layers and apply the *Center Horizontally* function.

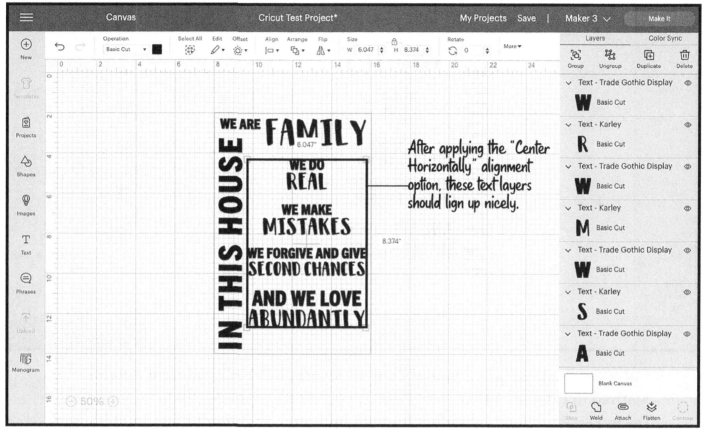

Clue #1: The *Align* function is only available from the Edit Bar (Chapter 4).

Clue #2: To select specific elements while ignoring others, you need to use your keyboard's handy SHIFT key (Chapter 3).

Clue #3: You *don't* want to make the "IN THIS HOUSE," "WE ARE," and "FAMILY" layers a part of the selection to apply the *Align* function here.

With the elements still selected, move the entire selection down a little bit. The goal is to create an equal amount of space above and below the selection, like you see in the screenshot on the next page.

Since this design is all black, we *could* simply go ahead and use the *Attach* function and move on to the Make It screen to start the cutting process. (Remember that attaching the layers keeps them in the exact position you see them on the Canvas when your Cricut cuts them out.)

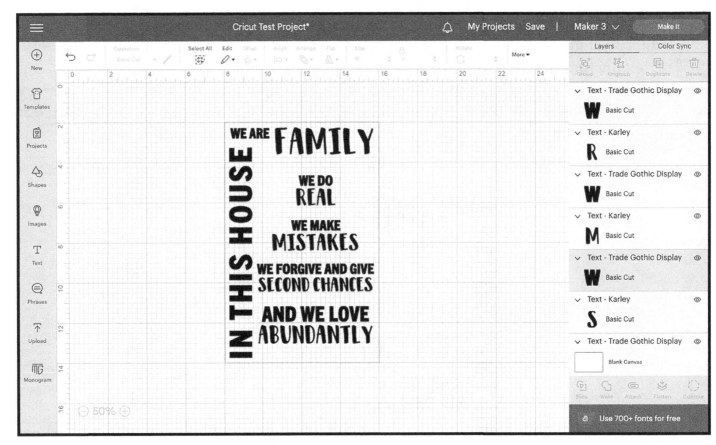

But what happens when you work with layers that have different colors? You learned in Chapter 3 that the moment you attach layers with different colors, Design Space will change everything to one color and your Cricut machine will cut it all on a single mat. To get your Cricut to cut different colors, it needs to understand that certain layers will be cut on one mat, while others will be cut on a different mat. So, the *Attach* function should *not* be applied to all the layers on the Canvas. But, at the same time, you certainly don't want to spend all your time rearranging every single word and decorative element to represent your original design after the cutting process. And—thank goodness!—you don't have to do that. The whole idea of Cricut crafting is to make the process smoother, easier, and faster, after all!

To see the solution in action, let's go to the *Images* library and look for something to add to the design. Type in "decorative line" in the search bar and tick the box next to *Free*. Also, choose *Cut Only* for the *Operation Type* filter. Scroll through the results until you see the swirly line (or something similar) in the illustration on the next page.

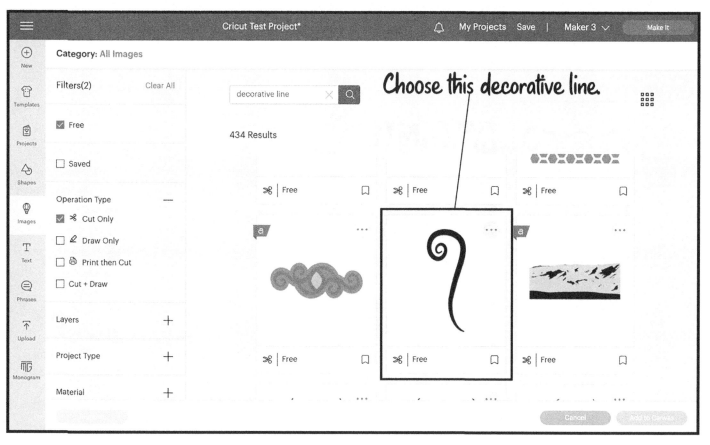

Back on the Canvas, do the following:

1. *Rotate* the swirly line 90 degrees.
2. *Flip* the swirly line vertically.
3. *Duplicate* the swirly line.
4. *Flip* the copy of the swirly line horizontally.
5. Position the two swirly lines so their ends meet each other.
6. Apply the *Align Top* function to make sure the two swirly lines are the same height.

When you're done with the above adjustments, you should see the same results as shown in the screenshot on the next page.

Clue #1: The *Flip* action can only be done via the *Edit Bar* (Chapter 4).

Clue #2: You can zoom in and out of your Canvas to make sure your swirly lines meet each other perfectly (Chapter 1).

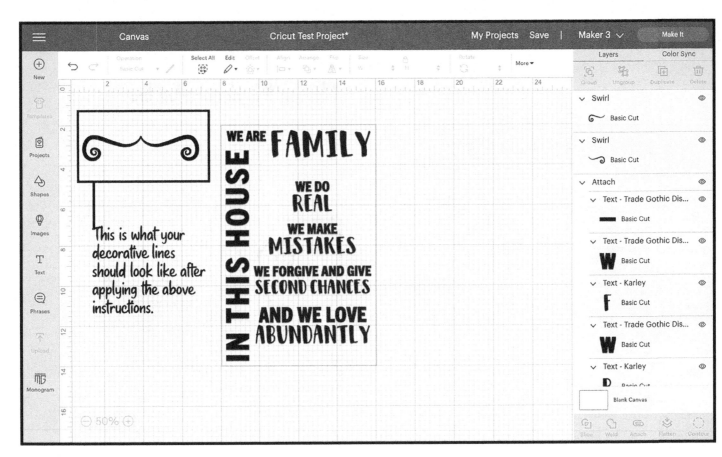

Next, let's do the following:

1. *Duplicate* the swirly line on the right.
2. Position the copy so the wavy part toward its end meets the wavy part of the original right-side swirly line.
3. *Duplicate* the swirly line on the left.
4. Position the copy so the wavy part toward its end meets the wavy part of the original left-side swirly line.

Check out the screenshot on the next page for guidance on what you should be seeing after making the above adjustments.

Pro Tip: If you feel like there's not enough space on the spot you're working, feel free to move things around, but remember to use the SHIFT button on your keyboard to select multiple layers so you can move them at the same time. (You can let go of the SHIFT button when you're ready to move the selection, but it will still move even while you're holding the SHIFT button down.)

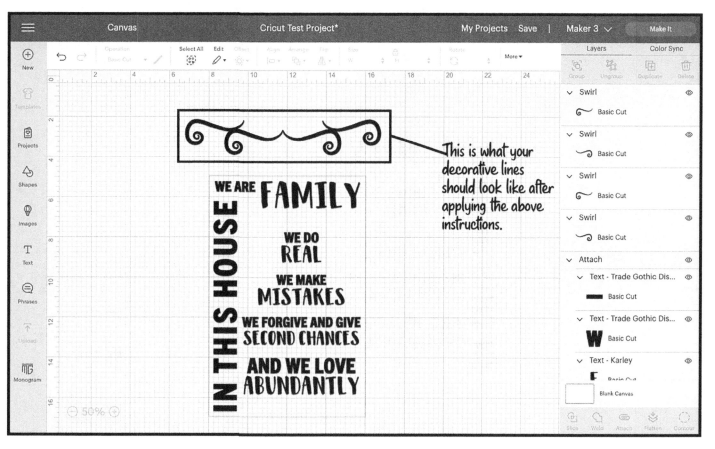

Let's continue:

1. Select all the swirly lines.
2. Use the *Group* function to turn the lines into a unit you can easily tweak and move around without affecting their positions relative to each other.
3. Change the swirly lines' color to anything you like.
4. Reduce the group's width to 6 inches (the height will adjust automatically).
5. Move the group down to the rest of the design so it sits in between "FAMILY" and "WE DO."

The screenshot on the next page shows you more or less what you should see now:

Clue: The *Group* function is an "all-rounder" function you can apply via the Canvas, Layers Panel, or Edit Bar (Chapter 3).

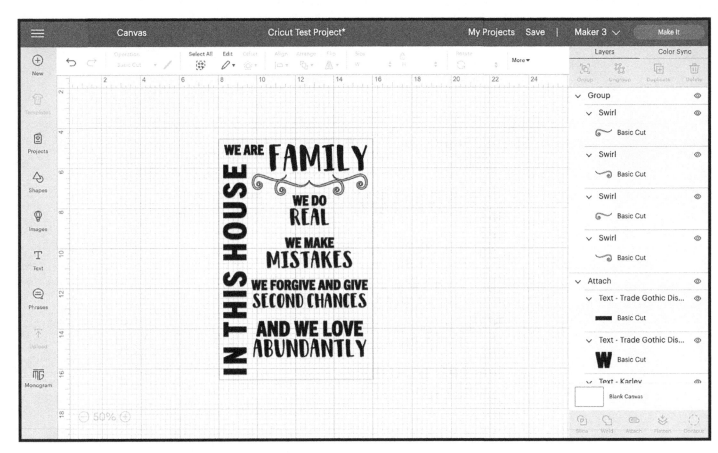

Let's apply the *Weld* function so these lines form a new, single element.

Clue: *Weld* is another "all-rounder" function (Chapter 3).

Finally, let's duplicate our newly-formed swirly decorative line, *Flip* the copy vertically, and move it down so it sits underneath "ABUNDANTLY" on the Canvas. (See the screenshot on the next page.)

Pro Tip: Your swirly decorative line may overlap with your "ABUNDANTLY" text layer. If so, you can nudge the text layers a bit so everything fits in nicely. On the other hand, you might like the overlap and decide to keep it. Let your creativity guide you.

At the moment, you should see your decorative lines lying at the top of the Layers Panel. Let's leave them there for now.

Now we come back to the big question: how do you keep this design intact for the cutting process, all while helping your Cricut machine understand you have two different colors to cut out?

Luckily, the answer is straightforward and easy to implement.

First, always remember that the *Attach* function can be used as many times as you want on a single Canvas, which means there can be two, three, five, or any number of attachments, as long as the design elements' colors in those attachments are the same.

Pro Tip: Design Space will not warn you if you accidentally attach layers with different colors to each other. It will simply change the colors of everything you want to attach to a single color. So, always be mindful of this and double-check yourself. If you notice a blunder, hit that *Undo* button and restart the process of attaching the right elements to each other.

Second, when working with different colors for a cut project, you should learn to see your design as a whole made up of different, independent units. Depending on your design, you can define these units according to shapes, words, colors, or whatever makes sense to you. In my experience, I have learned that defining the units according to colors makes the most sense when dealing with less complex designs like the one we're making in this tutorial.

Since we're dealing with two colors, our task is to make two separate attachments. Let's start with the text. Select all the text layers on the Canvas and apply the *Attach* function.

Pro Tip: While you can select multiple layers directly on the Canvas, you'll have much better control over the process via the Layers Panel. Each element you select turns gray in the Layers Panel, so it's easier to see if you accidentally missed a layer. (Just remember to hold in that SHIFT button if you want to select multiple layers!)

After applying the *Attach* function, you'll see a single selection box around all the text layers on the Canvas. In the Layers Panel, you'll see "Attach" at the top, followed by all the layers that are a part of the attachment. If you scroll down in the Layers Panel, you'll see that applying the *Attach* function has automatically pushed the two decorative lines below the attachment. (See the two screenshots on the following page.)

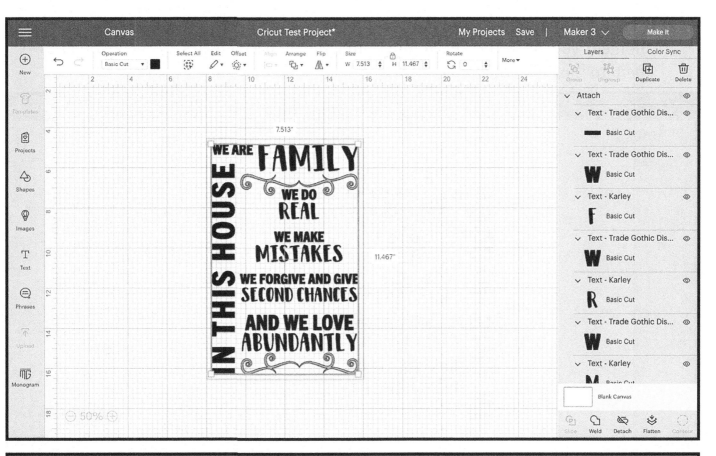

Now let's select the two decorative lines and attach them to each other. The moment you apply the *Attach* function, Design Space pushes the new attachment to the top of the Layers Panel.

You can keep it there, or rearrange it so it sits below the attachment containing the text layers for a more logical flow. Earlier, I mentioned that you can either let your decorative line at the bottom overlap the last word, "ABUNDANTLY," or nudge the text layers so nothing overlaps. If you opted for the overlapping effect, you'll have to decide whether you want the decorative line over the text, or the text over the decorative line. Whichever one you want on top should be on top in the Layers Panel.

My lines and text do not overlap, and I prefer a logical flow in my Layers Panel, so I'll go ahead and put the decorative lines attachment below the text attachment. (Remember that changing the order of layers in the Layers Panel will not affect the way the design looks on the Canvas when those layers don't overlap each other.)

That's it! You have just successfully created a layered design in Design Space from scratch *and* applied many Design Space functions that probably had you nervous back in Chapter 1.

But that's not all—your design is actually 100 percent ready to be cut out and applied to an 8 by 12-inch Canvas or art-board. Why not go ahead and start the cutting process? Do it just for fun. Above all, do it to prove to yourself that you have conquered the mighty beast that is Design Space.

And yes, you may do your happy dance now.

A Closer Look at the Layers Panel Functions

With everything you've learned so far, you've actually already conquered most of the Layers Panel's functions in Chapter 3. These functions include:

- *Group/Ungroup*
- *Slice*
- *Weld*
- *Attach*
- *Flatten/Unflatten*
- *Edit functions (Copy, Cut, Paste, Duplicate, Delete)*

There are two more things you can do via the Layers Panel, but you will not really use these functions until you become more versed in Design Space and Cricut crafting. They are *Color Sync* and *Contour*.

Color Sync is a quick way of changing a layer's color to match that of another color. According to Design Space, the goal with the Color Sync function is to help you use fewer materials.

How so?

When all the elements that make up your design are the same color, your Cricut machine can use a single mat to cut out everything, meaning it can cut the entire design out of a single piece of material (depending on how large your design is, of course).

However, when the elements that make up your design are different colors, your Cricut machine will cut the elements out of more than one piece of material. In the case of the design we made, your Cricut will use one sheet of material for the text part of the design (black, for example) and another sheet of material for the decorative lines (gray, for example).

If we wanted to change the decorative lines to black via the *Color Sync* function, here is what we would do:

At the top of the Layers Panel, you'll see *Layers* and *Color Sync*. Click on *Color Sync*. The moment you do, the Color Sync Panel will open. This panel contains every color on your Canvas and indicates which layers are associated with which colors via thumbnails. In the case of our design, there are two colors.

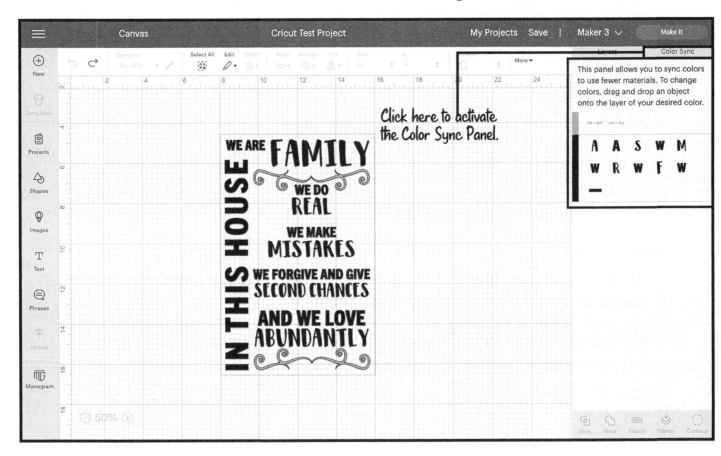

If we want to change the decorative lines to the same color as the text, all we have to do is click and drag their color (gray in my case, but yours can differ) into the text elements' color. When you do that, everything on the Canvas will show black, and the Color Sync Panel will no longer show two colors, but one (see the screenshot at the top of the next page).

The action we just performed is just a quick example of what you can achieve with the *Color Sync* function. If you want your entire design to be a single color, feel free to keep it as is. Otherwise, use the *Undo* button to revert to the design's previous state and click on *Layers* to go back to the Layers Panel.

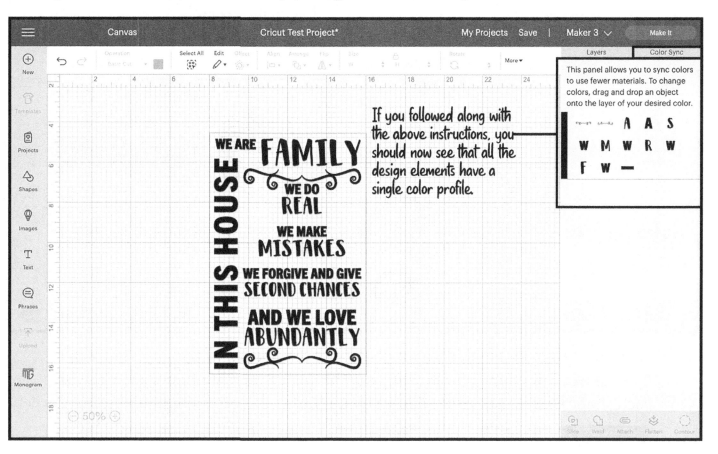

Contour is an advanced Design Space feature. With it, you can tell the program which parts of a layer you want to keep or discard for the cutting process. It's not exactly useful for less complex designs, but it might be something you want to use later in your crafting journey when dealing with more complex and intricate designs.

To give you a quick overview of how *Contour* works, I'm going to add a free design from the Images library to my Canvas. If you want to follow along (which I recommend), you can search for the element by its name, *Families*, or its unique ID, *#M2B0348EE*, using the search bar in your Images library. (See the screenshot on the next page.)

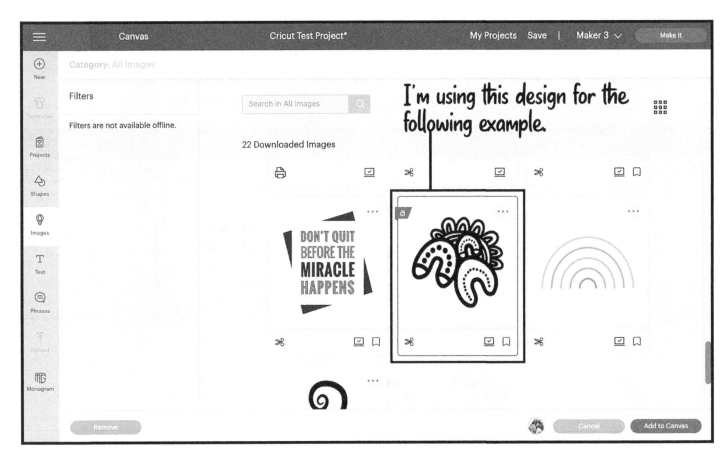

With the design selected, click on *Contour* at the bottom of the Layers Panel. A pop-up window will open, showing you the design on the left and a panel with each shape that makes up the design on the right.

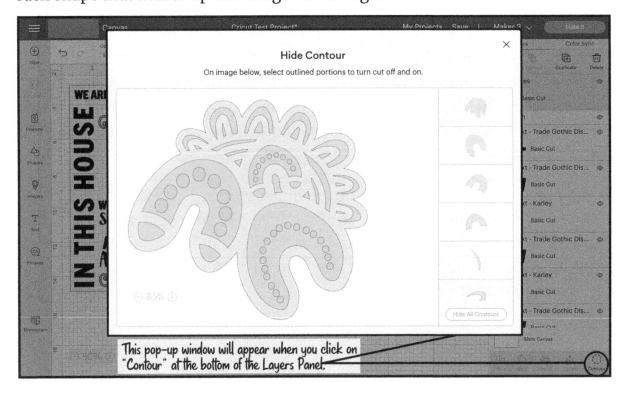

Now, if you click on any one of the shapes that make up the design, Design Space will remove it from the design, ultimately changing its character. Click on the shape that creates the outer edge of the design. See how the shape changes from a darker shade of gray to a lighter shade of gray? That tells you that you have removed that part from the design. You can also see it highlighted in the panel to the right, which is another indication that that specific shape has been removed.

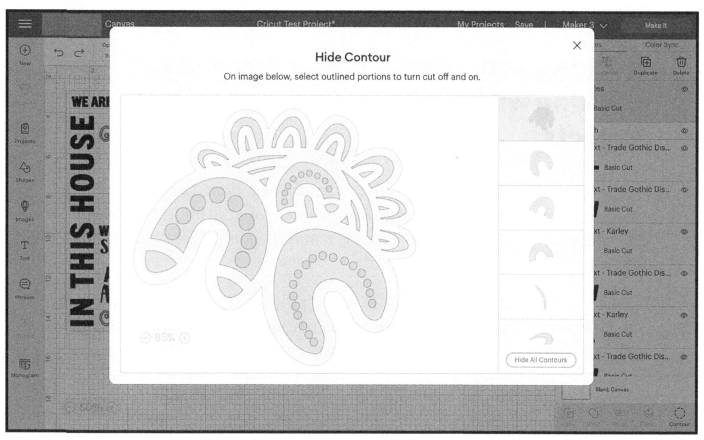

You can click on the shape again if you want to bring it back. However, to see how using the Contour function affects a design, let's keep the change we have just made. There is no "apply" button here, so you can simply close the *Contour* window. (See the screenshot at the top of the next page.)

As you can see, the thick outline we had around the design initially is no longer there. If you open the *Contour* window again, you can still bring back the outline you had removed by simply clicking on the shape again. Of course, you can play around with the rest of the design to see how it changes as you continue removing some of its parts.

Pro Tip: Don't confuse the shapes you see in the *Contour* window with layers. When using this function, you're working on a single layer, and the individual shapes you see are simply representations of where that layer's contour lines begin and end. The program can change the layer's appearance by manipulating its contour lines.

When you're done playing around with the *Contour* function, you can delete the image from the Canvas.

Working with Layers for Cut Projects vs Working with Layers for Print Then Cut Projects

The process of building a design from scratch for a *Print Then Cut* project is exactly the same as building a design from scratch for a *Cut* project, so your new knowledge of layers will come in very handy if you prefer *Print Then Cut* projects.

However, unlike *Cut* projects, *Print Then Cut* projects get flattened just before you move on to the next phase of the creation process (the cutting and application of the design). Flattening basically turns multiple layers into a single layer, just like a JPG or PNG image. This is important, as a printer cannot see or understand layers. It simply prints out the image given to it in black and white or color. That said, when you design your own *Print Then Cut* projects, you can always *Unflatten* a design and tweak its original layers to refine and change the design. But when you upload a JPG or PNG image for a *Print Then Cut* project, there are no layers to tweak, meaning you'll have to use the design 'as is.' If you want total design freedom to create unique projects, your best option will always be to create your own designs. The second best option (that even the pros use a lot) is uploading SVG files to Design Space. Although SVGs are ready-made designs, they consist of layers, and you can tweak those layers using all the functions you learned in this book to change the SVG into something unique. So, if you can, always opt for downloading SVG instead of JPG or PNG files, even if you plan on turning it into a *Print Then Cut* project.

Of course, if you come across a design you love and wouldn't change anything about it, you can absolutely download a JPG or PNG for your *Print Then Cut* project. When you download design files, always make sure you fully understand the license agreement that comes with it. Some files are free, but you can only use them for personal projects.

The Difference Between Cut Projects and Print Then Cut Projects

Right now, the design we created in this chapter is a *Cut* project (for the *Operation* settings tell us so). When your Cricut does a *Cut* project for you, it cuts out every visible layer on the Canvas (apart from Templates and Guides). How wide or long it can cut these layers depends on your Cricut model and the constraints of your cutting mats. However, with experience, careful planning, and creativity, you have the ability to create some pretty huge projects that can span across walls, windows, and other large surfaces.

A *Print Then Cut* project's size is limited to that of a standard printing paper (although you can print on any printable material supported by your printer). If we turn design into a *Print Then Cut* project (choose *Print Then Cut* as the *Operation* setting), Design Space will immediately tell us there is a problem. Next to "Attach" in the Layers Panel, a warning sign will appear (see the first screenshot on the next page).

When you click on the warning sign, you'll be met with a message that says the image size is too large for the *Operation* settings (see the second screenshot on the next page).

Whenever you see this sign, Design Space is telling you that there is an issue with the layer/group/attachment.

If you click on the warning sign, Design Space will tell you what the problem is.

Not supported by Maker 3:

Image too large. Reduce image size to 6.75" x 9.25" or less.

OR

Change Page Size

Because Cricut is so focused on making their crafters' lives as convenient as possible, the warning message even tells you to what size you should reduce the design if you want it to work as a *Print Then Cut* Project. In the case of our design, we should size it down to at least 6.75 inches wide by 9.25 inches high. Let's do that and see what happens.

If we adjust the width to 6.75 inches, there is *still* a problem with the height.

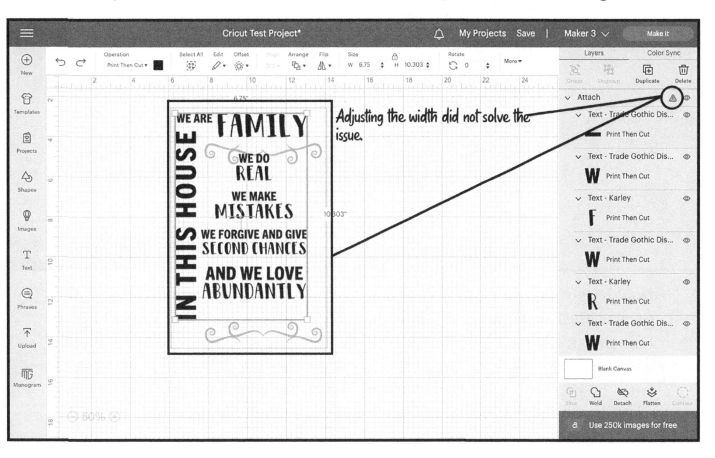

Should we unlock the padlock and change the height to 9.25 inches? We could, but then we risk pulling the text out of proportion, and we don't want that in this case. The solution, then, is to hit the *Undo* button and change the design's height instead. This solves the issue, as you can see the warning sign is no longer there in the screenshot on the next page.

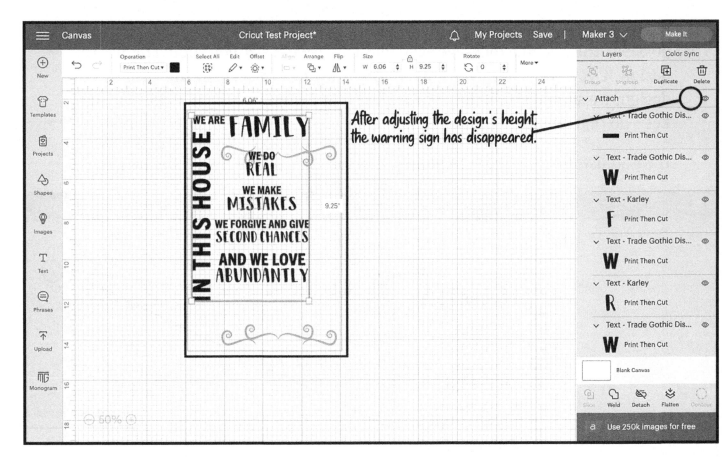

Now let's move on to the decorative lines. When you click on them in the Canvas, the Layers Panel will show them, too, and give you the same warning—that the size is too big. If we change their height to 9.25 inches, the overall design will not align, as the decorative lines covered a smaller piece to start with. To get them right, use the selection box around them to reduce their size until they're in line with the rest of the design as before, like you see in the screenshot on the next page.

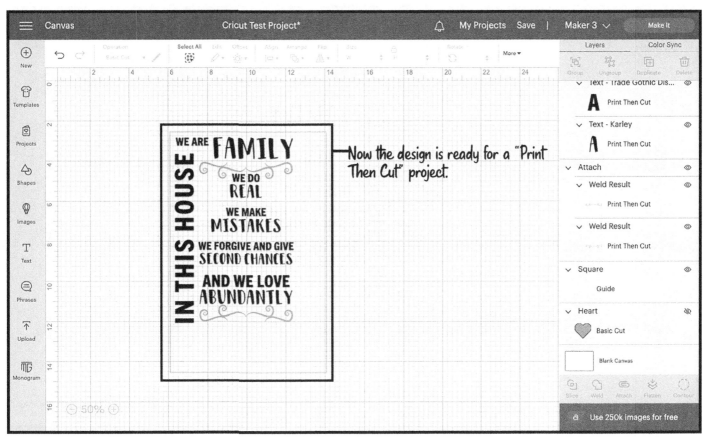

Now the design is ready for a "Print Then Cut" project.

Now you can flatten the layers (using the *Flatten* function) and you can move on to the Make It screen and start the printing and cutting process. The visible guide (the rectangle) gives you a good idea of how much the design has shrunk from how we had it originally.

Let's head over to the Make It screen. On the preview mat, there is a thick, black border around the design (see the screenshot at the top of the next page).

This is not the rectangular guide we had on the Canvas. You'll see the border on the Make It screen, called *registration marks*, every time you work with *Print Then Cut* projects. Before cutting a design, your Cricut machine scans the design to get its alignment perfect so it can make the most accurate cuts. The *registration marks* around a *Print Then Cut* project assist your Cricut with this alignment process.

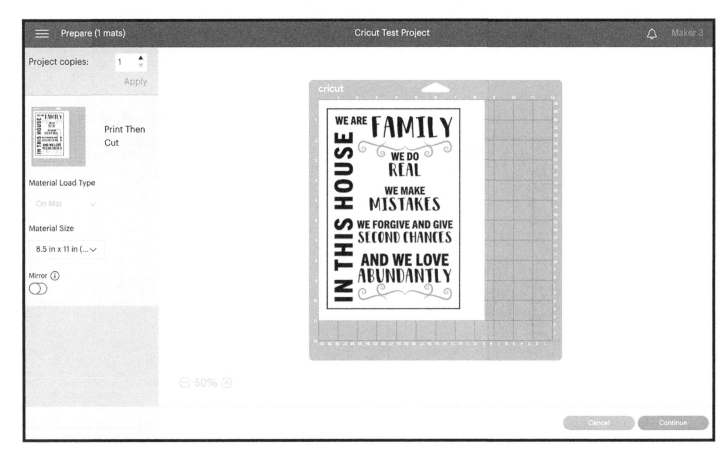

Another factor that distinguishes *Cut* projects from *Print Then Cut* projects is how your Cricut treats contour lines around the designs it cuts out. With *Cut* projects, each layer's borders (or contours) sets it apart from other layers, and whether they overlap or not, your Cricut will cut each layer individually. With *Print Then Cut* projects, your Cricut treats the entire design as a single layer and will only cut around the outer borders it sees. To better understand this difference, let's track back to the shapes we had stacked on top of each other earlier in the book. On your Canvas, hide the rectangular guide and the design we worked on in this chapter, and make the stacked shapes visible again (see the first screenshot on the next page).

If we treat these shapes as a *Cut* project, Design Space will separate each layer onto its own mat (because we're working with different colors) and cut out an individual square and three individual hearts. Even if all these shapes were the same color, your Cricut would still cut out the individual shapes (the only difference being that it would prompt you to use one cutting mat). (See the second screenshot on the next page.)

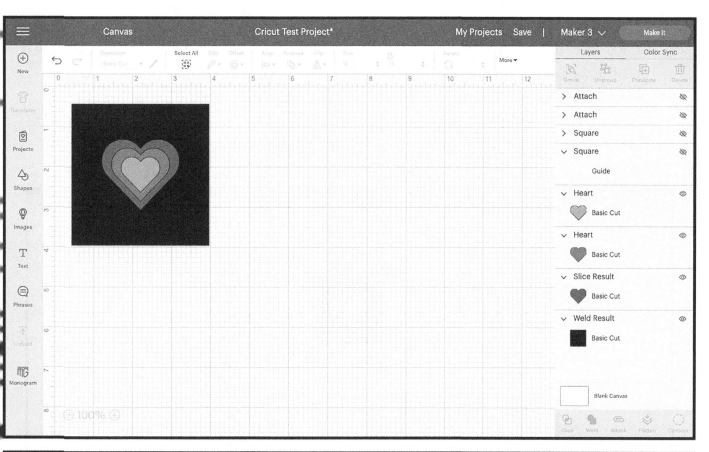

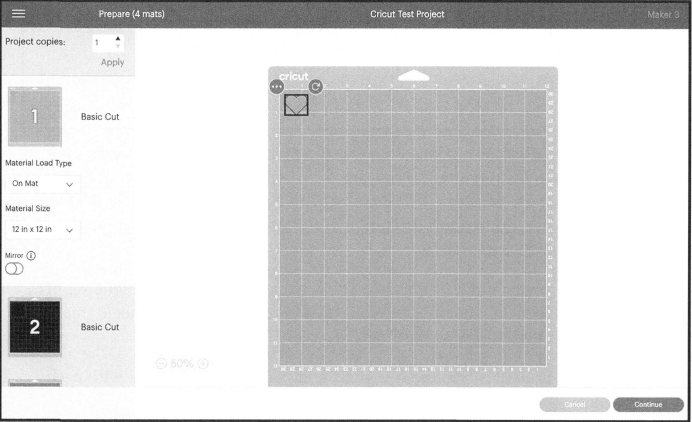

On the other hand, if we treat these shapes as a *Print Then Cut* project, Design Space will flatten the design, effectively turning it onto a single layer. Your printer will recognize the different colors and print out what you see on the screen. But when it comes to the cutting process, your Cricut will only recognize the design's outer edge (the square) as something to be cut out. In this case, it will not attempt to cut out an individual square and three individual hearts.

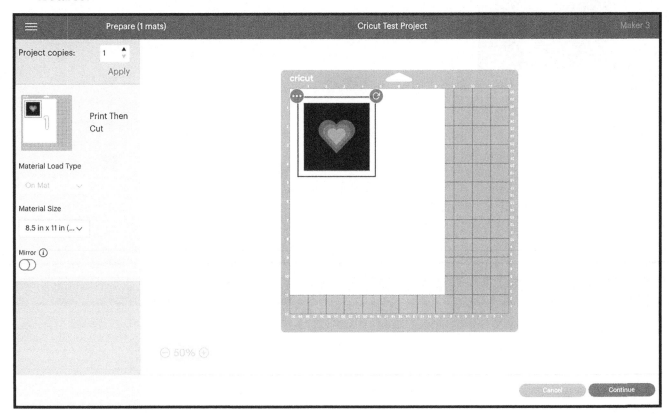

The design we created in this chapter (the text design) has no overlapping layers. So, in this case, whether you choose to make it as a *Cut* project or a *Print Then Cut* project, your Cricut will cut around the individual borders it sees. Here, the major difference is the output of the size and, of course, the goal you want to achieve with the design.

While *Cut* projects and *Print Then Cut* projects each come with a unique set of pros and cons, there is no right or wrong answer to the question, *"Should I make this design a Cut project or a Print Then Cut project?"*

In the end, it all depends on your goals and personal preferences with each design.

Layers & Layers Panel Self-Assessment

How would you describe layers in your own words?

_____

_____

_____

_____

_____

True or False: Design Space automatically turns any element you add to the Canvas into its own layer.

_____

Why are layers useful in digital design?

_____

_____

_____

_____

_____

True or False: While layers work on a hierarchical basis, two or more layers can occupy the same level.

_____

What would you say is the purpose of the Layers Panel in Design Space?

_____

_____

_____

_____

_____

True or False: Your Cricut machine can see hidden layers, so it's best to delete layers when you're not sure whether you want to use them or not.

_____

When creating a design where layers do not overlap each other, it's easy to forget that each layer still adheres to a hierarchical order when moving elements around on the Canvas. Do you think it's useful to still rearrange layers so they follow a logical flow when layers don't overlap each other? Why or why not?

_____

_____

_____

_____

_____

How can you easily identify a specific layer via the Layers Panel?

_____

_____

_____

_____

True or False: It's a bad idea to attach layers with different colors to each other because attaching them will give them all a single color, leading your Cricut machine to cut them all on a single piece of material.

_____

How do you keep a design intact for the cutting process, all while helping your Cricut machine understand you have two or more different colors to cut out?

_____

_____

_____

_____

Are there hard and fast rules when choosing between a Cut project and a Print Then Cut project? Explain your answer.

_____

_____

_____

_____

BONUS SECTION
Late 2022 Software Updates

Toward the end of 2022, Design Space announced a major update to their Layers Panel, as well as a new feature to the Design Panel, called *Editable Images*. Let's check out the Layers Panel update first.

The Layers Panel has a new function, called *Combine*. With this function, you have more control with overlapping layers. Think of it as an enhanced version of *Slice* and *Weld*. *Combine* lies right next to *Slice*.

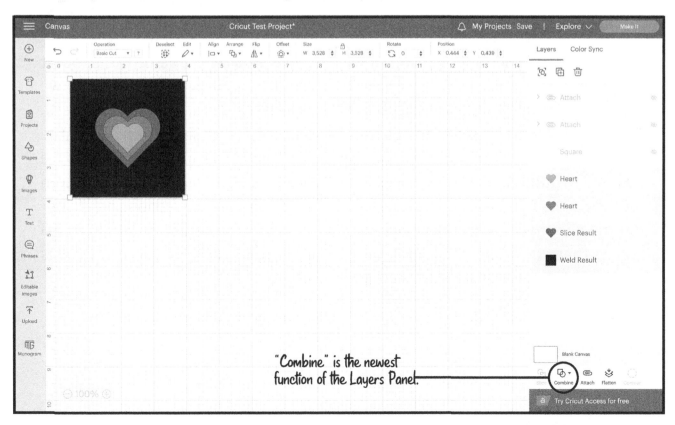

"Combine" is the newest function of the Layers Panel.

To see what we can do with it, let's move the three hearts of our stacked shapes to the side, increase their size, and click on Combine to see our options.

With the stacked hearts selected, click on "Combine" to activate the options.

You're already familiar with the first option, *Weld*, so let's move on to the rest.

Unite is a like a friendlier version of *Weld*. It does exactly the same thing, but it is much more forgiving because you can undo the action at a later stage. If we apply the Unite function to the hearts, it will have the same effect as *Weld*. However, as you can see in the Layers Panel in the screenshot at the top of the next page, this action produces a *Unite* group instead of a *Weld* group. Also, if we wanted to undo the action, all we'd have to do is click on *Combine* at the bottom of the Layers Panel and select the *Undo Unite* option (see the second screenshot on the next page). The option below *Undo Unite*, *Merge Layers*, will tell Design Space that you want to commit the change permanently. If you use it, it is basically the same as *Weld* and cannot be undone.

If you are following along, use the *Undo Unite* function before moving on.

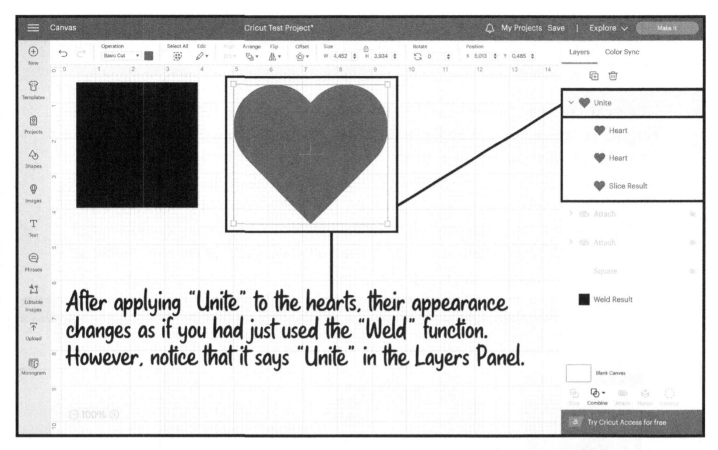

After applying "Unite" to the hearts, their appearance changes as if you had just used the "Weld" function. However, notice that it says "Unite" in the Layers Panel.

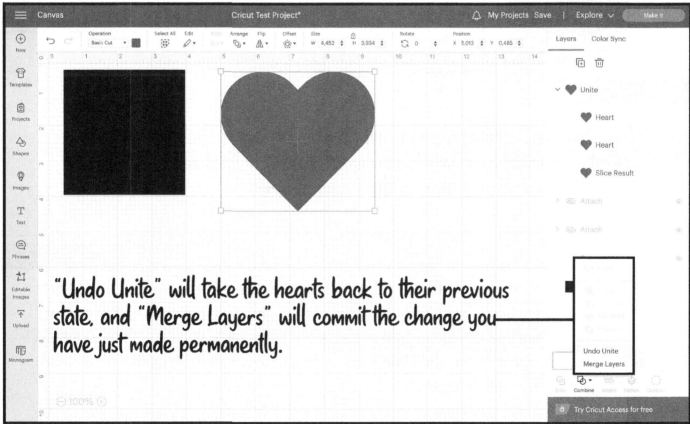

"Undo Unite" will take the hearts back to their previous state, and "Merge Layers" will commit the change you have just made permanently.

Pro Tip: When you undo the *Unite* action, the shapes you initially applied the action to will revert back to the standard Cricut gray color. Be sure to change them back.

The next *Combine* function action is *Subtract*. It works a lot like *Slice*, but the difference is that you can apply *Subtract* to more than two layers at a time. In the case of our hearts, we can apply the action to all three of them at once. Remember how we had to drag two hearts away from the square before we could see what the *Slice* action actually did? Well, with the *Subtract* action, Design Space automatically hides the layers that create the "cookie cutter" effect. With the three hearts selected, click on *Combine* and then go ahead and choose *Subtract*. This is the result you should see:

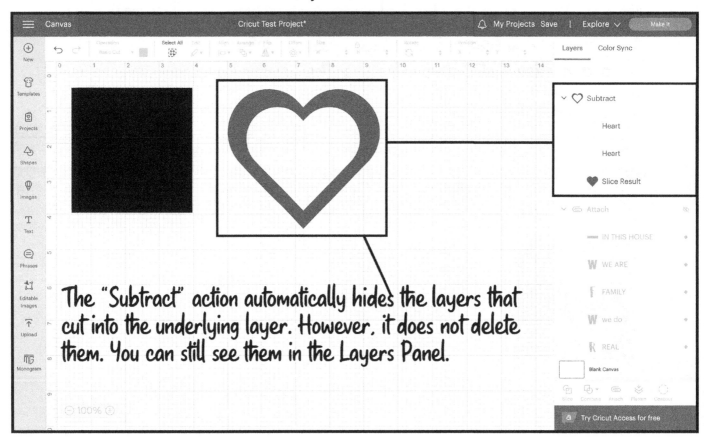

Pro Tip: The *Subtract* action is versatile. Play around with the *Show* and *Hide* icons next to each of the layers that you used to apply the action and see how the image changes according to what you hide and show. (Do you still remember what the *Show* and *Hide* icons are? They're the little eyeballs next to each layer in the Layers Panel.)

As with the *Unite* action, you can also undo the *Subtract* action or commit the change permanently by using the *Merge Layers* option.

Pro tip: Don't be too keen to use the Merge Layers option. It's a way safer bet just leaving the action you applied as is. If you leave it, you can always go back later to make changes if you want to, but if you merge those layers and you decide there's something you'd like to change later on, you'll have to do everything from scratch.

Let's see what else we can do with the Combine function. First, use the *Undo Subtract* action. You need not change the shapes' colors back every time we undo an action now, but don't forget to do it when you're working on an actual project.

Next up is *Intersect*. This action identifies the parts where all the selected shapes intersect each other and makes a cut-out of that intersection. Typically, it ends up being a little piece. In the case of our hearts, because they're so neatly stacked, the Intersect action simply cuts out the smallest heart (the one on top), as that is the point where all the hearts meet.

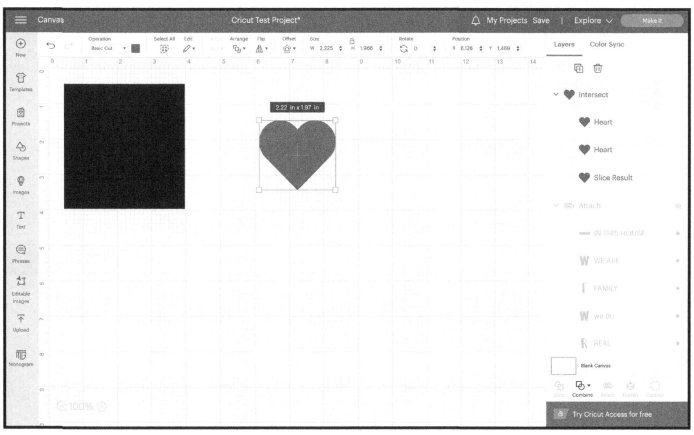

Pro Tip: As with the *Subtract* action, the *Intersect* action does not delete the layers you used to apply the action. And, also like *Subtract*, *Intersect* is versatile and allows you to play around with different results with the help of the *Show* and *Hide* icons.

The last *Combine* action is *Exclude*. (If you're following along, remember to undo the previous step before you continue.) Whereas *Intersect* gives you the bit where layers overlap each other, *Exclude* gives you a sort of in between result. The results will differ depending on how your layers overlap each other. In the case of our stacked hearts, the *Exclude* action removed the middle heart. However, if you play around with the Show and Hide icons, you will see varying results.

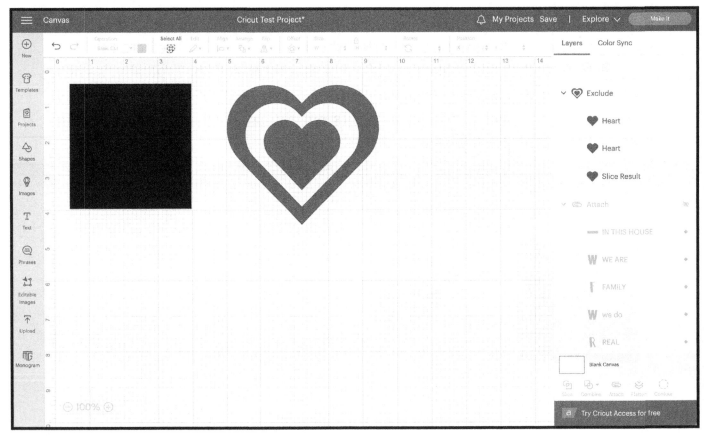

The Combine function opens many new creative opportunities, but to exploit those opportunities, you have to dig in and play around. The above examples are just touching the surface of what's possible.

The screenshot on the next page illustrates the four actions side-by-side.

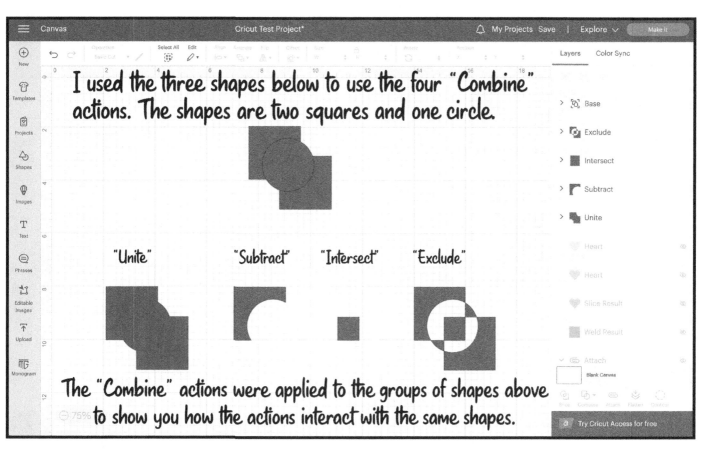

Pro Tip: You can new rename items in your Layers Panel to make identifying individual layers or groups of layers with more ease. To rename a layer, double-click on its name in the Layers Panel, type in whatever you want to name it, and hit the ENTER key on your keyboard.

Editable Images

Editable Images are a new Design Panel feature. It gives you access to a library of images that contains editable components, which you cannot do with regular images.

Open the *Editable Images* library, click the box next to Free in the left-hand panel, and look for something you like. The screenshot on the next page shows my choice.

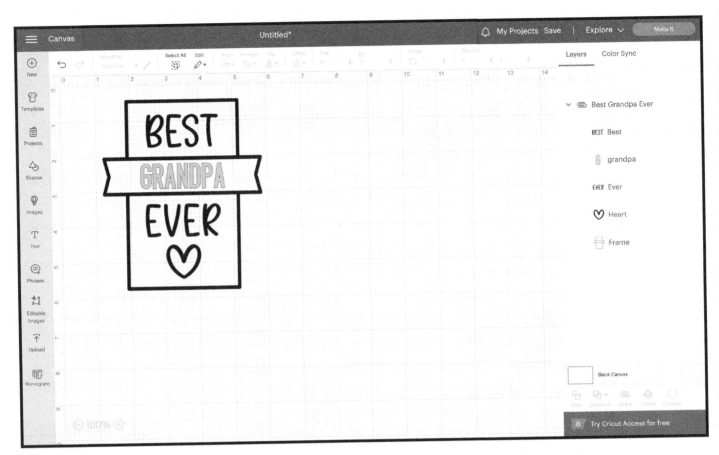

Typically, there is one editable area in these images. To find the editable area, click on each layer until you see the font menu appear beneath the Edit Bar. In the case of the above image, "Grandpa" is the editable part.

Pro Tip: For the most part, the gray text is the editable component of any *Editable Image*.

Change the editable part to anything you'd like. You can also change the font, the font style, and even the color. The editable part is a text element, so you can do anything with it that you'd normally do with a text element.

The screenshot on the next page shows the change I've made to the editable part of the image I chose.

Pro Tip #1: Remember that if you want to change an element's color if it is within a group, you'll have to ungroup the selection before you can do it.

Pro Tip #2: The new Layers Panel actions and the Editable Image feature is only available on the desktop app at the moment.

Chapter 5 Notes

Use this space to jot down the best take-aways you learned from Chapter 2. Use these notes as your personal quick-reference guide whenever you want to refresh your memory ons something specific.

_____

_____

_____

_____

_____

_____

_____

_____

_____

_____

_____

_____

_____

_____

_____

_____

_____

_____

_____

_____

_____

_____
_____
_____
_____
_____
_____
_____
_____
_____
_____
_____
_____
_____
_____
_____
_____
_____
_____
_____
_____
_____
_____
_____
_____
_____
_____
_____
_____
_____
_____
_____

Conclusion

You did it! You have conquered Design Space. Give yourself a pat on the back—not for conquering this beast—but for believing in yourself. Without your determination, you would not be reading these words. Many, many people *dream* of doing stuff. Few actually *do* the stuff.

You're one of the few, and you can be pretty damn proud of yourself.

Let's do a quick recap to see what you've learned in the *Cricut Design Space Handbook for Newbies*. Besides the fact that you know Design Space has a desktop and mobile app, you can navigate both with confidence. You also have a clear understanding of the difference between the two and know what you can and can't do with the iOS (Apple) and Android mobile apps. You discovered that Design Space's Canvas interface is so much easier to understand and use when you approach it by looking at its different parts:

- The Canvas
- The Design Panel
- The Edit Bar
- The Layers Panel

You know which types of elements you can add to the Canvas (like shapes or text), and you know that you can tweak each element from various parts of the interface. Some tweaks can be made from more than one part of the interface ("all-rounder" functions), while other tweaks can only be made from certain parts (like specifying the *Operation* settings in the Edit Bar or using *Contour* in the Layers Panel).

Above all—you now have a firm grasp on how to work with layers in Design Space.

All that's left now is to practice what you have learned—every day if you can. Remember that knowledge is not power. It only becomes power when we apply it.

Looking back on my own journey as a Cricut Newbie, I've learned that the right mindset goes such a long way. At first, I was convinced there was no way I could learn to use my machine or Design Space. It looked too hard. I was scared of failing, and that fear prevented me from trying. When I finally tried and failed miserably, you know what I realized? It was OK. The sun was still shining. My home was still standing. And my Cricut machine hadn't exploded.

My point?

Your journey has only just started. This book is not your fail-safe guarantee that nothing will go wrong from here on out. You're going to continue learning, and you're going to check, double-check, and triple-check yourself. Frustrations will come and go, but you have to accept every bump in the road as part of the learning process toward becoming a crafting master.

In all your learning and experimenting, take those mistakes lightly. Shake your head and turn it into a dance. Laugh. Have fun.

If a new challenge arises, never, ever say *never*!

And if at first you don't succeed, consult your Design Space handbook—it will always have your back.

Now go craft.

Glossary

There are few things in life that can cripple your enthusiasm for a topic like the distinct feeling of being an outsider. I bet you've been in your fair share of "this is way over my head" conversations.

You know how it goes.

You ask a sincere question, get even more excited because the person you asked gets excited, start listening intently, and then... they lose you. Sure, you nod along with a sincere smile and all, but you have no idea what they're saying. When the conversation is finally over, you usually end with, "Wow... That's so interesting."

I experienced that a lot as a Cricut Newbie.

The more I learned, the more I realized how the Cricut pros had forgotten that they, too, were once Newbies. To be fair, though, this phenomenon is not limited to the world of Cricut. It seems a natural thing that happens as you develop your skills in any craft, industry, or topic of interest. The more knowledgeable you become, the larger the gap grows between how your thoughts were processed as a beginner versus how you process them as an experienced user.

When I became a pro and realized I had an intense desire and passion for teaching others Cricut crafting, I promised myself I would never forget what it was like to discover Cricut for the first time. And that brings us to this glossary.

Looking back, I now know why the pros lost me when they tried explaining things: the lingo.

Every time a term I didn't understand was thrown my way, my brain froze right there and wondered, "What is that?!" while the pro continued chatting happily. Of course, most Newbies—myself included back then—feel too awkward to ask questions. You don't want to look stupid. Worse, you don't want to be laughed at because you don't know the answer. But, rest assured, the Cricut Community is really, really helpful. You might get the odd rude person, but the rest will always have your back and welcome any questions you have.

Still, it sucks to feel like the odd one out.

That's why I want to empower you with your very own crafting lingo glossary. Not only will this knowledge help you feel less anxious when you engage in conversations with fellow, more experienced crafters, you'll also be able to help other Newbies better understand the lingo.

The following terms are not exhaustive, and new ones will probably always come your way. So, at the end of the glossary, there are a few pages for you to continue adding new terms you learn on your crafting journey.

Have fun!

Common Crafting Terms that Pop Up in the Cricut Community

Acid Free

When materials, like paper and pens, are acid free, they last much longer than materials that contain acid. This is an important consideration, especially when working with paper crafts and making gifts you want to last a long time.

Adhesive

Any sticky substance that makes objects cling to each other. Adhesives can come in the form of wet glue, tapes, sprays, heat-activated particles, and so on.

Adobe

The name of a world-famous company that offers a suite of design programs. Most crafters use two Adobe programs: Adobe Illustrator and Adobe Photoshop, but may simply refer to "Adobe" when talking about the software they use.

Since you probably won't use any of the two as a complete beginner, we won't delve into the details. However, it is useful to know that Adobe Illustrator is a vector-based program that helps you create SVG files from scratch (we'll cover SVG further down), whereas Adobe Photoshop is mostly used to create and manipulate bitmap files (basically the opposite of vector files).

Rest assured, you do not need to know the technicalities of vector-based files and bitmap files to use them. I certainly don't, and I'm not about to learn, either. What is important, though, is knowing when to use which file type. In the project chapters, I'll guide you through the file types we'll be using for each project.

App

An abbreviation for "application," which can refer to any mobile or desktop computer-based software program that offers specific functions and features. For example, Cricut Design Space is an app.

Archival

If you hear someone speaking of materials being archival, they mean that it was made to last, as it is very durable. The best example of this type of material is archival ink, which is acid free and fade resistant.

Backing

In the sewing community, backing usually refers to the reverse side of a quilt. But in the general sense, backing refers to the carrier sheet behind materials like permanent and temporary vinyls.

Blank

When someone says they're looking for blanks or know where you can find blanks, they're referring to base materials that have no decorations on them. You can embellish blanks with your own designs. Examples include tote bags, t-shirts, mugs, keychains, tumblers, and hoodies.

Bluetooth

You might hear this term when engaging in online crafting communities, especially when people ask questions to help others. An example is, "Did you try sending it via Bluetooth?"

Bluetooth is a technology that allows devices which are relatively close to each other to communicate and share files. All the latest Cricut machines are Bluetooth-enabled. The Cricut Joy works with Bluetooth only, while the other machines can be connected to your computer or mobile device with either Bluetooth or a cable.

BMP

Also called a bitmap image file. You can upload BMP images to Design Space, but the chances that you'll come across these files are rare.

Brayer

A brayer is a small, hand-held roller that was first used in printmaking, then became a popular rubber stamping tool, and then made its way into the crafting world as a convenient way to make sure materials stick evenly to surfaces.

Burnish

The process of rubbing an adhesive material so it adheres properly to the surface you want to transfer it to. This also helps to remove air bubbles that might otherwise ruin your craft project. While a brayer is useful for making sure materials even-out as you apply them, it does not necessarily give you enough pressure to burnish. In Cricut crafting, we like to burnish with the Cricut scraper.

Butcher Paper

This is paper that has no coating, which we normally use when doing heat-transfer projects. The butcher paper protects your base material (the blank), crafting material, and heat plate (whether an iron or heat press machine) from accidental transfers of the crafting material. If there is excess moisture in the base material, the butcher paper can absorb it, as well.

If you hang around in crafting communities, you'll soon hear a horror story of how some heat-transfer material landed on an iron plate or heat press plate. It's not pretty... So, always have butcher paper handy when working with heat transfer materials.

Other materials crafters use for the same purpose include parchment paper and pressing cloth.

Cardmaking

A specialized craft of making cards by hand, which includes the help of die-cutting machines like Cricut.

Cardstock

A durable, light-weight to heavy-weight paper material used in the craft of cardmaking. It also comes in different colors and patterns.

Cutting Blades

Sharp-edged tools that help you cut out your crafting projects. Cutting blades can be handheld, or specialized ones that work with machines like Cricut.

Cutting Mat

Not to be confused with the Cricut (and other die-cut) cutting mats, this mat refers to a relatively thick sheet of protective material on which you can cut and do other craft works that can damage your regular working surface. Cutting mats come in different materials and sizes.

In the crafting world, when you hear "cutting mat," it is probably in reference to the mats you stick a material onto when you want to cut it with a machine like Cricut. You will also see me using the term in this context throughout the book.

Deboss

A method you use to make a permanent impression into material such as paper, cardstock, leather, chipboard, and more.

Decal

Decorative designs that can be transferred to various surfaces, like windows, mugs, or outdoor signs. You can make decals of permanent or removable materials.

Design Space

Cricut's proprietary design software. You need this program to give your Cricut machine instructions to cut your designs. You might come across its short form, DS, in social media conversations.

Digital Mystery Box

Many crafting communities, including Cricut, offer mystery boxes and digital mystery boxes. Essentially, it is a crafter's lucky packet. When you buy a mystery box (physical or digital), you do not know what's inside until you open it. Digital mystery boxes can include project folders, design files, fonts, licensed images, and more.

Die

A tool used in many industries the world over. It is shaped in a specific form and is typically made of a hard, durable material like metal. A die is an important and efficient way to cut out consistent shapes and sizes of whatever the user needs. In crafting, a die can be anything from star to letter shapes. The company that started Cricut revolutionized what is possible with dies when they down-scaled the technology and brought it into households during the late 1900s.

Die-Cutting

The process of using dies to cut shapes out of a sheet of material like paper or leather.

Die Cut Machine

Originally, industrial-sized machines that could be fitted with dies to cut out the desired molds. These days, the term is very popular in the crafting community and refers to machines that can cut out any imaginable shape with the help of sophisticated design software, like Design Space. Your Cricut is a digital die cut machine.

DXF

A type of vector file you can upload to Design Space. However, you'll rarely come across it, as the more popular format is SVG.

Embellish

Any feature you add to a surface to make it more attractive. For example, if you make a vinyl decal and stick it on your Cricut machine, you have embellished your machine.

Emboss

When you emboss something, you do the opposite of debossing. That is, instead of making an impression, you raise up a part of your craft material to create a three-dimensional effect.

Engrave

Whereas you typically deboss soft to medium materials, you will engrave hard materials like wood and metal to make a permanent design impression. For example, you can engrave bracelets with personalized names, words, or shapes.

Faux Leather

A synthetic alternative to genuine leather.

Foiling

A popular method used in crafting to transfer foil to craft projects, especially in card making. There are different ways to transfer foil, like heat or adhesive. Cricut has its very own Foil Transfer tool to make the process smooth and easy (and super satisfying).

GIF

A type of image format you can upload to some design programs, including Design Space. However, this format mostly gets used on the internet, and you'll probably never use it in your design projects.

Guillotine

Another tool that has its origin in the past—though it has scary beginnings... I'll let you look that one up on your own! After its invention, the guillotine made its way into some households as a convenient way to slice bread and vegetables.

These days, it's a handy and precise tool to have if you work with a lot of paper crafts. Also known as a trimmer, it basically helps you to cut off unwanted edges or even slice paper and other materials in the size you need. It's a lot quicker than scissors, for sure.

Hot Mess Canvas

This crafting technique is fairly new and has gained a lot of traction the last couple of years—for good reason. It is an easy and fun way of making a reverse stencil design with a beautifully messy and colorful base. Most hot mess canvas designs are memorable quotes. We'll cover a hot mess canvas in one of the project chapters.

Mixed Media

A crafting creation that consists of different materials. For example, if you use wood as your base material and transfer a picture onto it using Mod Podge and round it off by painting a frame around the picture, you are busy with a mixed media project.

Heat Pressing

The process of transferring a heat-activated material to a surface using a tool that produces the right amount of heat. You can do heat pressing with a household iron, but it's not the best method. Many crafting companies offer specialized heat press machines to do the perfect job. For example, Cricut has a range of heat press machines called EasyPress.

HTV

"HTV" stands for Heat Transfer Vinyl, an adhesive material that needs heat to adhere to a surface. HTV is typically used to put designs on tote bags, hats, and t-shirts.

JPG

Also called JPEG. It is one of two popular image files you'll mostly upload to Design Space for Print Then Cut projects. The other format is called PNG.

Kerning

When you hear people discussing kerning, they're talking about the spaces in between individual letters, numbers, and characters of text.

Kiss Cut

A term used when a material is cut in a way that leaves its backing intact while the material itself gets cut through.

Layering

When you create a single design that is made up of more than one layer of material. For example, you can create a layered heart-shaped design by cutting out three to four hearts that are proportionally different in size and then sticking them on top of each other.

Machine Mat

The adhesive mat onto which you stick craft materials you want to cut with a digital die cut machine like Cricut.

Mirror

Also known as image mirroring, this is the act of flipping an image you have designed on a software program, like Design Space, just before you give your digital die cut machine instructions to cut it out. When you flip the image, it will basically display the wrong way around. Mirroring is important for projects that you do with HTV, or when you want to protect the good side of a material like faux or genuine leather.

Oracal

A brand name you'll hear quite often in crafting circles. Oracal vinyl, especially, is very popular. We'll talk more about which Oracal vinyls are similar to specific Cricut vinyls in Chapter 5.

OTF

A type of font file, called Open Type Font. The other font file you'll usually come across is TTF, or True Type Font. If you have a choice when downloading fonts, always opt for OTF, as it offers more font features than TTF.

Paper Weight

Paper weight, or just weight, refers to how thick paper, cardstock, and similar materials are. If the weight is heavier, the material is thicker and vice versa.

Perforation

The process or piercing a row of tiny holes into a material so you can tear it with ease and without damaging the material. Raffle tickets, for example, need to be perforated.

Permanent Material

If an adhesive material is permanent, its adhesive properties are very strong and meant to last. It is difficult, if not impossible, to remove permanent material without damaging the surface it was stuck on.

PNG

One of two popular image files you'll mostly upload to Design Space for Print Then Cut projects. The other format is called JPG or JPEG. If you have a choice, always opt for PNG files, as their backgrounds have already been removed. With JPG files, you'll go through the extra step of removing the white (or other color) background in Design Space before you can use it for your craft project.

Pretty-Side Down

We mostly use this term when preparing material for a cut. In most cases, it refers to the act of placing a material upside down on a machine mat before the cutting process starts.

Pretty-Side Up

In most cases, the act of placing a material the right side up on your machine mat for the cutting process.

Quilling

A specialized papercraft art that involves rolling, shaping, and gluing strips of paper together to create unique designs, from flowers to cats, to anything you can imagine.

Removable Material

If an adhesive material is removable, it is possible to take off of a surface without damaging the surface.

Reverse Weeding

When you reverse weed, you stick transfer tape over your design immediately after the cutting process, burnish it, and then proceed to weed the excess bits. This is especially useful when working with intricate designs or designs made up of words, where you do not want individual parts of the design to move disproportionally to the rest of the design.

Rotary Cutter

A specialized tool for cutting fabric. Basically, it is a round blade that can rotate and move easily in any direction without tearing fabric materials.

Scoring

The process of creating indented lines to mark where a craft material should be folded. These lines are known as score lines or fold lines. A good example would be the line that goes in the middle of a greeting card to show you where to fold it over.

Scraper

A handheld tool with a flat edge that makes it easy to remove excess bits of material from a machine mat after the cutting and weeding process. Scrapers are also popular to use when burnishing materials like vinyl.

Shiny-Side Down

Whenever you hear this term, it is almost always in the context of cutting heat transfer vinyl. HTV should always be cut upside-down. A characteristic of HTV is that its pretty side is, in most cases, shiny. That is the side you want to stick to your machine mat for the cutting process.

Siser

Another popular brand name you'll come across. Siser's heat transfer vinyl, Easyweed, is quite popular among crafters.

Spatula

A handheld crafting tool with a thin, flat metal edge that helps you lift material off the machine mat. It helps prevent materials from tearing and curling as you remove them. It normally has an angled edge, which makes it easy to slide the spatula underneath the material on the mat.

Stencil

Shapes, letters, or complete designs cut out of a thin sheet of material, typically vinyl or plastic, which you can use multiple times or once-off for a specific project. The idea is to place the stencil on the surface you want to decorate with the design and then use ink or paint to fill the gaps in the stencil. Once you lift the stencil, you will have a perfect design made with ink or paint.

Sublimation

A process that infuses a design into a base material through chemical reactions, usually activated by heat. Sublimation comes with benefits, such as being waterproof. Sublimation is only possible with specific ink, so always be sure to ask if you're getting the right stuff when you have sublimation in mind for a project.

Substrate

For sublimation to work, the surface it gets applied to must be sublimatable. To achieve this, a thin coat is applied to non-sublimatable surfaces. The coat is called a substrate. However, you need not always apply this coat yourself, as sublimatable blanks are available.

SVG

Shorthand for Scalable Vector Graphic, the standard file most crafters use for Cut projects. SVGs mostly consist of layers.

Taco Method

A way to apply transfer tape to vinyl and application surfaces with as few bubbles and wrinkles as possible. It entails cutting a piece of transfer tape a little larger than your design, bending it in a u-shape with both hands (to make it look like a taco), and carefully placing it against the design, starting in the middle. Next, use your scraper to apply the transfer tape from the center outward.

Template

An existing design you can use as the base for your own design. Template files are usually pre-formatted in some way so you can jump in and make tweaks quickly. Depending on the license you get when downloading the template, you may be able to use it as is for personal or commercial projects.

Transfer Tape

A clear, adhesive film you can use to pick up a vinyl design from its backing and transfer the design to the surface you want to decorate. Transfer tape works best with smooth vinyls (in other words, vinyls without a textured finish).

TTF

A type of font file, called True Type Font. The other font file you'll usually come across is OFT, or Open Type Font. If you have a choice when downloading fonts, always opt for OTF, as it offers more font features than TTF.

Tweezers

Crafting tweezers help you to pick up tiny bits of material or small objects. Together with a weeder, it can make the weeding process quick and smooth (and, I might add, therapeutic on some days).

UFO

A creative term used by crafters for "unfinished projects." (Though, you might hear this more among quilters and sewers than in other communities, as I suspect that is where it started.)

Unzip

When you extract digital files from a ZIP file on your computer or mobile device, it is called unzipping.

USB

A universal serial bus (USB) is a specialized cable that allows you to connect an external device to your computer or laptop. Cricut's Explore and Maker series machines can connect to your computer or laptop via a USB connection.

USB may also refer to an external memory source, better known as a memory stick, which stores files that can be accessed once the memory stick is plugged into a computer or laptop.

Vinyl

An adhesive crafting material that comes in many colors and patterns. It is very popular and can be used for anything from window decals to car decals, to personalizing your favorite tumbler or coffee mug.

Washi Tape

A non-destructive adhesive tape that comes in various colors and patterns printed on it. It is easy to remove and restick, so it works well for decorating crafts made with paper and similar materials.

Weeder

A handheld tool with a sharp hook at the end, perfect for picking up excess and unwanted materials around your design after the cutting process. As the name suggests, a weeder is the perfect tool for weeding.

Weeding

The process of removing unwanted parts from a craft project. We typically weed just after cutting out a papercraft or vinyl project. If the term confuses you, just think of the weeds you need to remove from your garden. You also use this term to refer to the process of removing a material from its backing.

Weeding Ring

A silicone ring with a little holder on top of it. The holder's top has slits in it so you can scrape off excess vinyl from your weeder while weeding your design. It's a convenient way to avoid getting your fingers sticky and having a lot of sticky scraps lying around all over your working surface.

Wet Method

A technique to transfer vinyl to a smooth and non-porous surface. Examples of such surfaces include glass and tumblers. The wet method works best with permanent vinyl and requires slightly soapy water and some patience. Vinyl is notoriously difficult to position and place on surfaces, and this method makes it a little bit easier. It is also excellent in helping you do a transfer without forming wrinkles and bubbles.

WIP

Another creative term used by crafters for "work in progress."

ZIP File

A digital file that, once unzipped, contains folders with various usable files, from designs to fonts, to instruction manuals.

Cricut-Branded Terms

Adaptive Tool System

The Adaptive Tool System is unique to the Cricut Maker series. Maker machines have a special housing for tools, called the QuickSwap housing, onto which you can fit Cricut's growing range of adaptive blades and tool tips. Other Cricut machines' tools and blades come with their own housings, and those tools and blades are limited. The idea with the Adaptive Tool System is that you'll be able to use new Cricut tools with it as they get released.

Bonded Fabric Blade

A specialized precision cutting blade made especially for bonded fabric. It comes with a special pink housing and can make intricate cuts.

Brightpad

The brightpad is a working surface that lights up. You can use it to trace or make the weeding process easier when working with intricate designs.

Card Mat

A specialized cutting mat for making cards with your Cricut machine. The card mat has a special divider on it to protect the back of folded cards while your Cricut cuts or writes on the front.

Carriage

The movable part in your Cricut machine into which you insert blades and tools.

Cricut Joy Blade

The standard cutting blade that comes with your Cricut Joy. When the blade becomes dull, you can replace it.

Cricut Joy Foil Transfer Tool

A specialized tool that allows your Cricut Joy to transfer foil particles onto surfaces like cardstock.

Cricut Mug Press

Cricut's specialized tool that allows you to transfer heat-transferable materials, like Iron-On and Infusible Ink, to mugs.

Debossing Tip

A specialized tool that allows your Cricut to impress a design into certain materials like leather and coated paper.

Deep Point Blade

This blade has a steeper angle than the standard Cricut Fine-Point Blade, allowing for more intricate cuts.

Dial

The Cricut Explore machines have Smart Dials, also known simply as Dials. It is a knob on top of the machine that allows you to choose which material the machine should cut. The Cricut Explore 3 does not have the dial.

EasyPress

Cricut's very own heat press. With the EasyPress, you can transfer Iron-On, HTV, and other heat-transferable materials onto surfaces like t-shirts and tote bags.

Engraving Tip

A specialized tool that allows your Cricut to carve out a permanent design in materials like acetate, heavy cardstock, wood, and leather.

FabricGrip Mat

A specialized cutting mat for various fabrics. It has enough grid to hold the fabric in place but is still gentle enough to prevent tearing when removing the fabric from the mat.

Fine-Point Blade

The standard cutting blade that comes with all Cricut machines. Once it becomes dull, you can replace it with a new blade.

Foil Transfer Tool

A specialized tool that allows your Cricut machine to leave foil particles on designs. The Cricut Joy has its own version, called the Cricut Joy Foil Transfer Tool.

Foil Transfer Sheets

The special foil sheet you use with the Foil Transfer Tool to impress foil particles on designs.

Go Button

The button you press when your Cricut machine is ready to start the cutting process. Older Cricut machines have the Cricut logo on the button, while newer machines have a play sign on the button. The Cricut Joy has no buttons, so you control the entire process via your desktop or mobile Design Space app.

Grid

The crossing lines you see when looking at the Design Space Canvas. By default, the grid's measurements are in inches.

Housing

The tube-like gadget into which your Cricut blade goes. When you replace blades, you remove the old blade and insert the new one into this housing.

Infusible Ink

A specialized heat-transfer ink that gives professional results when applied to surfaces.

Infusible Ink Transfer Sheets

The sheet of material on which you cut out your design for an Infusible Ink project. After the cutting process, you will use this sheet to transfer the design onto the intended surface. These sheets come in a variety of colors.

Insert Cards

Specialized cardstock that has already been folded to make greeting cards. Insert Cards were originally designed especially for the Cricut Joy, but since the release of the new Cricut Card Mats that can fit into the larger machines, it is possible to use Insert Cards with all the latest Cricut machines.

Iron-On

Cricut's branded heat transfer vinyl (HTV).

Knife Blade

A specialized blade that allows your Cricut to cut denser and heavier materials like wood. The Knife Blade only works with the Cricut Maker series.

Pause Button

A button on your Cricut machine that allows you to pause the cutting process midway.

Perforation Blade

A specialized blade that creates perforation marks for easy tearing.

Premium Fine-Point Blade

A more durable version of the Cricut Fine-Point Blade. The Premium Fine-Point Blade can resist wear and tear better than the standard blade all Cricut machines come out with.

QuickSwap Housing

The housing for Cricut's Adaptive Tool System blades and tools.

Ready-Made Projects

Done-for-you craft projects you can access on Design Space. If you have a Cricut Access subscription, you can access premium Ready-Made Projects in addition to free ones.

Roll Holder

A specialized holder for Smart Materials to keep them secure and organized while your Cricut does its cutting magic. The holder also helps to guide Smart Materials as they feed into the Cricut machine.

Rollers

The thick, black rubber rollers on your Cricut's roller bar. These rollers help to move cutting mats in and out of the Cricut machine with ease during the cutting process.

Roller Bars

The steel bar you see when you open your Cricut machine. The roller bar houses the carriage and allows the carriage to slide from side to side as it cuts out your projects. It also helps move cutting mats forward and backward in the machine during the cutting process.

Rotary Blade

A specialized blade with a rolling and gliding ability made especially for cutting fabric with ease. Because of its design, it can also handle intricate cuts very well.

Scoring Stylus

A tool for Cricut Explore machines that allows you to make fold lines for various materials.

Scoring Wheel

The scoring wheel is a part of Cricut's Adaptive Tool System for Cricut Maker machines. It allows you to make fold lines for various materials.

Sensor

A component inside your Cricut machine that allows it to scan cutting mats and sensor marks (or registration marks) around Print Then Cut projects before the cutting process starts.

Smart Materials

Cricut's range of Smart Materials have a special backing that allows your Cricut machine to cut the material without needing a cutting mat.

SnapMat

SnapMat is a special feature of the Design Space iOS app. It allows you to take a photo of the cutting mat with material on it so you can visualize the placement of design elements on the mat. You can also reposition elements on the virtual mat according to your liking.

SportFlex

A specialized Iron-On (HTV) made for sportswear. It lasts longer on materials like nylon and polyester because it can stretch with the fabric.

Star Wheels

The white rings you see on your Cricut machine's roller bar. They help to keep materials in place by preventing them from shifting during the cutting process. They can be moved to the sides of the roller bar when necessary, like when you're cutting thicker materials like felt.

TrueControl Knife

A precision cutter you use by hand. It's useful for trimming materials, finishing cut lines if necessary, and checking if your Cricut machine had cut all the way through a material before removing it from the machine. You can also use the TrueControl Knife for craft projects that do not involve your Cricut machine.

Wavy Blade

A specialized blade that gives your cut projects stylized edges. The Wavy Blade is a part of Cricut's Adaptive Tool System for the Cricut Maker machines.

Cricut Design Space Terms

Align

A function that lets you align a selection of elements relative to each other. Alignment options include Align Right, Align Left, Align Top, Align Bottom, Align Horizontally, Align Vertically, and Align Center.

Attach

The Attach function groups a selection of elements together so that their positions stay intact for the cutting process, allowing your Cricut machine to cut the design out exactly as you see it on the Canvas. If you do not apply the Attach function, the program will distribute the design elements in the best way to limit material wastage.

Arrange

You can change the order of layers using the Arrange function. It lets you move a layer forward one position at a time, all the way to the front, backward one position at a time, or all the way to the back.

Bleed

Design Space automatically adds a small border around images when you do Print Then Cut Images; this border is called a bleed. It helps your Cricut achieve more precise cuts, but you can turn it off before starting the cutting process.

Bubble Letters

Letters that look like thick outlines, kind of like cartoon fonts. This happens when your Cricut traces the outlines of letters only and does not draw complete letters, leaving you to fill in the rest by hand. The best way to prevent bubble letters is by using Cricut's range of writing fonts when you want your Cricut to draw letters.

Calibrate

A quick process your Cricut machine goes through to ensure accurate cutting. Depending on the Cricut model you own, you can do calibration for Print Then Cut projects, cutting with the Knife Blade, or cutting with the Rotary Blade.

Canvas

The large workspace on which you can see a preview of your craft project as it takes shape. The grid is visible on the Canvas.

Canvas Interface

Also called the Design Interface. This is the part of Design Space where you create designs from scratch or upload existing designs. The Canvas Interface comprises the Canvas, Edit Bar, Design Panel, and Layers Panel on the desktop app.

Color Sync

A quick way to change elements' colors to the same color of any other element on the Canvas. You apply Color Sync via the Color Sync panel.

Collections

Collections allow you to organize your craft projects into groups so you can find them more easily. For example, you can have a Collection called "Greeting Cards" in which you save all your greeting card projects, and another one called "T-shirts" in which you store all your t-shirt projects.

Color Tolerance

An advanced feature when uploading JPG images for Print Then Cut projects. Color Tolerance controls how many different colors get selected and deleted when erasing the background of a JPG image. The higher the Color Tolerance value, the more colors will be removed. You'll have to play around with this setting quite a bit to get the right parts of the image to stay while deleting everything you don't want.

Contour

A function that helps you hide parts of a design element to change the way it looks. The program uses the element's contour lines (visible borders) to help you control what to show or hide.

Cricut Access

Cricut's subscription program that gives you access to all their premium design content for your own projects.

Cricut Fonts

Fonts designed by Cricut to work with their range of smart cutting machines. You can access Cricut Fonts via Design Space while creating your projects.

Custom Material

Design Space sorts materials by popularity when prompting you to choose which material you'd like to use for your project. These popular options (like cardstock and vinyl) come with pre-programmed settings for your convenience. However, if you want to work with another material, like leather, Design Space considers it a custom material, which you can access when you click on Browse All Materials. The program offers pre-programmed settings for most custom materials, too, but you can tweak their settings and even add new materials with your own settings.

Curve

A function that allows you to bend single lines of text.

Design Panel

The left-hand panel you see on the Canvas Interface.

Edit Bar

The bar you see above the Canvas on the Canvas Interface.

Fast Mode

A setting that allows your Cricut Explore or Maker series machine to cut certain materials at twice the speed of previous Cricut models.

Fill

Allows you to fill up a design element with colors or patterns. The most popular fill mode is color. Pattern Fill is an advanced option and mostly used for Print Then Cut projects.

Flatten

A setting you apply to the layers on your Canvas before moving on to the Make It screen for a Print Then Cut project. The setting turns multiple elements into a single, flat layer for printing purposes.

Flip

This function allows you to instantly mirror an element or an entire design. Mirroring is important for Iron-On projects, especially.

Group

Create a unit out of a selection of design elements or layers. Once grouped, you can move the entire selection around without worrying about affecting each element's position relative to the other elements in the selection; you can also change all the elements' colors and their sizes at the same time. You cannot tweak individual elements within a group. To do that, you have to Ungroup the selection.

Hide

A feature that makes a layer invisible on the Canvas without deleting it.

Layers Panel

The right-hand panel you see on the Canvas Interface when using the desktop version of Design Space. From here, you can see every layer that makes up your design and apply various layer-specific functions like Group/Ungroup, Slice, and Attach. You can also rearrange the order of layers from here.

Matless Cutting

A term we use to refer to the cutting process of Smart Materials, since there is no need for a cutting mat when working with them.

Mat Order

When you move on to the Make It screen and you have a design that consists of different colors, all the design elements will be sorted according to those colors and each color will be placed on a separate mat. Each mat, in turn has a mat order, which determines in which order your Cricut will cut out the elements. The order is determined by numerical values in the panel to the left of the Make It Screen, with 1 being first in line.

Multi-cut

A setting that determines how many times your Cricut should cut the same design on a single mat. When working with thicker materials, multi-cuts are very useful to ensure the project gets cut all the way through.

Offset

A function that creates a proportionally larger or smaller silhouette layer of a design element.

Operation (Formerly Linetype)

Determines what your Cricut will do with your design project. The options are Cut, Draw, and Print Then Cut. There is also a Guide option, which turns any element into a template on which you can visualize your actual design.

Pattern Fill

An advanced fill option mostly used for Print Then Cut projects. It fills shapes, images, or text with patterns and backgrounds as opposed to solid colors.

Position

A function that determines where on the Canvas a design element sits. Position works on an X and Y axis, with X controlling the left and right position and Y controlling the up and down position.

Print Then Cut

An Operation setting. Print Then Cut specifies that you will print a design on your home printer before loading it into your Cricut machine for the cutting process.

Registration Marks

The black border Design Space creates around Print Then Cut designs. Your Cricut uses this border to scan the image with ists sensor so it can cut the design with accuracy.

Rotate

A function that determines the angle of a design element.

Shapes

Basics shapes, like squares and circles, you can use to create designs for your craft projects.

Size

A function that allows you to increase or decrease the size of design elements.

Slice

A function that allows you to split overlapping layers into new forms. When applying the Slice function, Design Space uses the edges of elements to slice into the other elements that overlap with it and vice versa.

System Fonts

The fonts installed on your computer or mobile device that you can access via Design Space to use them in your craft projects. Not all system fonts are compatible with your Cricut machine.

Text

A design element that allows you to type letters, numbers, and words for your craft projects. The text element comes with unique editing functions, like choosing the font, changing its size, and curving single lines of text.

Ungroup

If you used the Group function on a selection of elements and would like to dissolve the unit so each element in the selection can be edited and moved on its own, you can apply the Ungroup function.

Ungroup to Layers

A function applicable to text layers. If your text element consists of more than one line, you can apply the Ungroup to Layers function to split each line into its own layer.

Ungroup to Letters

A function applicable to text layers. It allows you to split each letter of a word in a text element into its own layer.

Ungroup to Lines

A function applicable to text layers. It basically does the same thing as Ungroup to Layers, allowing you to split two or more lines of text into individual layers.

Weld

A function that allows you to merge two or more overlapping layers into a single form. Once applied, the individual layers disappear and the new form's name in the Layers Panel becomes Weld Result.

My Cricut Crafting Glossary

Term

_____

Definition

_____

_____

_____

_____

_____

Term

_____

Definition

_____

_____

_____

_____

_____

Term

_____

Definition

_____

_____

_____

_____

_____

Term

_____

Definition

_____

_____

_____

_____

_____

Term

_____

Definition

_____

_____

_____

_____

_____

Term

_____

Definition

_____

_____

_____

_____

_____

Term

_____

Definition

_____

_____

_____

_____

_____

Term

_____

Definition

_____

_____

_____

_____

_____

Term

_____

Definition

_____

_____

_____

_____

_____

Term

_____

Definition

_____

_____

_____

_____

_____

Term

_____

Definition

_____

_____

_____

_____

_____

Term

_____

Definition

_____

_____

_____

_____

_____

Term

_____

Definition

_____

_____

_____

_____

_____

Term

_____

Definition

_____

_____

_____

_____

_____

Term

_____

Definition

_____

_____

_____

_____

_____

Term

_____

Definition

_____

_____

_____

_____

_____

Term

_____

Definition

_____

_____

_____

_____

_____

Term

_____

Definition

_____

_____

_____

_____

_____

Term

_____

Definition

_____
_____
_____
_____
_____

Term

_____

Definition

_____
_____
_____
_____
_____

Term

_____

Definition

_____
_____
_____
_____
_____

Term

_____

Definition

_____

_____

_____

_____

_____

Term

_____

Definition

_____

_____

_____

_____

_____

Term

_____

Definition

_____

_____

_____

_____

_____

Appendix
Self-Assessment Answers

Chapter 2

Text Element Self-Assessment Answers

1. Font, Cricut, System, Bookmarks

2. Style

3. Font Size

4. Letter, Line

5. Alignment, Left, Center, Right

6. No

7. Advanced, Actions, Ungroup

Upload Process Self-Assessment Answers

1. SVG

2. PNG or JPG

3. A PNG image's background has already been removed, so the upload process is much quicker than it is with a JPEG image.

Design Panel Self-Assessment Answers

1. Click on the "New" icon at the very top of the Design Panel.

2. From the home page, tap on the green "plus" icon at the bottom of the screen. You can also tap on "Canvas" at the top-right corner of the Home page. However, if you were busy with a design you have not yet saved, the

Canvas will open with that design.

3. No

4. No

5. True

6. A ready-to-make project's settings are already in place and the project comes with special instructions to help you with the entire process. It's as easy as choosing a project you like and clicking or tapping the "Make It" button.

7. Desktop app: Choose "Shapes" from the Design Panel.
Mobile app: Choose "Shapes" from the bar at the bottom of the Canvas screen.

8. Projects are ready-to-go designs with specific applications in mind. For example, a t-shirt or a tumbler. Images, on the other hand, are just design elements with no predefined settings and no specific applications in mind. While you can use an image 'as is,' you'll probably end up tweaking it and adding other elements to build a unique design.

9. No. Some Projects, Images, and Phrases are premium design assets that you need to pay for. You can buy individual assets at a once-off price, or subscribe to Cricut Access for a monthly fee.

10. Scissors: Indicates a file your Cricut will cut with a blade.
Printer: Indicates a file that you'll print out with your home printer and then let your Cricut cut it out with a blade.
Pencil: Indicates a file that our Cricut will write or draw with a Cricut Pen.
Scissors and Pencil: Indicates a file that your Cricut will cut with a blade and write or draw with a Cricut Pen.

11. The Upload function.

12. The Text function.

Chapter 3

Select All Function Self-Assessment Answers

1. You have a choice between "Edit Bar," "Directly on the Canvas," and "Layers Panel"

2. Press on the Canvas and drag a box around everything. Once everything is inside the box, you can let go. This will form a selection box around all the elements.

Edit Function Self-Assessment Answers

1. False. To find the Duplicate action on your mobile device, you should use the Actions function.

2. Duplicate and Delete

Size Function Self-Assessment Answers

1. When the Size function's padlock is locked, you can resize an element's width and height proportionally. In other words, if you adjust the width, the height adjusts automatically with it, and vice versa. When the Size function's padlock is unlocked, you can change the width of the element without affecting the height, and vice versa.

Rotate Function Self-Assessment Answers

1. The Rotate function allows you to tilt a design element to the right or left, giving you more design freedom to create unique artworks for your Cricut crafting projects.

Position Function Self-Assessment Answers

1. Desktop app: Click and drag the element or elements to the spot you want it directly on the Canvas.
Mobile app: Tap on the element or elements you'd like to move and drag them to the spot you want with your finger.

Arrange Function Self-Assessment Answers

1. Physical position: This is the actual spot where you can see an element on the Canvas.

2. Hierarchical position: This refers to whether the element is on top or underneath other elements on the Canvas. For example, if you stack the elements on top of each other, you'll see that they're all on different 'levels,' and none of them can be on the same 'level.'

3. Use the "Bring Forward" Arrange option.

4. Use the "Send Backward" Arrange option.

5. "Bring to Front"

6. "Send to Back"

7. False. You can see the order of elements when looking at the mobile app's Layers Panel, but you can't rearrange their orders from there.

Slice Function Self-Assessment Answers

1. The Slice function allows you to cut out parts of design elements that overlap each other on the Canvas, allowing you to create a cut-out effect, like when cutting a shape of cookie dough.

Weld Function Self-Assessment Answers

1. The Slice function cuts parts out of design elements, while the Weld function fuses design elements together. However, both create new and unique shapes.

2. False. There is no "unweld" function in Design Space, so applying the Weld function is a permanent change.

Group/Ungroup Function Self-Assessment Answers

1. The Group function is useful because it allows you to treat elements as a unit. It's a quick and easy way to make minor adjustments to grouped elements, like moving their position on the Canvas, resizing them, or

adjusting their colors at once.

2. True. Design Space turns the Group function into the Ungroup function once you have grouped elements into a unit. Unlike the Slice and Weld functions, the Group function does not combine different elements into a single element, but instead treats them as a unit of elements.

Attach/Detach Function Self-Assessment Answers

1. False. The Group and Attach functions seem to do the same thing at face value. However, the Attach function only determines how your Cricut machine sees each element it needs to cut, whereas the Group function allows you to bulk-select units of elements and make minor bulk adjustments to them.

2. False. Whether you Attach a design before the cutting process depends on your goals with that design. For example, if you're going to cut out elements that are different colors, you don't want to attach them.

Flatten/Unflatten Function Self-Assessment Answers

1. You should use the Flatten function when you want to use the design elements on your Canvas for a Print Then Cut project.

Chapter 4

Operation Function Self-Assessment Answers

1. The Operation function contains options that allow you to specify what our Cricut machine should do with your project. For example, if you want to write out a message, you have to set the Operation settings to Pen Draw. And if you want to cut out a vinyl decal for your car, you have to set the operation settings to Basic Cut.

2. False. It's possible to have your Cricut machine apply different operation functions to the same project. For example, it can cut out a greeting card and write in it.

Material Colors Function Self-Assessment Answers

1. You can find a design element's color settings in the same place as its operation settings. Click on "Operation" in the bar at the bottom of the screen, choose "Material Color, and then pick the color you'd like to apply to the element.

2. False. The color options in Design Space are just to help you visualize the final design. If the blue on your screen is different from the blue cardstock you have, it will not make a difference to the actual design once the cutting process starts.

Offset Function Self-Assessment Answers

1. The offset function creates an additional layer of a design element that is proportionally larger or smaller than the design element itself. It's like a silhouette of the original and creates outlines for design elements to help them pop.

Align Function Self-Assessment Answers

1. Center Align

Flip Function Self-Assessment Answers

1. The Flip Horizontal function keeps a design upright but flips it so the left and right sides switch.

2. The Flip Vertical function turns a design upside-down.

Chapter 5

Layers and Layers Panel Self-Assessment Answers

1. The various elements on the Canvas that make up the overall design are layers. Each layer can be edited on its own without affecting the other layers on the Canvas. For example, if there is a word, a square, and an image on the Canvas, each one of those are individual layers.

2. True. However, it's good to keep in mind that Design Space is a unique program when it comes to layers, as you can usually add more than one element to a layer in other design programs.

3. Layers give you the ability to tweak specific parts of a design; so, if mistakes slip in, it's easy to fix it without worrying about losing the entire design or having to restart the design from scratch. Layers also give you total design freedom and allow you to test limitless possibilities with options like Slice, Weld, Duplicate, and Delete. It's also important to understand layers, as most Cut projects work with them.

4. False. Each layer occupies its own space in the hierarchical order. You can rearrange the order of layers, but no two layers can be on the same level.

5. The Layers Panel gives you a bird's eye view of all the layers on the Canvas and tells you which layers are where in the hierarchical order. You can also use it to rearrange the order of layers and perform other functions like Group and Flatten.

6. False. If a layer is hidden, your Cricut machine can't see it. If you're not sure whether you want an element as part of your design, it's better to hide it as opposed to deleting it.

7. Arranging layers according to a logical flow is useful, as the human brain likes order. However, you might feel differently. At the end of the day, it's your call.

8. Each layer is represented by a thumbnail in the Layers Panel to help you identify specific layers more easily. For example, if there is a text layer that says "Total Craft Addict," the text layer's first letter will also be the layer's thumbnail in the Layers Panel (a "T" in this case). If there is a heart on the Canvas, its thumbnail in the Layers Panel will show a little heart.

9. True. If you are working on a design that has different colors, you can't attach all the layers together without losing the different colors.

10. Your solution is learning to see a design as a whole made up of different units, and different colors can represent those different units. Instead of attaching the entire design, you can attach the different elements that have

the same colors. For example, if you have a design that has blue, pink, and red elements, you can attach all the blue layers together, all the pink layers together, and all the red layers together. After the cutting process, you can bring those units back together to make up the entire design again.

11. There are no hard and fast rules when deciding on the type of project you want to do. It all depends on your personal goals with a design.

Index

S

T

Share Your Honest Opinion of this Book

If you haven't done so already, I'd really appreciate it if you could take a few minutes to tell fellow crafters what you thought of the *Design Space Handbook for Newbies*. Your opinion matters immensely, and the only way others will know if this book can change their lives is with your help.

Please head over to Amazon or your favorite book review platform and share your honest opinion of how this book has influenced your personal journey as a Cricut Newbie.

Join the Cricut for Newbies Facebook Group

This is goodbye, but by no means is it farewell. There's an entire community of fellow Cricut Newbies waiting to meet and encourage you, and I'm first in line. Since we're practically crafting besties now, there is so, so much more I want to share with you, from unique project tutorials to little-known Cricut secrets even many pros still haven't figured out. Join the Cricut for Newbies Facebook Group now to connect with like-minded people and be part of a community who believes in you and what you can achieve.

https://www.facebook.com/groups/cricutfornewbies

Have You Claimed Your FREE Gift?

If you haven't done so already,
head over to www.cricutfornewbies.com to claim your
FREE copy of *The Must Have Design Space Cheat Sheet for Cricut Newbies*

Happy crafting!

Acknowledgements

Zabed, I've said this before, and I'll say it again: no wife has ever loved her husband more than I love you. Thank you for being you and for all your love and support.

Aliya, you're still too young to read this, but every day, every week, you're getting closer. Time flies, baby girl. Cherish every moment and always remember you're the best thing that has ever happened to us.

Mom & Dad... How can a child ever properly express her grattidute in words? You're the best. I love you.

Ela, Luna, and Rida, you're still the best sisters anyone coul ask for. **Forhad**, thanks so much for everything! **Ayaz**, Auntie hopes you'll enjoy this book when you're old enough to read it. Love you!

To ALL my in-laws: I wish I had space to mention every one of you, but you're in my heart and I appreciate you all from the bottom of my heart. Love you all!

And a BIG heartfelt thank you for always being the best support group:

Matthew, you are awesome!

Renee, you're pretty incredible!

Melissa, you're a dime and the best ever!

Izak, for being a great sport!

Tony, you'll always be remembered!

Jacob, you're pretty amazing!

About the Author

Delara Chowdhury is an unapologetic craft addict, smitten wife, adoring proud mother, and the author behind the Amazon best seller, *Cricut for Newbies*.

Delara grew up in Ontario, Canada, as the middle child amongst four sisters. The latest and coolest arts and crafts trends have always been a subject of fascination for her. From scrapbooking to paper-craft, to quilting, to glass-crafts, she's done it all. She is also a technology and design enthusiast. So, when she discovered the perfect combination of the two in the form of Cricut crafting, she was instantly hooked.

Delara's Cricut journey ensured many interesting, fun, happy, crazy, and sometimes down-right frustrating moments. Every one of those experiences prepared for her ultimate passion and purpose: helping Cricut Newbies conquer their machines and Design Space with confidence. Today, she specializes in Cricut crafts and pays it forward by sharing her knowledge in a way so easy to understand, even your grandmother could become a Cricut pro! The *Design Space Handbook for Newbies* is Delara's second book.

You can connect with Delara by joining her Facebook Group at https://www.facebook.com/groups/cricutfornewbies or by writing to her at delara@cricutfornewbies.com

Made in the USA
Monee, IL
16 April 2023

31967684R00210